Teaching and Learning in Multicultural Schools

BILINGUAL EDUCATION AND BILINGUALISM

Series Editors
Professor Colin Baker, *University of Wales, Bangor, Wales, Great Britain*
Professor Nancy H. Hornberger, *University of Pennsylvania, Philadelphia, USA*

Other Books in the Series
Becoming Bilingual: Language Acquisition in a Bilingual Community
    JEAN LYON
Building Bridges: Multilingual Resources for Children
    MULTILINGUAL RESOURCES FOR CHILDREN PROJECT
Child-Rearing in Ethnic Minorities
    J.S. DOSANJH and PAUL A.S. GHUMAN
Curriculum Related Assessment, Cummins and Bilingual Children
    TONY CLINE and NORAH FREDERICKSON (eds)
Foundations of Bilingual Education and Bilingualism
    COLIN BAKER
Language Minority Students in the Mainstream Classroom
    ANGELA L. CARRASQUILLO and VIVIAN RODRIGUEZ
Languages in America: A Pluralist View
    SUSAN J. DICKER
A Parents' and Teachers' Guide to Bilingualism
    COLIN BAKER
Policy and Practice in Bilingual Education
    O. GARCIA and C. BAKER (eds)
Multicultural Child Care
    P. VEDDER, E. BOUWER and T. PELS
Teaching Science to Language Minority Students
    JUDITH W. ROSENTHAL
Working with Bilingual Children
    M.K. VERMA, K.P. CORRIGAN and S. FIRTH (eds)

Other Books of Interest
Encyclopedia of Bilingualism and Bilingual Education
    COLIN BAKER and SYLVIA PRYS JONES

Please contact us for the latest book information:
Multilingual Matters, Frankfurt Lodge, Clevedon Hall,
Victoria Road, Clevedon, BS21 7HH, England
http:/www.multilingual-matters.co.uk

BILINGUAL EDUCATION AND BILINGUALISM 13
Series Editors: Colin Baker and Nancy Hornberger

Teaching and Learning in Multicultural Schools

An Integrated Approach

Elizabeth Coelho

Multilingual Matters Ltd
Clevedon • Philadelphia • Toronto • Sydney • Johannesburg

Library of Congress Cataloging in Publication Data

Coelho, Elizabeth
Teaching and Learning in Multicultural Schools: An Integrated Approach/Elizabeth Coelho
Bilingual Education and Bilingualism: 13
Includes bibliographical references and index
1. Minorities–Education–Canada. Multicultural education–Canada. 3. Inclusive education–Canada.
4. Teaching–Canada. 5. Minorities–Education. 6. Multicultural education. 7. Inclusive education.
8. Teaching. I. Title. II. Series.
LC3734.C64   1998

British Library Cataloguing in Publication Data

A CIP catalogue record for this book is available from the British Library.

ISBN 1-85359-384-2 (hbk)
ISBN 1-85359-383-4 (pbk)

Multilingual Matters Ltd

UK: Frankfurt Lodge, Clevedon Hall, Victoria Road, Clevedon BS21 7HH.
USA: 1900 Frost Road, Suite 101, Bristol, PA 19007, USA.
Canada: OISE, 712 Gordon Baker Road, Toronto, Ontario, Canada M2H 3R7.
Australia: P.O. Box 586, Artamon, NSW, Australia.
South Africa: PO Box 1080, Northcliffe 2115, Johannesburg, South Africa.

Copyright © 1998 Elizabeth Coelho

Typeset by Archetype IT Ltd (http://www.archetype-it.com).
Printed and bound in Great Britain by WBC Book Manufacturers Ltd.

Contents

Acknowledgements

Many of the ideas in this book are based on the experiences, insights, and creative endeavours of the many teachers with whom I have worked over the last 25 years. Thank you for allowing me into your classrooms and sharing your ideas with me. I hope I have represented you well in this book.

I would also like to thank the teachers I have met as students in the courses I have taught at the University of Toronto. Our discussions on policy and practice in multilingual and multicultural education have helped me to develop my ideas.

In addition, the helpful staff at the F.W. Minkler Professional Library at the Toronto District School Board have provided invaluable assistance. Thank you.

I wish to thank my friends and colleagues who contributed their time and thoughtful advice as readers of various drafts of this material: Tara Goldstein, Marjatta Holt, Susanne Holunga, Irene McKay, Stephanie Paulauskas, Joan Speares, Chau Tran, and Debbie Zakus.

Many thanks to editors Colin Baker and Nancy Hornberger, who provided expert advice and assistance as they read earlier drafts, and gave me ongoing support over the two years it took to shape the manuscript for publication.

The photographs in this book, unless otherwise credited, were taken by Al Weinberg of Special Events and Media Production Services at the Toronto District School Board. The photographs were taken in two Toronto District schools: R.J. Lang Elementary and Middle School, and Sir Sandford Fleming Secondary School. Thanks to the staff and students at both schools, and to the Toronto District School Board for permission to use the photographs in this book.

Finally, I wish to thank the many students from many different linguistic and cultural backgrounds whom I have taught at schools in England, Bulgaria, and Canada. I have learned so much from all of you.

Foreword

by Jim Cummins

In urban centres across North America and in many other contexts, culturally and linguistically diverse students constitute the mainstream school population in an increasing number of schools. Despite the fact that diversity is the norm in these schools, there has often been strong resistance among policy-makers and some educators to implementing the changes in pedagogy, school organization, and professional development required to address the changing demographic realities of the school and community.

While calls for school reform ring out from both the right and left of the political spectrum and occasion often acrimonious debate, little attention is generally paid to the learning needs of students whose knowledge of the school language is limited or whose culture, 'race', religion, or sexual orientation are stigmatized in the wider society. At best, these concerns have had the status of footnotes to broader and more urgent issues such as the need to boost accountability, academic standards, and literacy. The perception appears to be that the needs of these students are well taken care of by ancilliary provision such as teaching English as a second language (ESL) or, if that proves inadequate, special education. These 'satellite' programs revolve around the mainstream leaving the core provision intact and still largely reflecting the power structure of the society. The adoption of a smattering of multicultural rhetoric tends to reinforce rather than challenge this power structure.

Issues related to diversity are also outside the focus of most Colleges of Education. Even in cities such as Toronto where students from non-English-speaking backgrounds constitute at least half of the school population, pre-service teacher education relegates consideration of diversity and ESL issues to the status of an 'additional qualification'. Thus, newly-minted teachers emerge into the school with excellent qualifications in teaching subjects such as Science or Language Arts to 'the general population', but with little idea of how to teach these subjects to students whose command of academic English is still very limited. The expectation, particularly at the secondary level, is that these children's linguistic needs will be taken care of by the specialist ESL teacher. This expectation is clearly highly unrealistic not only because of the relatively short period of time that each student will receive ESL support during any particular school day but also because second language learners usually require at least five years to catch up academically to their native English-speaking peers. If subject matter teachers are not prepared (in both senses of the term) to teach language together with the content of their particular specialty then ESL students' academic difficulties are likely to be compounded.

It is for these reasons that I very much welcome Elizabeth Coelho's lucid account of what is required to teach and learn effectively in multicultural schools. The importance of integrating an antiracist perspective into all facets of instruction and school life is clearly stated as is the centrality of language issues to antiracist education. The knowledge base that this volume outlines must be internalized by all educators, and particularly by educational leaders, if educational reform is to have any impact on improving the quality of students' learning experiences.

The interactions that are going on between educators and students in multicultural schools today reflect the realities of the multicultural communities within which these schools operate. We have the opportunity in our schools to model and nurture the kind of cooperative, respectful and mutually affirming interactions that any society requires to function smoothly at a time when cross-cultural contact is at an all-time high in human history. Respect and affirmation imply that teachers must learn from their students in order to teach them effectively. I can think of no better starting point for educators in preparing for this learning process than reading this volume and discussing with colleagues its implications for policy and practice at a local school level.

Introduction

This book aims to provide examples of approaches and strategies that schools and teachers can adopt in order to provide educational experiences that meet the needs of all the learners in culturally diverse schools and classrooms. Many of the ideas will be especially helpful to educators in areas where new immigrants settle. The book is addressed to all teachers, administrators, and curriculum advisors in multilingual, multicultural, multiracial schools and school districts. Teachers in training, and the educators who help them to prepare for work in today's culturally diverse schools, will also find many useful suggestions and ideas for effective practice in this book. Some of the ideas and topics in this book may suggest themselves to educational researchers as subjects for study.

PERSPECTIVES

Although I have lived and taught in other countries, most of my professional life has been in Canada. Therefore, this book was written from a Canadian perspective, and uses many Canadian examples. Canada currently has the largest per capita immigration program in the world, and its largest city, Toronto, is the most multicultural city in the world. Although Canada has two official languages, English and French, multilingualism was a fact of life long before there was a Canadian nation. In addition to the Aboriginal languages spoken by the descendants of the country's first inhabitants, some of which are used as languages of instruction today, more than a hundred other languages have arrived over the last four hundred years.

Many of the lessons learned in the schools of Toronto, Vancouver, and other urban school districts in Canada can be generalized to other cities in other countries where immigration, past and present, has had an impact on schools, and to all schools in culturally diverse communities. This is not to say that Canada has found successful ways of dealing with all the issues — some of the lessons are about what not to do, as well as what has been successful. Nor do all the successful practices originate in Canada; Canadian schools have learned from the experience of educators in other countries, especially the United States and the United Kingdom.

There is unlikely to be a school in existence that already has in place all of the procedures and practices described in this book. The multicultural school I envision here is a composite ideal, and includes some ideas about what might be. Many of the approaches I recommend will require adaptation to conform to local policy and practice. For example, the suitability of some of the recommendations may depend on whether all, many, or only a few of the students are from cultural backgrounds other than the mainstream culture of the larger society. Therefore, I offer this book as a menu of options for teachers and administrators to choose from and adapt according to local needs, resources, and constraints.

A word about the title of this book: 'Teaching and Learning' are viewed as reciprocal, in that teachers in multicultural schools are also learners, and learners are also teachers. The term 'multicultural' is used in the title and throughout this book — as in 'the multicultural school', or 'a multicultural environment' — as a succinct way of encompassing cultural, linguistic, and racial diversity. The book is subtitled 'An Integrated Approach' because it is about the integration of students from diverse linguistic and cultural backgrounds into every facet of school life, through the adoption of a integrated whole-school approach that encompasses curriculum development, classroom practice, school policy, and school–community relations.

Some chapters in this book focus on the needs of students who are recent immigrants or the children of immigrants. In others, the discussion includes children of indigenous or historical minority groups such as Aboriginal peoples and African Americans.

It is important to examine the use of the word 'minority'. The term is especially common in the United States, where minorities include such groups as Native Americans, African Americans, Mexican Americans, and various immigrant groups. Expressions such as 'linguistic minority' or 'racial minority' are also common. However, according to Cummins (1996), the term may be viewed as pejorative among some educators and in some communities, and is inaccurate in terms of the demographic composition of some school districts. 'Minorities' actually constitute a numerical majority in many school districts in the United States and Canada, or soon will do so, but they are a minority among those who have power, status, and influence. In the educational context, they constitute a minority among teachers and school administrators, curriculum developers and textbook writers, and officials responsible for educational planning. As a result, their achievements, contributions, experiences, and perspectives are often under-represented in the curriculum that is offered to all students. In this book, I use the word 'minority' as a shorthand for 'groups other than the English-speaking white mainstream which constitutes the dominant social and cultural group in countries such as the United States, Canada, the United Kingdom, and Australia'.

An underlying assumption in this book is that schools can become agents of change in society. For example, some of the strategies and activities suggested in the book will transform the school into an important site of antiracist activity, where students, teachers, and parents can learn to recognize and counter inequities that result from existing power relationships in the school and in society.

CONTENT

Living in linguistically and culturally diverse communities is interesting and stimulating, and provides all students and teachers with valuable opportunities for cultural enrichment and global education. At the same time, this diversity poses special challenges for educators, especially those whose education and training did not prepare them to live in multicultural societies and work in multicultural schools. In this book I hope to support teachers by outlining some of the knowledge they need, with reference to relevant research, and describing some practical examples that build on that knowledge.

Note: Although many students in multicultural schools are learning the language of instruction, this book does not attempt to provide specific advice on how to teach English as a Second Language. To do so would make the book twice as long; therefore, I have put second language learning and teaching aside for another book.

ORGANIZATION

The book consists of nine chapters. The first chapter provides an overview of the sources of cultural diversity and describes some public policies that have a direct impact on the cultural composition of many classrooms. Chapter 2 focusses on the special needs of students who have recently arrived from other countries, or who are the children of recent immigrants. The chapter describes the effects of the immigrant experience on families, and on children's psychological adjustment and eventual integration into the academic and social life of the school. Chapter 3 suggests some practical ways of receiving and welcoming all students and helping them to get off to a positive start in their new educational environment. The chapter includes detailed practical advice on the assessment and placement of recently arrived students and children who start learning English when they start school. Chapter 4 suggests some ways of helping everyone — immigrants and the children of immigrants, indigenous minorities, and members of the mainstream cultural group — to feel valued and included in the multicultural school community. Chapter 5 describes how each teacher can create a positive and inclusive classroom environment, where students learn to work together and appreciate each other's linguistic and cultural backgrounds. Chapter 6 describes important elements of an inclusive instructional style in the multicultural classroom. Chapter 7 provides an overview of antiracist education as a context for Chapter 8, which examines the content of the curriculum, and recommends specific actions that schools and individual teachers can take to develop a curriculum that is inclusive in orientation and equitable in effect. The final chapter discusses issues related to assessment reform, and provides advice on curriculum related assessment in the multicultural school.

Throughout the text there are graphics and text boxes consisting of quotations, commentaries, instructions, and examples that explain, expand on, or illustrate a key point or suggestion in the main text. At the end of each chapter there is an annotated list of resources for teachers who would like to explore some of the ideas in more detail. Several chapters also provide checklists that educators can use to assess progress in implementing some of the approaches and strategies suggested in this book.

HOW TO USE THIS BOOK

Use this book as a 'menu' of information and suggestions, selecting topics and strategies as and when they seem appropriate to your school and your needs. Although the chapters may be read selectively and in any order, some chapters may refer to some concepts introduced in another chapter. For example, some of the strategies suggested in Chapter 3, 'Getting Started in the Multicultural School', respond to the needs of recently arrived immigrant students as described in Chapter 2, 'The Immigrant Experience'. Throughout the book, reference is made to other sections or chapters that may be relevant to a particular topic.

I address many of the ideas and suggestions in this book directly to teachers, giving practical advice on what 'you' can do in your classroom or in your role as a teacher-counsellor. If you are a school administrator, curriculum advisor, or teacher educator, these ideas are suggestions on what to encourage, expect, and look for in the classrooms where you have influence.

Elizabeth Coelho
Toronto, September 1997

CHAPTER 1

Melting Pots and Other Metaphors

INTRODUCTION

Educators in English-speaking countries are increasingly aware of cultural diversity as a significant factor in schooling. In Canada, for example, school populations may include children of First Nations ancestry as well as children with ancestral roots in Europe, Africa, or Asia. Children may live in anglophone or francophone communities, or belong to one of over a hundred other language communities. In the major urban areas, large numbers of students have recently arrived from other countries. There are also many Canadian-born children whose parents have immigrated from other countries, and whose first major exposure to English is at school.

This chapter provides an overview of the historical and contemporary sources of diversity in Canada, and describes contemporary policy on immigration. The chapter also discusses public attitudes towards cultural diversity, and describes different approaches to managing diversity such as 'the melting pot' and 'the cultural mosaic'.

Most of the examples in this chapter are drawn from Canadian sources. While the specifics of immigration history and policy differ in other countries, and the impact of immigration on schools may be less dramatic than in cities such as Toronto and Vancouver, the situations and experiences described in this chapter are illustrative of cultural diversity in many other cities and countries. The challenges faced by teachers in multicultural schools in the United States, Britain, Australia, and New Zealand are very similar to those described in this book, and lessons learned about multicultural education in Canadian schools can be helpful to all teachers working with immigrant and culturally diverse students. For example, whether the school receives one immigrant student per year, or several hundred, there is a need for a planned program of reception and support, as well as a need to educate the 'host community' for life in a culturally diverse community.

SOURCES OF DIVERSITY

Cultural diversity is a result of the movements of peoples over time and across continents and oceans. Migration from one region to another has been a phenomenon of human activity since the first humans are thought to have appeared in Africa. The variety of human language, culture, and physical appearance has evolved in response to the environments in which different groups settled, and in response to contact with other groups.

The dominant cultural groups in Great Britain, the United States, Canada, the English-speaking Caribbean, South Africa, Australia and New Zealand migrated to those countries from elsewhere and overwhelmed the indigenous populations, beginning with the Anglo-Saxon and Norman invasions of Britain. Thus English, derived from Anglo-Saxon, with the addition of thousands of words from Norman French and Latin, is the dominant language in many of those countries today.

Immigration to North America occurred in several overlapping stages: colonization and conquest, early European settlement and African slavery, several boom periods in immigration during the late 19th and early 20th centuries, and new sources of immigration in the last three decades.

Colonization and conquest

Immigration history in Canada begins with the colonization of the territory and the conquest of the people who were already living there.

Canada's indigenous peoples, also referred to as Aboriginal People and Native People, are thought to have arrived from Asia in two major movements widely separated in time. Archeological work in the 1980s suggests that the first people may have been in what is now known as Canada at least 100,000 years before the Europeans — much longer than the 10,000–20,000 years suggested in many history texts (Herberg, 1989). By the time John Cabot arrived in Newfoundland, in the service of the British crown, in 1497, there were more than 50 distinct cultural and linguistic groups, such as the Cree, Ojibway, Huron, Beothuk, Mohawk, and Haida peoples. To the Europeans, these were all 'Indians'; today, the preferred term is 'First Nations' or the name of the specific group. In the far North, the Inuit (once called 'Eskimo', which means 'eaters of raw flesh' in Cree) arrived more recently, about 2000 years before the European colonists. 'Inuit' is an Inuktitut word meaning 'The People'.

It is estimated that 250,000 to 300,000 indigenous people were already in Canada when the first explorers and colonists arrived from Europe (Herberg, 1989). Each group had a distinct social, political, economic and material culture; Canada was a multicultural and multilingual country long before the arrival of new languages and cultures from Europe, Africa, and Asia.

At the beginning of what Herberg calls 'the Anglo-European era in Canada', most of the land was already occupied or claimed by various indigenous groups (Herberg, 1989: 34). From their perspective, the arrival of the first Europeans, often referred to as a 'discovery' in history texts, might more accurately be described as an 'invasion'. The effects of this invasion were devastating. Having taught the first traders and colonists how to survive and how to exploit the rich resources of the land, the Aboriginal People were dispossessed of the land, decimated by European diseases, and culturally overwhelmed by the combined effects of alcohol, the fur trade and Christianity. By the mid-19th century, Canada's indigenous peoples had been reduced to a population of about 23,000 within the boundaries of the new nation. Massive expropriation of the land in favour of European settlers — most of whom were British — and, later, the effects of schools designed to eradicate Aboriginal culture, caused the Aboriginal peoples to become 'numerically inferior and a socially conquered, culturally ravaged and suppressed group, until well into the 1970s' (Herberg 1989: 36).

Today, Canada's indigenous peoples are experiencing a renaissance of cultural pride and identity. Many Aboriginal groups have become politically active in demanding more control over education, the courts, and local government. For example, First Nations groups were instrumental in the government's failure to win agreement to proposed constitutional changes in the 1980s — changes that many First Nations people felt would not take into account their special needs and rights. First Nations groups have also challenged the provincial and federal governments over issues such as land rights and the use of natural resources. In the 1990s several confrontations drew the nation's attention to Aboriginal concerns, and in 1996 a Royal Commission on Aboriginal Peoples, which included strong representation from Aboriginal People themselves, issued a comprehensive report which included recommendations on self-government.

Early European settlement

Early settlement policies in Canada and many other British colonies had permanent effects on the linguistic and cultural composition of the colonies, establishing a language and a culture that remain dominant today. As the British government established a military presence in new colonial territories, administrators and settlers were recruited from Britain to supervise trade and taxation, control Aboriginal populations, farm the expropriated lands, and boost the British presence against other colonial contenders such as the French.

After defeating the French in 1763, the British gained dominion in Canada and encouraged the settlement of large numbers of new immigrants from Britain in order to increase the English-speaking population and maintain the minority status of the French, thus ensuring loyalty to the British crown. The French-speaking Acadians were expelled from Nova Scotia and dispersed among other British colonies on the coast. Many ended up in Louisiana, a French possession at the time, where 'Cajun' culture survives to this day. After the American War of Independence, the arrival of the United Empire Loyalists from the former American colonies, including many African Americans, helped to increase the proportion of English-speaking people in the Canadian population.

In the early colonial period, there were no immigration laws to control the flow of people into what is now known as Canada. According to Malarek, 'the British government viewed emigration to the colonies as a release valve for chronic unemployment, misery and poverty at home rather than as a means of advancing the colonies' (Malarek, 1987: 1). There was plenty of work in the colonies, most of it hard manual labour clearing the land for farming, building railroads, and developing resource industries such as forestry and mining. Thousands of people were encouraged, assisted, and sometimes even forced to leave Britain for Canada and the United States.

In addition to fit and healthy people seeking their own piece of land to farm, early arrivals included paupers, indentured labourers, and deported criminals. Moreover, conditions on board the ships were so appalling that many would-be immigrants died en route or arrived sick from smallpox, typhus, and other contagious diseases. When several American states introduced measures to control immigration, many ships were diverted to Canada. In 1831 and 1832, about 20,000 people arrived in Canada having been denied entry to the United States (Malarek, 1987). Colonial administrators began to protest against the dumping of the sick and destitute in Canada, and began to demand more control over who came to the new land. In some colonies, a head tax was imposed on every new immigrant in order to offset the costs of caring for the sick and helping immigrants to travel to their final destination.

Slavery

In the earliest days of European settlement in North America and the Caribbean, the indigenous peoples were enslaved. However, this source of labour was not available for long. In the Caribbean, almost all the Aboriginal People were exterminated within a generation after the arrival of Columbus. The causes included the rigours of slave labour, European diseases, and suicide, as well as armed conflict. Meanwhile, in North America the indigenous people were pushed further and further away from areas of European settlement. Colonists in the New World turned to Africa as the major source of slave labour.

During the colonial period — and beyond, in the United States — the African slave trade was an important source of capital and labour. The forced emigration of millions of enslaved Africans to the United States and the British West Indies provided capital and labour that financed the Industrial Revolution, made further expansion of the British Empire and the United States possible, and developed plantation economies in the Caribbean and the United States.

Although plantation slavery was never a feature of the Canadian economy, African slaves were present in colonial Canada, mainly as domestic workers. The first African slave in Canada was a six-year-old boy from Madagascar, who came as the 'property' of an English privateer. Until 1783, most Africans in Canada were slaves. Slave auctions were common, especially in Halifax, Nova Scotia, a major port of entry to Canada during the colonial period. Most arrived from other British colonies in the Caribbean and what is now the United States. According to Alexander and Glaze (1996: 41), 'blacks were preferred to indentured European servants, who could fade into the general population. Black skin was a badge of slavery'.

In 1783, the United Empire Loyalists, defeated in the American War of Independence, arrived in Canada. About 10% of the Loyalists were African Americans who had been promised land, freedom, and equal rights in exchange for supporting the British during the American War of Independence (Alexander and Glaze, 1996). The Black Loyalists settled mainly in Nova Scotia and New Brunswick. However, only a small percentage of the Black Loyalists received the land they were promised, and most land that was allocated to them was poor and unproductive. Moreover, the land was distributed in such a fashion as to create segregated districts of settlement. In 1792, discouraged by these and other incidents of racism, about one-third of the African population of Nova Scotia and New Brunswick sailed for Sierra Leone, another British colony in West Africa, where they hoped to pursue the dream of freedom, equality, and land.

Efforts to abolish slavery in Canada and other British possessions began in the late 18th century. In 1793 the colonial government in Ontario passed a law to prevent the importation of new slaves and to free the children of slaves after the age of 25. In 1834, slavery was abolished in Canada and throughout the British Empire.

Meanwhile, in the United States, runaway slaves who escaped to freedom in the northern states represented a loss of investment to slave owners. In order to protect their investment, the Fugitive Slave Act was passed. According to this Act, Africans anywhere in the United States who were suspected of being runaways could be captured and enslaved. The northern states no longer represented a safe haven for African runaways or even for free Africans; for this reason, African American refugees began arriving in Canada in increasing numbers. The 'Underground Railroad', a clandestine organization of Africans and Europeans, helped thousands of fugitives to travel to safety in Canada. The most famous 'conductor' on the Railroad was Harriet Tubman, an escaped slave who returned to the South on numerous occasions to help several hundred others to escape. Alexander and Glaze estimate that 50,000 Africans came to Canada as refugees from slavery between 1815 and 1816 (Alexander and Glaze, 1996). Other sources estimate that by 1860 there were about 40,000 people of African ancestry in Ontario alone (Ministry of Education, 1983).

During the American Civil War, about two-thirds of the African population of Upper and Lower Canada (now Ontario and Quebec) returned to fight for the Union and for the freedom of Africans throughout the United States (Ministry of Education, 1983). According to Alexander and Glaze (1996:79), 'The call to free their American brethren so moved black Canadians that some 30,000 took the Underground Railroad in reverse to join the Union Army'. After the American Civil War and the abolition of slavery in the United States, many African Americans returned to the United States to participate in the reconstruction of the country. Conditions in Canada also contributed to the exodus. There was strong public sentiment in Canada against the settlement of Blacks, most of whom lived in segregated communities and were denied equal access to schooling. As a result of the attraction to the United States and the rejection they experienced in Canada, 60–70% of the Africans in Canada left in the 35 years after the war (Alexander and Glaze, 1996). By the time Canada became a country in 1867, only 21,000 Africans remained (Malarek, 1987). The population continued to decline into the 20th century, and did not grow significantly until discriminatory immigration laws were changed and immigrants from the Caribbean began to arrive in Canada in the 1960s — partly as the result of well-researched and articulate political action by members of the African Canadian community (Alexander and Glaze, 1996).

The immigration boom

In 1867, the British government passed the British North America Act, uniting some of the British North American colonies as the Dominion of Canada; other colonies joined later. The 'National Dream' was a country united from coast to coast, linked by a great railroad and sufficiently populated to resist annexation by the United States. New immigration was encouraged as a way of settling the west and strengthening consumer demand for Canadian-made goods. New legislation was passed establishing immigration policies and procedures that excluded criminals, paupers, and the destitute.

This was a boom period in immigration. Between 1867 and 1895, nearly a million and a half new immigrants arrived in Canada. Immigration reached its peak between 1896 and 1914, when nearly three million immigrants arrived. Some came as contract labourers to build the railway; many of these were viewed as a short-term solution to a labour shortage rather than permanent settlers. Many others came in response to advertising campaigns designed to attract settlers from Britain and other European countries.

The preference was for British immigrants, who would uphold the institutions and cultural values of the dominant culture and maintain English as the majority language. Other Europeans, including many Italian and Finnish immigrants, were admitted to fill labour needs as construction began on the railway. As the railroad pushed west, another 17,000 labourers were imported from southern China as a source of cheap labour. The work was back-breaking and dangerous but many believed they would make enough money to return wealthy to China. However, few realized this dream; they were paid considerably less than other workers, many of whom resented cheap Chinese labour for keeping all wages low. Many Chinese in Canada remained after the completion of the railroad, doing a variety of menial and manual work, still at wages lower than those offered to Europeans. Resentment against them became so strong that in 1885 the government restricted Chinese immigration by imposing a 'head tax' of $50 on every Chinese immigrant entering the country.

The railroads opened up the territory to increased immigration, mainly from Europe. In the last decade of the 19th century, there was a major change in immigration policy. Clifford Sifton, as Minister of the Interior, developed ambitious plans to populate the prairies with new settlers. Advertisements offering free land to new settlers were placed in newspapers in Britain and, when this failed to attract people in sufficient numbers, similar advertisements appeared in Eastern Europe. Sifton is famous for his claim that 'a stalwart peasant in a sheepskin coat, born on the soil, whose forebears have been farmers for ten generations, with a stout wife and half a dozen children, is good quality' (cited in Malarek, 1987: 6). By the turn of the 20th century 75,000 Ukrainians had arrived in Canada. In spite of Sifton's praise of them, they were not usually welcomed by more established groups. Like the Chinese, they were employed in gruelling labour, underpaid, and often fiercely resented. Some French Canadians feared that the government intended to over-whelm the French minority by importing large numbers of people into English-speaking Canada (Malarek, 1987).

In the early years of the 20th century, new restrictions were placed on the immigration of non-Christians and non-Europeans. It was argued that these groups could not assimilate readily and could not adapt to Canada's climactic conditions (even though the Chinese and the Africans had already demonstrated that they could). The head tax on Chinese immigrants was increased to $100 in 1900, and to $500 in 1903. Meanwhile, racist interpretations of the theory of evolution were used to justify the exclusion of Blacks from immigration to Canada (Alexander and Glaze, 1996).

New sources of immigration included Japan and India. Most immigrants from these countries sailed to British Columbia, on the West Coast, where anti-Chinese feelings were already strong. In Vancouver, 2000 marchers whose banners included the messages 'Keep Canada White' and 'Stop the Yellow Peril' sparked a race riot which resulted in several deaths. The government began to take action to exclude non-European immigrants. A new regulation was passed, requiring all Asian immigrants to have $200 in their possession on arrival. This put immigration to Canada out of reach for all but a few Asian immigrants. In addition, the government negotiated an agreement with Japan to restrict immigration to Canada to 400 persons per year. In 1923, this figure was reduced to 150. In the same year, the Chinese Immigration act was passed; this legislation virtually closed the door to 'persons of Chinese origin or descent, irrespective of allegiance or citizenship' (cited in Malarek, 1997: 9).

It was more difficult to exclude immigrants from India because technically they were citizens of the British Empire. However, the government was able to keep out most Indian immigrants through devising the 'continuous journey' regulation requiring that new immigrants arrive on a ship that had made a non-stop journey from the country of origin. As there were no shipping lines operating non-stop routes between India and Canada, this strange rule had the desired effect.

In 1914, in an effort to get around this regulation, an Indian businessman chartered a Japanese ship, the *Komagata Maru*, anchored in Hong Kong harbour, to transport Indian residents of Hong Kong directly to Vancouver. The ship arrived in Vancouver in with 376 Indian passengers, almost all of whom were Sikhs. They were denied entry to Canada, and after months of legal argument and racial conflict, during which time the Indians remained on board and the ship was placed under guard, the ship was escorted out to sea.

Immigration declined sharply during the First World War and, in 1919, new immigration regulations excluded those whose cultural and linguistic backgrounds were deemed to make then unassimilable: that is, non-Europeans. In addition, 'preferred' and 'non-preferred' source countries were identified. Immigrants from Britain and the United Sates were preferred; next in order of preference were immigrants from northern and western Europe, and after them immigrants from central and eastern Europe. Southern Europeans were less desirable, and Jews were treated as a separate category, regardless of their countries of origin (Malarek, 1987). Some of these restrictions were eased during the 1920s in response to local economic needs, although the restrictions on Asians were not removed.

During the Depression, only the wives and children of established residents, and those with sufficient money to establish a farm, were permitted to enter. Immigration all but ceased during the Second World War. During this period, xenophobia reached new heights and more than 22,000 Japanese Canadians were stripped of their property and interned in prison camps. Also during this period, Anti-Semitism was strong in Canada, especially in Quebec, and the Canadian government was very reluctant to accept Jews attempting to escape the Nazi terror in Europe. For example, in 1939, a ship carrying more than 900 Jewish refugees arrived in Halifax, Nova Scotia; the Jews were refused entry and the ship was turned back to Europe, where many of the passengers eventually became victims of the Holocaust (Abella and Troper, 1982). Other governments were more humanitarian in their approach: for example, the United States admitted 200,000 Jewish refugees, and Britain, fighting a war on its own doorstep, found room for 70,000. More than a 100,000 went to various countries in South America, and 25,000 were admitted to China. In contrast, Canada admitted fewer than 5000 Jewish refugees during the years of the Nazi terror in Europe.

During the post-war economic boom, large numbers of people from Europe left their ravaged homelands to seek a better life in 'the colonies' or in the United States. In Britain, meanwhile, people from the British Commonwealth, especially from the

Caribbean and from India, were recruited to run basic services, especially in health care and transportation, and to fill lower paid jobs in the manufacturing sector.

In Canada, Prime Minister Mackenzie King acknowledged Canada's need for more people in order to promote economic growth but reaffirmed the preference for Europeans:

> the people of Canada do not wish, as a result of mass immigration, to make any fundamental alteration in the character of our population. Large-scale immigration from the Orient would change the fundamental composition of the Canadian population. Any considerable Oriental immigration would, moreover, be certain to give rise to social and economic problems of a character that might lead to serious difficulties in the field of international relations. The government, therefore, has no thought of making any changes in immigration regulations which would have consequences of that kind. (cited in Malarek, 1987: 15)

A new Immigration Act in 1952 still allowed the government to restrict entry to persons on the basis of their country of origin or ethnic group and to exclude people of Chinese, Indian, and African origin or ancestry (Malarek, 1987). With a few exceptions, such as a program that admitted women from the Caribbean to enter as domestic servants, these restrictions remained in effect until the 1960s.

New sources of immigration

In the last three decades, immigration policy in Canada has gradually become less restrictive, partly in response to an increased awareness of human rights and social justice, but also because, as Europe recovered, people were no longer anxious to leave western Europe, while eastern Europeans were not always free to leave. Western Europe also began importing labour from other countries after the Second World War. Today, individual assets such as educational background, age, work skills, and financial wealth are more important than ethnicity in determining an individual's eligibility for immigration.

Canada currently seeks to attract immigrants through a variety of programs. Each year, a target for immigration is established. For example, in 1990 new higher targets of 250,000 per year were announced in a five-year plan. The target was not always reached: in 1994, 217,000 new immigrants were admitted to Canada (Citizenship and Immigration Canada, 1995a). The Immigration Plan for 1996 set a target of between 195,000 and 220,000.

Immigrants are carefully selected in several categories. Independent immigrants are selected for their ability to contribute to the economy and fill labour-market gaps. For example, there is a need for 'high-tech' workers, certain kinds of skilled labour, and for people who will fill service jobs such as child care and hospital care that many 'older' residents are no longer inclined to do. In addition, family reunification programs enable people who are already established to sponsor relatives to join them. Refugee acceptance procedures are also established to select a quota of refugees among the total number of immigrants accepted.

Current trends in immigration are based on 'an ambiguous mixture of compassion and pragmatism' (Fleras and Elliott, 1992: 44). Policies are formed and informed by the interplay between pragmatic considerations and altruism in Canada, and political and economic events and conditions in other countries. These policies have a direct impact on communities and on the schools that serve them.

A pragmatic approach

Immigration policy in Canada changes constantly, usually for pragmatic reasons. The chart shows Canadian immigration levels over the last century and a half, and relates them to some contemporary political and economic factors.

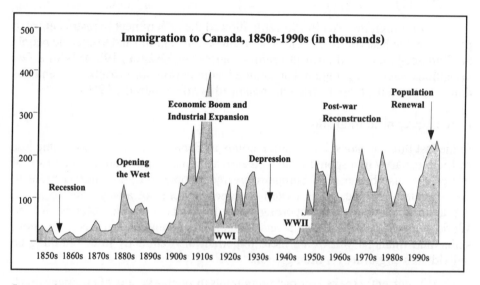

Source of immigration data: Employment and Immigration Canada, 1992; Citizenship and Immigration Canada, 1995a

During the late 1980s and throughout the 1990s, immigration to Canada increased in spite of the economic recession that began in the late 1980s. Higher immigration levels were established in recognition of the need to stimulate the economy and compensate for an aging population.

The pool of potential immigrants still consists of many millions of people. Today, as in the past, Canadian immigration policy is designed to select people who are perceived as likely to make the greatest contribution to the country. According to Fleras and Elliot, contemporary immigration policy in Canada reflects 'political calculation and economic expediency' (Fleras and Elliott, 1992: 44). For example, the acceptance of independent immigrants depends on current labour market demands. Immigrants are carefully selected for their ability to contribute to the economy and fill labour-market gaps. In order to be accepted as independent immigrants, potential immigrants must score a certain number of points allocated for such factors as level of education, knowledge of English or French, training and job experience, pre-arranged employment, and the current demand for the occupation in Canada. Labour-market demands are monitored very closely, and Canadian immigration officers all over the world regularly receive updated guidelines on high-demand and low-demand jobs. The age of the applicant is also significant. The preference is for those who have completed their education and training, and still have several decades to participate in the workforce and contribute to taxes. Recently, there has also been an emphasis on importing capital and entrepreneurial skills through the recruitment of immigrants who can transfer capital and invest in their new country. For example, during the 1990s, billions of dollars flowed into Canada from Hong Kong in anticipation of the colony's transfer to China in 1997.

The Canadian government views immigration as a means of revitalizing and expanding the economy. For example, the Minister of Citizenship and Immigration said in the House of Commons, Ottawa, on 1 November 1995:

> Canada needs immigrants. I can't put it more simply than that. Our country needs workers and investors to maintain and improve our standard of living. We need them to help us keep sparking our economy — and to create jobs . . . maintaining and improving the standard of living of every Canadian relies, in part, on keeping a vibrant and dynamic immigration system . . . Immigrants and refugees become some of the best, brightest, most self-motivated, hardest-working Canadians. And that's why we are actively promoting Canada as a place to come and settle. These are the people who will work with us to build a stronger, more economically dynamic country. (Citizenship and Immigration Canada, 1995b: 2)

Another pragmatic concern is the changing demographic composition of the Canadian population. The combined effects of a large post-war generation that is now aging, increased life expectancy, and a steadily declining birth rate have increased the proportion of the Canadian population over 65. Many economists and politicians have identified a need to counter this trend by bringing in new, younger residents. As Fleras and Elliott point out, 'the immigrants of today are likely to underwrite the costs of the delivery of social services in the future. For this reason alone, we are as dependent on immigrants as they are on us' (Fleras and Elliott, 1992: 46).

Altruism

Altruism also plays a role in contemporary Canadian immigration policy. For example, family reunification programs acknowledge family-based support for newcomers and encourage immigrants who might not otherwise have ventured away from home, or who might not have been accepted as independent applicants. Immigration policies also establish procedures for the admission of refugees from countries that are recognized as refugee-producing because of civil war, or because they are governed by corrupt or tyrannical régimes that violate human rights. The Geneva Convention defines refugees as those who have left their country of origin and have reasonable grounds to fear persecution if they return. The Convention recognizes persecution on the basis of race, religion, nationality, political opinion, or membership in a particular social group. In some cases, Canada also accepts claims by individuals who are threatened by persecution on grounds other than those recognized by the Convention, such as gender.

Events in other countries

Historically, immigrants left their homelands for a variety of reasons, such as to escape religious or political persecution, to flee from war, poverty, or famine, or to seek land ownership or increased economic opportunity. Today, people emigrate for the same reasons, but the patterns of emigration and immigration continually change. Whereas until the middle of the 20th century immigrants were predominantly from European countries, recent immigrants to Canada and other English-speaking countries are predominantly Asian, African, Caribbean, or Latin American. In the last few years, many thousands of Asian immigrants and refugees have migrated to North America and Australasia.

Top ten countries of birth for all immigrants and recent immigrants to Canada

All immigrants living in Canada		*Recent immigrants (arrived between 1981 and 1991)*	
Country	*%*	*Country*	*%*
UK	16.5	Hong Kong	7.8
Italy	8.1	Poland	6.3
USA	5.7	People's Republic of China	6.1
Poland	4.3	India	5.9
Germany	4.2	UK	5.8
India	4.0	Vietnam	5.6
Portugal	3.7	Philippines	5.2
People's Republic of China	3.6	USA	4.5
Hong Kong	3.5	Portugal	2.9
Netherlands	3.0	Lebanon	2.8

Source: Badets and Chui, 1994

**Top ten source countries of immigrants
to Canada: 1994**

Country	%
Hong Kong	20.0
Philippines	8.6
India	7.6
China	5.6
Taiwan	3.4
Sri Lanka	2.9
Vietnam	2.8
USA	2.8
UK	2.7
Bosnia-Herzegovina	2.2
Others	41.3

Source: Citizenship and Immigration Canada, 1995a

Immigrants are generally classified as voluntary immigrants and refugees. Voluntary immigrants usually choose to leave their homelands to make a better life elsewhere. The 'push factors' that propel them out of their homelands include limited economic opportunity and limited access to education. Prospective immigrants are attracted to countries that provide universal education, offer good health care and other social programs, have a high standard of living, are safe and peaceful, have an international reputation for respecting human rights, and have policies that promote and support immigration. These are often referred to as 'pull factors' that attract new immigrants.

Unlike voluntary immigrants, refugees leave their homelands not by free choice, but because they have no other choice. Refugees are fleeing for their lives and have little choice about where they will settle; they usually go to any country that will offer them a safe place to live and to bring up their children. The 'push factors' that drive refugees out of the country where they are living include war, religious persecution, and political oppression.

The following chart shows the top ten source countries of those accepted into Canada as refugees; events in these countries have been reported in newspapers and broadcasts all over the world.

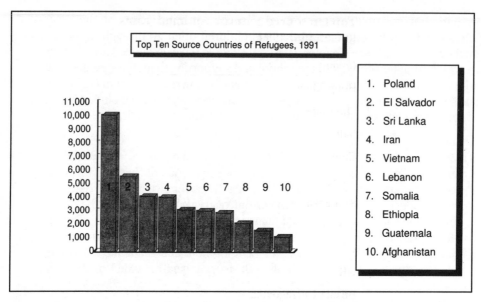

Source of immigration statistics: Employment and Immigration Canada, 1992

Implications for schools

Cultural diversity is a historical phenomenon, not a recent one. However, it is the increased diversity resulting from recent immigration trends that has caught the attention of many educators in Canada. For example, there is a changed awareness of human rights and equity, and the cultural domination of some groups is being challenged. Most school districts have developed policy statements indicating that one of the roles of the school is to provide all students with experiences that will help them to live well-adjusted lives in a multicultural society, and programs for multicultural and antiracist education have been established in various forms in most urban school districts in Canada. In addition, concern is frequently expressed about the differential performance of various groups in the education system. Aware that traditional pedagogy and curriculum content may not be effective with all students in a multicultural setting, many teachers are diversifying their methods of instruction (see Chapter 6) and incorporating multiple perspectives into the curriculum (see Chapters 7 and 8).

Immigration policies have a direct impact on schools in the areas where immigrants tend to settle: usually in urban areas and often, at least during the initial period of resettlement, in poorer neighbourhoods. In some areas of Toronto, for example, more than 50% of the students have arrived from other countries within the previous five years. In many schools, a language other than English is the home language of most of the students. While the experience may be less dramatic in other areas and in other countries, immigration clearly creates special challenges for the education system. For example, teachers need a special understanding of the process of adjustment that immigrant families and children often go through in the first few years after arrival (see Chapter 2). Many schools have developed a variety of ways of welcoming newcomers to the school and supporting them through the process of adjustment to a new cultural environment and a new school system (see Chapters 3 and 4). Teachers are exploring ways of helping everyone to feel included as members of the school and classroom community (see Chapters 4 and 5).

Schools that receive students from refugee-producing countries are directly affected by world political events. For example, in the 1980s, Somali refugees began arriving in Canada. Because of political upheaval and conflict in their homeland, and because many families had been in transit for several years, many of the children had experienced little or no schooling prior to arrival and had not had the opportunity to develop literacy in their first language. In many schools, existing English as a Second Language programs were not sufficient to help children learn English and catch up to their age peers in literacy development and academic knowledge and skills. Some schools and school districts reorganized or added to their existing resources in order to provide services such as special literacy classes or bilingual tutoring (see 'Support Services' in Chapter 4).

ATTITUDES TOWARDS IMMIGRATION

Official policy welcomes immigrants and pays tribute to their contribution, but immigrants may not be welcomed by some members of the host society.

Immigrants in Canada, as elsewhere, are often a target of prejudice and discrimination, especially in times of unemployment and economic recession. Among the many myths and misconceptions are the following: immigrants 'take people's jobs', 'cause pressure in the housing market' and are 'a drain on the social services', while refugees often 'jump the immigration queue' by making 'bogus claims' about persecution. Some established residents may regard immigration as a benefit to the immigrant only: an altruistic gesture of goodwill towards those unfortunate enough to have been born as citizens of 'less developed' economies, a humanitarian rescue of the victims of war and persecution, or a burden on the host society.

Public opinion on immigration is often founded on inaccurate or inadequate information. Many established residents are unaware of the ways that immigration continues to foster the growth and development of the country. It is important, then, that the education system take some responsibility for reducing prejudice through public education about immigration. To counteract the negative stereotype of immigrants, schools can help to create informed public opinion, and provide a welcoming environment for new residents. Teachers who work in multiracial schools can share unbiased information about immigration and immigrants, not only with the children of immigrants and the children who represent the host community, but also with parents and colleagues. For example:

- Immigration is an important resource to the host country: a workforce whose education and training were provided in the country of origin. For example, recent immigrants to Canada are more likely to have a university degree than Canadian-born residents (Badets and Chui, 1994). Middle class and professional immigrants are attracted by the opportunity to take up similar positions in developed countries, for much greater material reward. Many students educated abroad also apply for permanent resident status when their studies are completed. This creates a 'brain drain' from the home country, which has invested its scarce educational resources in the training of this group. The home country's lost asset is the host country's gain. The medical and engineering professions in North America include a high proportion of immigrants who were educated partly or wholly at the expense of a developing country. Therefore, a country's investment

Cartoon: Peter Pickersgill for the *Toronto Star*, 17 July 1994

in immigration, in terms of education, language training, and refugee resettlement programs, are outweighed by the benefits received. However, this rationale is repellent to those who would prefer to see immigration policies that help to equalize the world status quo rather than increase the economic advantage that affluent countries already have over the rest of the world.

• The media help to form public opinion by focussing on sensational cases and by using language in ways that alarm rather than inform. For example, the use of such terms as 'flood', 'wave', or 'influx' imply that the host society is in danger of being overwhelmed by newcomers. In addition, a tendency for some media sources to focus on sensational events involving members of various ethnocultural groups creates a distorted impression of the integration of those groups into Canadian society. For example, this appeared as the main headline on the front page of *The Toronto Sun* (10 February, 1997: 1):

FLOOD OF REFUGEES SWAMPING CANADA
Huge jump in claimants from peaceful countries chokes review process

On the inside pages of the same edition, photographs of would-be immigrants at Canadian immigration offices in Jamaica and Hong Kong accompanied stories with these headlines (p. 4):

Refugee claims jump 75%
More than 30,000 cases clogging system

Citizenship fraud feared

These headlines conjure up alarmist visions but careful reading of the stories suggests that the problems may be largely administrative in nature, rather than abuses of the system by would-be immigrants and refugee claimants. For example, the 'flood' of refugee claimants includes a 'backlog' of cases pending from previous years, and one of the country's 19 citizenship judges says the system of granting citizenship is 'open to fraud' because of cutbacks in the system.

Teachers can help students, parents, and colleagues become more critical consumers of the media by presenting alternative sources of information and points of view. Contrary to the impression created by some media reports, the flow of immigrants is controlled, and is designed to counteract population decline in major industrialized nations. For example, although Canada receives more immigrants per capita than any other country in the world, present immigration levels are not the highest in history, and current annual intake levels of about 1% of the total population are close to the average for this century. The proportion of Canadians born outside the country has remained more or less constant over time. The 1991 Canadian census shows that the immigrant population represents 16% of the total population of Canada; in 1951, this proportion was 15% (Statistics Canada, 1992). Also, between 50,000 and 75,000 individuals *emigrate* from Canada annually; so the net gain in population is considerably smaller than is shown by the immigration statistics alone (Kaprielian-Churchill and Churchill,

1994). Public perceptions, then, about the high numbers of immigrants are not based on fact; however, as the racial composition of the immigrant population has changed, immigrants have become more 'visible', and this is the real source of concern for many established residents.

- Immigrants contribute to the economy as consumers, taxpayers, and producers. Immigrants bolster consumer demand with the very first purchase they make, and create work when they use public services such as education. Immigrants in Canada pay sales tax on everything they buy, and contribute to property taxes or local rates through the first rent they pay. Immigrants pay income tax, and although an immigrant's first job is likely to be a low-paid one that established residents consider beneath them, over time, immigrants in Canada can catch up to the native-born population in earning power and revenue contribution. Some immigrants — especially males from 'traditional' (i.e. white European) sources — tend to do better than the native-born population, although females and persons of colour remain relatively disadvantaged (Fleras and Elliott, 1992). Immigrants aged 25 to 44 participate in the labour force at about the same rate as their Canadian-born peers, while immigrants aged 45 and older are more likely to be working than their Canadian-born counterparts (Badets and Chui, 1994). Immigrants generally receive less support from social services than other Canadians. This is because good health is one of the requirements for entry, and because most immigrants are young; 77% admitted to Canada during the 1980s were under 40, and 57% were under 30 (Employment and Immigration Canada, 1992). This healthy, youthful, immigrant population will contribute to the labour force and public revenue for an extended period of time.

- Most immigrants generally make law-abiding and loyal new citizens. Studies in the United States, Canada and Australia have consistently shown that immigrants commit fewer crimes than the native-born population (*Toronto Star*, 1994). In Canada, an increasing proportion of immigrants — about 81% of those eligible — demonstrate a commitment to their new country by choosing to become citizens (Statistics Canada, 1992).

Public and political attitudes toward cultural diversity have resulted in the adoption of various policies designed to manage diversity. Some of these are discussed in the next section.

MANAGING CULTURAL DIVERSITY

Cultural diversity has been viewed differently in different times and places, and various metaphors such as 'the melting pot', 'the salad bowl', or 'the cultural mosaic' have been used to describe different approaches to managing diversity. As cultural diversity becomes the norm in many industrialized countries and major urban centres, governments and educational planners have moved along a continuum from segregation, through assimilation, towards cultural fusion or cultural pluralism as a strategy for managing ethnocultural diversity. These strategies or approaches are not always clearly delineated in practice and elements of each approach often co-exist.

Segregation

Segregation entails the legally enforced separation of different cultural and racial groups. Policies of segregation are designed to limit the participation of minorities in decision-making — even when the minorities actually constitute a numerical majority — and serve to ensure the continuing economic and political dominance of some groups and the subordination of others. The best-known examples of this ideology in action are the racial segregation that was enforced in the southern United States prior to desegregation in the 1950s and 1960s, and the system of Apartheid that existed until recently in South Africa. Less known is the fact that segregated schools for children of African ancestry existed in Ontario and Nova Scotia until the 1960s.

Segregation also exists informally, without the sanction of the government: for example, when social clubs restrict the participation of certain groups, as was the case when Jews were refused entry to certain Canadian social and country clubs. Sometimes, institutions effectively exclude some minorities by setting up certain stipulations that appear neutral, but that serve to limit the participation of specific groups, as was the case when some branches of the Canadian Legion insisted that all members must bare their heads, including Canadian Sikh veterans of the second World War.

Few people in English-speaking countries today openly support segregation as an approach to managing diversity. However, some current practices do serve to segregate one group from another. For example, the provision of publicly funded separate or parochial schools for specific religious denominations can be regarded as segregated schooling. There is also *de facto* segregation in many urban and suburban areas, where the patterns of geographic and economic separation that exist in the community are reflected in the ethnic make-up of the school. In some jurisdictions in the United States, the way public funds are allocated to schools results in what Kozol eloquently describes as 'savage inequalities' in the distribution of resources, so that poor and minority children in inner-city schools receive an education far inferior to that of their white peers living in suburban or more affluent areas (Kozol, 1991).

Assimilation

Assimilation is a one-way process of absorption whereby minorities abandon, at least publicly, their ethnic identities. An assimilationist approach regards diversity as a problem, and cultural differences as socially divisive. In earlier decades, it was considered appropriate for immigrants and indigenous minorities, such as the Aboriginal peoples of Canada, to become completely assimilated, and education was regarded as one of the principal means of accomplishing this. For example, a

Canadian educator wrote in 1913 that 'the wisest method of teaching English will aim at eliminating for the time being from the learner's consciousness all memory or thought of his vernacular tongue' (Black, 1913: 106; cited in Cummins and Danesi, 1990: 10). According to Troper (1979: 9), one of Canada's great scholars of multiculturalism and ethnic history,

> The survival of active and distinct ethnic communities in Canada, especially before World War II, occurred in spite of public policy and sentiment not because of them. . . . Ethnicity, if tolerated at all, was seen as a temporary stage through which one passed on the road to full assimilation. Prolonged ethnic identification, especially among non-English speaking immigrants, not to mention their children and grandchildren, was seen as a pathological condition to be overcome, not as a source of national enrichment and pride.

Many established residents still feel that immigrants and ethnocultural minorities should drop their ethnic identities, including their languages, and assimilate into the mainstream. Assimilation was, and is, more feasible for some groups than others — for example, other white Christian Europeans, or those willing to adopt the external 'rituals and empty gestures of behavioural compliance' (Fleras and Elliott, 1992: 61). Some groups, especially those whose skin colour or other physical features marked them as 'minorities', could not assimilate as readily. In any case, as Banks points out, 'coerced assimilation does not work very well. [It] . . . is not authentic, is not perceived as legitimate by non mainstream populations, does not have moral authority, and is inconsistent with democratic ideals' (Banks, 1994: 4).

An assimilationist approach to education may be tolerated by some groups who do not see themselves as permanently changed if they adopt some of the outward behaviours of the dominant group. This tolerance is more prevalent among voluntary migrants (Ogbu and Matute-Bianchi, 1986). In contrast, some cultural groups were coerced into becoming became part of the society, through conquest, colonization, and enslavement (Ogbu, 1983, 1992, 1995). These oppressed groups were never given the opportunity to assimilate; instead, they were systematically denied equal opportunity over many generations, and had little hope of integrating into the mainstream culture or participating in society on an equal footing with the dominant group. Despite some progress towards equality of opportunity, groups such as African Americans and Aboriginal Peoples still constitute what Ogbu calls a 'caste-like minority' in their own country (Ogbu, 1983).

Some members of oppressed groups may resist assimilation into the culture of the oppressor and resist school as the agent of assimilation. For example, Solomon describes a group of Caribbean youth in Toronto who 'separate themselves from the dominant cultural group and no longer embrace the school as an avenue for making it in Canadian society' and who 'oppose the school structures they perceive as not serving their interest' (Solomon, 1992: 8 and 9). Some students are caught between a desire to gain the education they need in order to overcome oppression and marginalization, and a social identity that causes them to adopt an oppositional stance towards the school. The results may include further marginalization and even exclusion from the school, and a failure to gain the education that might have offered a way to counter oppression.

Cultural fusion

Cultural fusion differs from assimilation in that it involves a two-way process of adaptation and acculturation. Whereas assimilation is designed to eliminate diversity, fusion serves to incorporate diversity into the mainstream and, by so doing, change the mainstream. Education is an important means of creating a common cultural identity which merges majority and minority cultures. This is often referred to as *e pluribus unum:* out of many, one (Banks, 1993, 1994).

Cultural fusion has occurred many times in the past. The story of the English language is an example of the cultural fusion of Anglo-Saxons and Norman French speakers. Although there were, throughout the feudal period, clear status differences between the two groups, eventually the social distinctions vanished and the languages became one. Today, however, cultural fusion remains an ideal rather than a fact in most English-speaking countries. For example, the American version of this approach, often referred to as the 'melting pot' approach, has not resulted in a new cultural identity that contains elements of all the cultures present in the United States. Cultural diversity continues to exist and, while everyone has equal rights under the law, there are often large inequalities among the different cultural groups. In North America, there is still a dominant culture, which is fundamentally white, European, Christian, and English-speaking, and the curriculum in most schools reflects this perspective (see Chapters Seven and Eight for a discussion of this topic).

Cultural pluralism

This approach, like cultural fusion, is more of a concept than a practice at the present time. Often called multiculturalism, cultural pluralism involves creating a cohesive society where individuals of all backgrounds interact and participate equally, while maintaining their cultural identities. Unlike other approaches, which essentially view diversity as a problem, multiculturalism views diversity as an asset. For example, Canada's official multiculturalism policy 'openly promotes the values and virtues of diversity as a necessary, beneficial, and inescapable feature of Canadian society. It provides a framework that upholds the rights of minorities to retain aspects of their social past without loss of social equality' (Fleras and Elliott, 1992: 63). In Canada, this concept is idealized in the metaphor of the 'multicultural mosaic' where each culture contributes equally to the overall design, while retaining a distinctive identity. This is also referred to as the 'salad bowl' approach: each ingredient retains its own distinctive taste and appearance, but tastes better in combination with the others. This approach is perceived to be very different from the American 'melting pot' image in that official Canadian policy encourages cultural diversity rather than a cultural melding.

Whether the melting pot or the mosaic is the ideal, intolerance and inequalities still exist. In the school context, practice has not caught up to policy, and the education offered to most students remains Eurocentric (see Chapters 7 and 8 for more on this topic).

CONCLUSION

Teachers in multicultural schools need general background information on the sources of cultural diversity and on contemporary immigration policies and procedures, in order to understand how why their classrooms are becoming increasingly diverse. Teachers also need an awareness of public attitudes towards diversity, and of public policies aimed at managing diversity, because these have an impact on how students see themselves and each other. The information in this chapter provides this background knowledge. The chapter also establishes a historical and political context for the suggestions made in other chapters on how schools and teachers can include everyone in the school community and help to integrate diverse cultural groups into a just and harmonious society.

FURTHER READING

Abella, I. and Troper, H. (1982) *None is Too Many: Canada and the Jews of Europe: 1933–1948.* Toronto: Lester and Orpen Dennys. This book describes how the Canadian government turned away Jewish refugees, sending them back to Europe and almost certain extermination in the Holocaust.

Alexander, K., and Glaze, A. (1996) *Towards Freedom: The African–Canadian Experience.* Toronto: Umbrella Press. A rich source of information about 400 years of African history in Canada, this book links the past with contemporary events by exploring themes such as human rights, education, and immigration.

Cummins, J. and and Danesi, M. (1990) *Heritage Languages: the Development and Denial of Canada's Linguistic Resources.* Toronto: Our Schools/Ourselves. This book critically examines policy on linguistic diversity in Canada, especially in relation to the teaching of heritage languages in schools.

Cummins, J. (1996) *Negotiating Identities: Education for Empowerment in a Diverse Society.* Ontario, CA: California Association for Bilingual Education. This book is essential reading for all teachers in culturally diverse schools. Cummins views schools, teachers, and students as agents of social change: by challenging aspects of the existing power structure, and by valuing students' linguistic and cultural backgrounds, patterns of school failure among culturally diverse students can be reversed.

Ferguson, T. (1975) *A White Man's Country: An Exercise in Canadian Prejudice.* Toronto: Doubleday Canada Limited. The story of the *Komagata Maru*, a ship that arrived in Vancouver in 1914 with 376 passengers from India who hoped to immigrate to Canada. After months of legal argument, the Indians were refused entry to Canada and the ship was eventually escorted out to sea.

Fleras, A. and Elliott, J. (1992) *Multiculturalism in Canada: The Challenge of Diversity*. Scarborough, Ontario: Nelson Canada. The authors analyze past and present policy on immigration and multiculturalism in Canada.

Gilad, L. (1990) *The Northern Route*. St. John's, Newfoundland: Institute of Social and Economic Research, Memorial University of Newfoundland. This book is a case study of Canada's approach to resettlement. The author describes the journeys of refugees from six countries, through six more countries, to Newfoundland.

Herberg, E. N. (1989) *Ethnic Groups in Canada: Adaptations and Transitions*. Scarborough, Ontario: Nelson Canada. This book draws on more than a century of census information to describe how various groups in Canada have become integrated into Canadian society.

Kaprielian-Churchill, I., and Churchill, S. (1994) *The Pulse of the World: Refugees in Our Schools*. Toronto: OISE Press. This study reviews contemporary policy on refugees in Canada, and includes a case study of a Cambodian refugee camp. Contains recommendations for teachers, administrators, and government.

Kozol, J. (1991) *Savage Inequalities: Children in America's Schools*. New York, NY: Crown Publishers, Inc. A passionate and eloquent indictment of the *de facto* segregation that persists in America's schools, where educational resources are allocated unequally to children of different cultural and social class groups.

Malarek, V. (1987) *Haven's Gate: Canada's Immigration Fiasco*. Toronto: Macmillan of Canada. Written by a journalist, this highly readable book includes an overview of immigration history in Canada from the earliest colonial times to the present, as well as a critical look at current policies and procedures.

Matas, D., with Simon, I. (1989) *Closing the Doors: The Failure of Refugee Protection*. Toronto: Summerhill Press. The authors describe how immigration policies in Western countries deny refugees protection, and argue for changes in the refugee determination process.

Skutnabb-Kangas, T. and Cummins, J. (eds) (1988) *Minority Education: from Shame to Struggle*. Clevedon, England: Multilingual Matters. The articles in this book critically examine policies and models for minority education, especially assimilative models of education, and describe some alternatives to reverse patterns of school failure among many cultural groups.

Solomon, P. (1992) *Black Resistance in High School: Forging a Separatist Culture.* Albany, New York: State University of New York Press. An ethnographic study of Black students in Toronto, describing the conflict between their aspirations for the future and their resistance to assimilation.

CHAPTER 2

The Immigrant Experience

INTRODUCTION

Teachers in schools that receive students who have recently arrived from other countries, or whose parents are immigrants, need an awareness of the immigrant experience, and how the experience may affect the students and their families. This chapter provides an overview of the stages of acculturation that most newcomers go through as they adjust to life in a new country and a new cultural environment. This is followed by a description of some factors that may have an impact on the adjustment process, and on students' academic and social integration into the school. Next there is a description of some of the additional stresses that refugee families and children have to cope with, and some case studies of students in Toronto schools. The chapter concludes with a reminder that immigrants, like other groups, have strengths as well as needs.

A note of caution

Immigrant children and families are as diverse as children and families in every community. The information in this chapter is not intended to stereotype immigrants as a group, or to create the impression that all immigrants react to their new environment in the same way. While there are some experiences that many immigrants have in common, others have experiences that are completely different. Therefore it is very important not to view the information in this chapter as applicable to every family or all children, and not to expect all immigrant students to react in the same way or to have the same needs. The information is provided so that teachers have some awareness of and sensitivity towards the special needs that some immigrant families and children may have.

THE NEW ARRIVAL: STAGES OF ACCULTURATION

Immigrants arriving in a new country have already passed through several stages of transition from one life to another. For those who come directly from the home country to the new country, having planned and prepared for the move, the transition is relatively smooth. For others, the transition includes traumatic experiences of war or persecution, imprisonment, the murder or disappearance of family members, and flight. Many refugees arrive after a sojourn in another country, often in a refugee camp. It is important for those receiving new immigrant families in the school to be aware of the circumstances surrounding a family's decision to leave the home country, and the conditions experienced en route. For example, it is especially important to know if students have spent time out of school.

On arrival in the new country, immigrants begin a new period of transition as they adjust to their new environment and come to terms with their new circumstances. Immigrants commonly pass through four stages of acculturation and adjustment after arrival in their new country (Kim, 1988; Brown, 1992). However, it is important not to overgeneralize this process. Different individuals — even members of the same family — may pass through these stages at different rates, or even skip a stage. The stages are not always clearly delineated; sometimes they overlap, so that an individual may appear to have reached a certain stage of acculturation in one area of life, but remain at an earlier stage in another. For instance, children who enter welcoming and supportive classrooms may become comfortable and confident at school long before they are comfortable interacting with strangers or in less familiar contexts in the wider society. Some immigrants report feelings of great optimism and seem to experience little or no difficulty during the transition period, while others experience great pain and frustration and sometimes become 'stuck' in the second stage.

The stages of acculturation are:

• Arrival and first impressions
• Culture shock
• Recovery and optimism
• Acculturation

The following descriptions of each stage are illustrated by students' own recollections (Porter, 1991) and anecdotal reports from a research study (Yau, 1995).

Arrival and first impressions

During the first few days and weeks there may be a feeling of adventure, optimism, and even euphoria, during which many immigrants celebrate their good fortune in having embarked on a new phase in life, or in having escaped from a desperate situation in the home country. At the same time there is a good deal of anxiety. The family is very busy dealing with practical problems such as finding a place to live, finding work, or registering the children in school. Some newly-arrived children may behave as observers rather than participants in classroom situations as they try to figure out what is going on.

First days

Most immigrants have clear recollections of their first days in the new country:

When I first saw Toronto from the airplane, it seemed so green. I remember looking out at the blue sky and feeling happy, excited, and a little scared. We had come prepared with our coats handy, waiting to face the 'frozen country' outside . . . We walked out on a June summer day with our coats on . . .

Since then, Canada has held many surprises. The frozen country in my old geography book has come to life. Caroline Moraes (Porter, 1991: 24)

I still remember the day I first arrived in Toronto from my country, Korea. I said to myself with my swollen heart that it was the place where my new life would begin and imagined my bright future.

Everything was surprising and exciting to me from the first day. Everybody was friendly and kind, as I had heard they would be. Especially in my uncle's store, customers always said 'Thank you,' to me every time I finished serving them. I was very happy.

. . . When summer came, it was more surprising. Most people walked almost naked and I found it fascinating that young couples kissed on the street, or even in school, and nobody seemed to be aware or care. However, it became usual and casual to me and I got used to seeing it. Joseph Park (Porter, 1991: 21)

Culture shock

Culture shock involves feelings of discomfort, dislocation and alienation as the newcomer begins to identify aspects of the new environment that are intimidating or distasteful, at odds with the individual's previous experience, values, and world view. The individual may experience great emotional fluctuation between feelings of curiosity, adventure, and optimism, and feelings of sadness, loss, and despair. Even voluntary immigrants experience feelings of grief in response to the loss of family and the loss of the culture that sustained them and gave them a sense of identity. The experience of immigration has been compared with that of bereavement in terms of its traumatic impact on the individual (Disman, 1983). This is a period of anxiety and frustration during which difficulties in communication make the task of learning to live in a new culture seem insurmountable. Individuals may feel that the majority culture is a threat to their sense of identity and completeness, and may seek support by bonding more closely with members of their own ethnic group. Others who are able to may return to the home country or migrate to another.

It is often the case that different members of a community or a family have different experiences during this stage. Some may feel the loss so intensely that they can feel no optimism about the future; they may become clinically depressed. Meanwhile, others may be more inclined to believe that things will get better and that this is a transitional period.

Living through culture shock

When I first came to school I had the most terrible time because of the language problem. I was surprised and happy to see how each teacher was nice to me whenever I asked something. However, I noticed that many ignorant students discriminated against me because of the colour of my skin and my poor English. I felt miserable and began to miss my country very much .... I went half crazy as I hardly said a word in school and understood none of what the teachers were saying. I didn't dare ask questions of the teachers because I was scared I would make mistakes. I began to hate our immigration to Canada. I hated my poor English. I hated school and I hated myself. It was much like living in hell.
Steve Lee (Porter, 199: p.57)

A number of adult Chinese students described how anxious and worried they were at the beginning because of the new environment and the language problem. They were all alone when they first arrived, and were afraid to go outside Chinatown. (Yau, 1995: 37)

Three young Vietnamese students who came recently reported that for a period of time they were frustrated and unhappy. For some time, one of the girls cried every day when she got home from school. (Yau, 1995: 42)

The school can play a role in supporting families through this period. The more positive experiences the school can provide for the newcomer, the more positive the child will feel about the future. For many parents, knowing that their children are adjusting well and that their educational future is assured can be a great comfort during this difficult period of their lives.

Recovery and optimism

Recovery from culture shock brings a renewed sense of optimism and autonomy. Immigrants and refugees are often extraordinarily resilient. The stresses that they have experienced and overcome may actually help them to develop coping skills and problem-solving strategies that will stand them in good stead throughout their lives. At this stage, although there are still feelings of pressure, the individual begins to feel competent in overcoming difficulties, including those associated with learning the new language. Students are able to communicate adequately for most day-to-day purposes with their peers and their teachers, and begin to feel they are making progress at school. Some may begin to make friendships with students outside their own cultural or linguistic group.

Looking forward to the future
After spending about a year feeling weak and grieving, I decided to console myself by studying hard and getting good marks. This made my classmates and

my teachers aware of my vivid existence in the class. I began to feel self-confident and become vivacious. My family was really delighted to see me doing fine in school and I became their hope. Now, all I had to do was keep studying hard, go to university, and become a 'big' man, so that my family would think that, after all, our immigration to Canada had been worthwhile. Steve Lee (Porter, 1991: 58)

At this stage individuals often have a clearer sense of the future and begin making long-term plans. For many, this is the point at which they accept that they are in the new country to stay, and adults apply for citizenship. Individuals begin to adopt cultural values and behaviours of the mainstream or dominant culture. The children usually do so earlier and to a greater extent than their parents.

Adapting to a new life
It seems to me that my immigration to Canada has changed me a great deal. It makes me feel independent when I compare myself to other Canadian teenagers. Because it is a struggle for me to become fluent in English, I am more quiet than I used to be or would like to be. Coming to Canada has also made me more mature than I used to be because I have to worry about many things which I never had to worry about in my native country. For example, I have to worry about my mother. Will she be able to keep her job? I worry about my father. Will he be able to leave Vietnam and join us soon? I worry about our finances. How can we save more money? These questions have gradually made me into a more serious person. Donna Phung (Porter, 1991: 15)

Acculturation

After a period that may last a year or two, or many years, most newcomers resolve internal conflicts by re-creating their identities. This resolution may take the form of assimilation into the mainstream, in which the original culture is discarded and the individual may abandon the first language, choosing to operate in English only.

Social psychologists suggest that complete assimilation may represent a total disjuncture between different parts of one's life, a rejection of one's former self, and a denial of identity; in fact, according to M. Freire, 'too complete an assimilation' has 'a negative adaptive value and would indicate an incomplete process of adaptation' (Freire, 1989: 3). This is not the goal of education in a multilingual, multicultural society.

Acculturation, on the other hand, involves acceptance of the new culture in a more integrated way. Many immigrants integrate both their realities by adopting some of the values and practices of the new culture while maintaining some aspects of the original culture. Many children adopt different cultural styles depending on the context and the relationship between themselves and the others in that context. This is highly adaptive behaviour, and children who can move comfortably between languages and cultures have learned to be flexible and socially responsive. In a multicultural society, everyone needs to develop this kind of sensitivity to cultural diversity, at school, in the workplace, and in the community. Schools can support successful integration by offering an inclusive curriculum that celebrates and validates the languages and cultures of all the students in the school community, as well as effective programs to teach the language of instruction.

A new identity

Integration is an attainable goal. For example, these high school students have succeeded in creating new bilingual, bicultural identities for themselves (Porter, 1991):

. . . now I find that being an immigrant is an added advantage, because I know at least two cultures and two languages. This means I have more choices in daily entertainment and job opportunities than do native-born Canadians.

Although I have been in Toronto for six years now, I still miss my native country occasionally, but I know I would also miss Canada tremendously if I went back. Slowly I have built around me a world which is part of me and of which I am a part. Ephrem Shui (Porter 1991: 296)

To be Canadian I simply have to be myself. If I cannot accept myself or appreciate others, how can I expect to live in this multicultural nation? To make my life in Canada worthwhile, I must share my unique heritage. Winston Loui (Porter 1991: 296)

I like the political freedom in Canadian society. Anyone can openly discuss international or domestic politics and politicians. This was not the case in my motherland, China. I also enjoy personal privacy in this society with regard to life-style and personal belongings such as bank accounts.

However, I feel that in some respects Canadians get carried away with freedom of expression. For instance, we, especially the younger generation, are exposed to excessive violence, obscene language, drugs, sex, and infidelity in movies, television programs, magazines, radio, and books. As a result, we may question our family values and weaken in our sense of responsibility towards others and towards society as a whole.

I cannot help but remember my golden years as a teenager in China. Unlike many teens in Canada who are in too much of a hurry to be like adults without fully realizing the implications, I loved my childhood. In those green years I learned many new ideas and enjoyed invaluable experiences in a safe and innocent environment where drugs and sex were never heard of. I grew up in a society with strong moral values and strong family ties. These I believe are very important to keep in my family in Canada. Belinda Binhua Wang (Porter 1991: 288)

I am lucky and grateful to experience two countries with different societies, cultures, and customs, and to be able to speak two languages. I think it is

wonderful because it helps me understand human relationships. I have learned
something which I could never have learned in any other way. I enjoy life better
because there is more colour in my life. I have two countries at the same time —
Canada and China. Gary Que (Porter 1991: 273)

Integration is also manifested in the development of bilingual competence. This
may not mean that the individual is equally proficient in both languages in all
contexts. Many bilingual children use each language in different domains. For
example, the home language may be the first language while the student uses English
for academic purposes, or for interaction with friends from different cultural
backgrounds. Many bilingual children think in the first language for specific tasks,
such as counting or calculating in mathematics. Some bilingual people feel that one
language is just 'better' than the other — more flexible or more expressive — for
some concepts or activities.

Immigrant parents may have less opportunity than their children to become
bilingual and bicultural, depending on their access and exposure to mainstream
culture through their participation in the workplace or in adult education. Schools
can help by providing programs specifically designed for adults in the community
who have recently arrived from other countries (see 'Parental Involvement' later in
this chapter and in Chapter 4).

FACTORS IN ADJUSTMENT AND ACCULTURATION

Individuals pass through the stages of adjustment and acculturation at different rates,
and may combine elements of each stage, or remain at a 'plateau' at one or more
stages for many years. Immigration and adjustment to a new culture is experienced
differently by individuals of the same cultural background, and even by siblings in
the same family, because there are many other factors such as age, social class,
family dynamics, and personality involved as well. The extent to which the 'host'
society and its institutions are responsive to the needs of recently arrived immigrants, and the effects of other stress factors that may exist, will have an effect on
the adjustment and acculturation process.

The stress of moving from one country to another does not, by itself, threaten
individual well-being or mental health; however, mental health is threatened when
a number of other 'risk factors' are added to those of immigration and resettlement
(Canadian Task Force on Mental Health Issues Affecting Immigrants and Refugees,
1988). These additional stress factors determine how much additional pressure a
family or an individual may have to cope with, which in turn will have an impact
on the academic and social integration of immigrant students into the new school
system.

Teachers and administrators who have an understanding of the process of
acculturation, and who are sensitive to the many additional pressures on their
immigrant communities, 'can provide the 'ounce of prevention' needed to ensure

that most newcomers will have as much chance as Canadian-born persons of maintaining their mental well-being, despite the stress of migration' (Canadian Task Force on Mental Health Issues Affecting Migrants and Refugees, 1988: i). Some of the 'risk factors' that teachers need to be aware of are outlined later in this chapter.

Family separation

It is quite common for immigrant families to arrive in stages. Often, one parent will arrive first, and send for spouse and children once he/she is established in a job and a place to live. This may be a matter of months, or of years.

Family reunification after years of separation is often extremely difficult for parents and children alike. If a family arrives as a unit, all members experience adjustment at the same time. There is a commonality of experience to help bind the unit together. However, if parents and children are adjusting to each other as to strangers whom they barely remember, there is an additional stress: one that some immigrant families never fully overcome. Spouses who have been separated have often adopted new roles and may have difficulty negotiating new ways of relating to each other.

Even when families arrive as a unit, the loss of extended family can have far-reaching effects. At a time of acute stress, family support systems are no longer available. Immigrant children and parents may be very reluctant to confide in teachers or guidance counsellors the problems they may be having at home or at school, particularly if they perceive the cultural gap between the teacher or counsellor and themselves to be so wide that there is little possibility of mutual comprehension. These feelings of isolation make many immigrant children feel very helpless.

Choice

It is much easier to adjust to a new situation if it is a situation of one's own choosing, while lack of choice and feelings of powerlessness may impede the adjustment and acculturation process. Voluntary immigrants choose to make this change in their lives, and generally feel positive about the new opportunities they hope to find. However, it is extremely rare for dependent children to have any involvement in the decision, and in some families the adult women have no say either. Refugees have little or no choice; most would not have chosen to leave but for catastrophic events in the home country, and most who leave have little or no choice about which country will offer them asylum. Refugees sponsored by non-governmental organizations have no choice about their destination in the new country, and may end up in a location where there are no members of their own linguistic or cultural group to help ease the transition.

Preparation and support

Those who choose to leave their countries and emigrate to another have time to prepare themselves financially and emotionally. Sponsored immigrants have relatives in the host country to help ease the transition, and are usually quite well-informed about the new country. However, some immigrants have little opportunity to prepare themselves for their new country. Refugee families, in particular, lack the time and resources that might enable them to prepare for the transition.

Immigrants who are joining an already established community often have access to resources and orientation services, as well as informal networks that serve a variety of important needs. These networks often stand in for the extended family networks that existed in the home country. For example, community networks help newcomers to find jobs, accommodation, and marriage partners, and provide 'insider' information on Canadian culture and the workings of Canadian institutions (Kaprielian-Churchill and Churchill, 1994). However, communities in exile are sometimes divided by the political or socioeconomic differences that separated them in the country of origin. These divisions are sometimes evident in school, where children may display hostility that originates in the home country, or parents may refuse to attend meetings where the other faction is present.

International students

International students or 'Visa students' are not permanent residents, but are included here because they experience many of the strains of adjustment that immigrants do, and often with fewer resources to support them. Foreign students may stay in the country as long as they have a valid student visa, which is given or extended after acceptance (and payment of fees) to an educational institution. In the last ten years there has been a significant increase in the number of visa students in public high schools in North America, mostly in the senior grades, preparing for entrance to a North American post-secondary institution.

Although they are fee-paying students, international students are not always from affluent families; in many cases, the extended family will make sacrifices to contribute to the support of a student and provide an education that might not be available at home because of intense competition for fewer spaces. Many international students, on completion of their studies, will return home in order to work and sponsor another relative for education overseas. Such students are under immense pressure to do well and honour their families, and are often anxious to complete their studies in the minimum amount of time. Because most international students are here only temporarily, they are unlikely to reach complete acculturation; were they to do so, the return home might be another difficult transition.

Most international students are away from home for the first time, dealing with shopping, cooking, laundry and other domestic chores, as well as with loneliness and homesickness. They often create their own support networks and spend many hours studying together. School personnel often express concern about the one-dimensional life many international students lead, and some schools form social organizations to meet their non-academic needs. Some schools and school boards provide individual and group counselling services to assist these students with personal and academic problems they may experience.

Environmental factors

Most immigrants settle in large cities in the new country. For many, this is their first experience of life in a large urban centre, and their first experience of apartment life. This kind of transition represents a major lifestyle change even when it takes place within the same country; with the additional stress of being in a strange country, many immigrants have difficulty in adjusting to the new environment. They may be anxious about activities that other residents do as a matter of course, such as using public transit. Parents may worry about the safety of their children on the way to and from school, or about the safety of the elevator in the apartment building.

Apartment-living isolates families from each other in a way that living in a house in a neighbourhood does not. Immigrant women in particular, especially those who maintain a traditional role, 'may become increasingly isolated, secluded in thousands of apartment cells, often yearning for a country to which they can never return' (Canadian Teachers' Federation, 1990: 6). Moreover, apartment life requires each family to spend much more time together in very close quarters, and if relationships are strained this becomes another source of stress.

Adjusting to a different climate is also physically stressful. The first winter may be very difficult for immigrant families from warmer countries. Weather forecasts of temperature and wind-chill factors mean little to those who have not experienced them, even if they understand the language in which they are broadcast. Wearing so many clothes feels awkward and bulky, and the cost of buying different clothes for different seasons creates financial difficulty as well.

Cultural isolation

Many immigrant families have very limited opportunities for social interaction with the mainstream culture. Many adults work in 'ghettoized' occupations such as textile work or contract cleaning, where the workforce is predominantly immigrant and often predominantly one language group. Children at school often socialize within their own cultural group; the older they are the more evident this is. It is difficult for newcomers to integrate socially when they don't speak English, don't know current adolescent jargon, don't know the rituals and symbols of the peer culture, and may even prefer not to be noticed at all for the first few months.

Immigrants rarely receive invitations into the homes of their co-workers or classmates unless they are of the same cultural and social class background. This may not be because the host community is cold or unfriendly, as many immigrants perceive it to be, but because the social structure of the workplace or classroom provides insufficient opportunities for different groups to get to know each other and recognize commonalities.

Current practices in organizing English as a Second Language (ESL) programs may promote or impede social and racial integration among schoolchildren. In some jurisdictions, ESL learners are placed in ESL or bilingual programs for all or most of the day. This may seem to be an effective way of meeting the needs of the learners and their teachers, but the fewer opportunities the ESL learners have for interaction with their English-speaking peers, the more socially isolated they are likely to be. In other jurisdictions where a program of 'ESL integration' is implemented, ESL learners are placed in the mainstream program for most of the day, with support for the student and for the classroom teacher from an ESL teacher. An effective program of supported integration can provide newcomers with opportunities for social integration as well as second language acquisition (Handscombe, 1989).

Unless the school and classroom program is structured in such a way as to promote positive intercultural interaction, students who do not belong to the dominant or mainstream cultural group have little opportunity to find out first-hand about mainstream and other cultures; similarly, members of the mainstream culture have little opportunity to develop non-stereotypical views of other cultures, and may develop a distorted view of reality that exaggerates the importance of their own group.

Proficiency in English

Children who have had some exposure to English in their own countries, or whose language is related to English through Germanic or Latin roots, may feel relatively more confident about learning English. However, increasingly large numbers of immigrants are arriving from very different language backgrounds, where the script may not use the Roman alphabet. These students may be relatively less confident about learning English.

Learning English

Students describe their feelings about themselves as learners of English (Porter, 1991):

After arriving in Canada, it seemed to me that the most important challenge for me was the new language, English. I had no English background in my native country. The first step in learning English was the alphabet. In the beginning, I wrote very slowly, and my handwriting was awful.

I went to elementary school in a special class which was for students from other countries to learn English. But all the other students were better than I in English, and I was the only one who spoke no English. This made me nervous and lonely. Fortunately, there were some Chinese students in the class. I did not know what to do when the other students spoke to me because I did not understand them. I was forced to use signs with my hands to communicate with people, just as if I were deaf and dumb. I hated the students who spoke to me. When the teacher wanted to speak to me, he had to get the other students to translate. Sometimes there was a joke, and I had to laugh with the others even though I did not know what the joke was, because I was afraid of being laughed at. I hated myself for being in such a situation, and I wondered when I would be able to understand what the people were talking about! Gary Que (Porter, 1991: 56)

The feeling of exclusion and isolation from the life of the school and the community of the classroom is one of the most painful memories for many young immigrants, as this poignant comment attests:

Sometimes a teacher makes jokes and students laugh a lot, but I just sit in my seat like a stone. How embarrassed I am. Hau Yu Wong (Porter, 1991: 52)

Previous educational experience

Learners who have been to school in their own countries, whose education has been uninterrupted, and who were experiencing at least average success, are likely to make a smoother transition to school in the new country. The new school system may be very different from the previous one, but the experience is still recognizable as schooling.

However, some immigrants are coming from countries where educational opportunities are extremely limited, or where education has been totally disrupted for a number of years by war and civil turmoil. Children with little or no educational experience, who may not yet have learned to read and write in their own language, or who have not yet developed some notion about schooling, books, and study, are likely to have a difficult time understanding what is required of them, and may be very afraid of the whole school environment. Some may be almost pedagogically paralyzed by culture shock.

The culture of the school

The culture of the school is the whole 'way of life' of the school, and includes the way the adults and children behave towards each other, the way children are expected to learn, the content of the curriculum, and the images and events that are celebrated in the school.

Student–teacher relations in most North American schools are very different from student–teacher relations in many other parts of the world. Some immigrant children and parents may be accustomed to schools where all the children wear uniforms and the teachers follow a dress code; where the students stand when the teacher enters the classroom, and whenever they are called on to answer a question; where teachers are addressed respectfully by name or title; where students seldom ask questions or initiate discussion, but wait to be called on. These and other symbols of 'respect' are highly ritualized and visible, and discipline is often strict and severe. Many immigrant students and their parents have a genuine respect for teachers, and many teachers find this refreshing in comparison with the way the profession may sometimes be regarded by students and parents of the majority culture.

'Just like a god'
This student expresses an opinion held by many recently arrived students:

One major difference I have seen is that Canadian students have no respect for the teacher. The teacher is just like a person who shouts all the time in the class, but in Pakistan, the teacher is just like a god or a prophet to the student. (Student from Pakistan)

In contrast, immigrant and minority children in North American schools may find an almost total lack of the symbols of respect that they recognize. Some newcomers are extremely uncomfortable with a classroom culture that allows students to leave their seats, work in groups, initiate discussion with the teacher, and joke with their peers or the teacher. They may be unable to discern the 'invisible discipline' that informs the other children how far the informality can go, and often conclude that there is no discipline or classroom structure at all. Some may withdraw from interaction in an unpredictable, incomprehensible environment. Others may become boisterous and playful, testing the limits of this new and strange classroom environment. For example, according to the teachers from one elementary school, their newly arrived Vietnamese students stood out because of maladaptive behaviour in class — 'creating chaos in classrooms', 'being aggressive and street-wise', 'showing little respect for teachers', 'often saying 'No' ', 'failing to obey rules', 'refusing to remain seated or do what the teachers asked', 'wandering around the classroom', 'doing their own thing', or 'shouting across to each other openly' (Yau, 1995: 43).

Another source of difficulty is the miscommunication that sometimes occurs when language and non-verbal behaviour communicate messages that were not intended. These cultural 'miscues' include cultural differences about how far apart speakers should stand; when and with whom it is appropriate to make eye-contact; how loudly one should speak; how directly one should express requests, warnings, advice, or refusals, or how to use tone to change or add meaning. Such miscues are the cause of much frustration in cross cultural communication.

The curriculum may be a source of cultural dissonance for recently arrived students. For example, the content of the curriculum may not reflect their presence, or may not relate to their experiences and values. Aspects of the 'hidden curriculum', such as the images and events that are celebrated in the school, also give strong messages about the relevance or importance of the different racial and cultural groups in the school. Chapters 7 and 8 explore these issues in detail. Also, learning styles may vary within and among various social and cultural groups; Chapter 6 includes suggestions on how teachers can diversify their instructional style to meet the needs of all the students in culturally and socially diverse classrooms.

Identity

For most immigrants, resettling in a new country involves coming to terms with a changed identity, which often includes membership in a cultural minority group. This is especially true for persons of colour. In their own countries they were likely to be able to identify with the majority population, and children were presented with authority figures (teachers, the judiciary, the medical profession, politicians, and other public figures) with whom they could identify as role models. In their new environment they may be presented with few positive images of people like themselves, and be in contact with few people of their own background who are in positions of respect and authority in the mainstream society. This can have a very negative impact on self-esteem, and damage a child's motivation to learn.

'Who am I?'

Some children may begin to question their own identity (Porter, 1991):

> *Of course, I am not Canadian. But it seems I am no longer Chinese either. Then, who am I? Who will I be? I feel so confused.* Xuan Cen (Porter, 1991: 23)

Others try to assume a new identity in order to fit in with their peers at school:

> *It was four years ago when I suddenly became a different person. I don't mean that I physically changed or anything, but my personality changed because I had been known as Khan and then I became Chris. When I came to school, I wanted the teacher to call me Chris because it was easy for them.* Chris Truong (Porter, 1991: 61)

Some students are given English names by their teachers; others take English names for themselves in order to save themselves and/or their teachers embarrassment. In both cases this may represent a denial or rejection of the student's identity.

The quest for identity is a normal part of adolescence; for students whose lives have been uprooted, this may be especially difficult (Kaprielian-Churchill and Churchill, 1994).

Socioeconomic status

Many skilled and professional immigrants are unable to find employment in their fields on arrival in the new country (Burke, 1992). There is often a systemic problem in that persons educated and trained overseas, and accepted as immigrants because of their education and training, have difficulty in getting their qualifications recognized by professional or trade organizations in the new country. Sometimes the immigrant cannot find appropriate work because adequate language training is not available, or because the individual needs updating and retraining in the field (for example, in the use of computers), or because many employers routinely discriminate against immigrant applicants (Henry and Greenberg, 1985). Many well-qualified immigrants find themselves forced to take low-paying service or manufacturing occupations where lack of English is not a problem — and where they will find little opportunity to improve it. For many, these jobs can become a dead end rather than a transition to the kind of employment they expected. Many working adults are emotionally exhausted from the frustration of being trapped in occupations for which they are overqualified and which do not provide the stimulus, challenge, or satisfaction they hoped for.

Downward mobility
Stories like this are common:

A teacher described one of his former students — a young refugee doctor. She was studying English each morning . . . , working as a cashier in a local store in the afternoon and pumping gas each evening. Her immediate goal was to save enough money to help her family in a camp. The prospect of her practising medicine in Canada seemed to him remote. (Kaprielian-Churchill and Churchill, 1994: 60)

This kind of underemployment represents a tremendous waste of human resources, and the effects on the family can be devastating. Children may begin to view their parents as diminished because of their loss of status. They may also feel responsible for what has happened to their parents, who are willing to sacrifice themselves for the sake of their children's opportunities in the new land.

We arrived at the airport where my father, who had come to Canada three years previously, greeted us. Unfortunately, my first impression of Canada was not a pleasing one because of my father, who looked weaker and older than he should have. It seemed to me that hard labouring work had taken away the strength, confidence, and dignity which he used to have when he was a colonel in Korea. Well, it might have been our fault because he had been working so hard to bring us to Canada, but that was the way I felt then. Steve Lee (Porter, 1991: 18)

Although immigrants as a group eventually catch up economically to their Canadian-born peers, this may take years. For older professionals, it may never happen. They do not have the time and may not have the flexibility to learn large amounts of technical terminology, or to learn the cultural nuances of a professional environment that may function in a very different way from a similar environment in the home country. Other immigrants, especially some refugees and family-sponsored immigrants, arrive with limited education or job training, and may never be able to rise far above the menial jobs they take on arrival. They perform important functions in the host society, especially in the service sector, but for much less material reward than they may have expected, and often less than most non-immigrants would accept.

As a result of these difficulties, many immigrant families experience extreme poverty, especially in the first few years after arrival. In Canada, for example, 31% of immigrant children are in low-income families, compared with 19% of Canadian children overall (Burke, 1992). Poverty is related to academic failure for children of all racial and cultural backgrounds, including those of the white majority culture. Growing up in poverty increases the chances that children will fail, drop out of school, and therefore be unprepared as adults to do the kind of work they will be expected to do in the changing economy of the new century (Lincoln and Higgins, 1991). Poverty does not make people stupid, but it does make it extremely difficult for families to provide the kind of environment and support that helps children to become successful at school (Hess, 1989). Recent studies in Canada confirm that children from lower income families are three times as likely to be in remedial classes as those from higher socioeconomic levels (Carey, 1997). At the same time, governments continue to cut programs that provide the social services, early childhood experiences and school funding that can make a difference (Carey, 1997; Philp, 1997). This does not mean that schools should blame the children and their families for their difficulties at school, and give up on these children as a lost cause; on the contrary, schools have to make special effort to provide the environment and support that poor children need in order to succeed. In addition, teachers have a special responsibility to promote informed discussion with colleagues, neighbours, and politicians about the long-term costs to society of cutting social services, pre-school education, and educational funding.

Shifts of power in the family

In some immigrant families, a power shift occurs between the genders and between the generations after arrival in the new country. Few families can exist on one income, and many immigrant families have to make the adjustment to both parents' going out to work. Traditional male/female roles may begin to break down; women have less time to give to domestic responsibilities, and in the workplace they often become exposed to different sets of societal values about gender roles or the rights of women and children. These values may be in conflict with those of the traditional culture, and may entail for some males a loss of power and status within the family and the community. This loss of status may result in anger and frustration, and occasionally this anger may be acted out in family violence.

Another power shift may occur between parents and children as the family adjusts to new roles and relationships. One source of intergenerational conflict is the sometimes marked difference in child-rearing practices between the new culture and the old culture. In some families — not only in immigrant families, but in many families of the mainstream culture as well — children and parents are not regarded as equals, and physical chastisement, or the threat of it, is one of the methods of discipline. Children are exposed to different child-rearing practices and family roles through their interaction with other children at school, and through the models presented to them through such media as television and movies. In the new culture, children may have more rights and often begin to assert them. Some parents are shocked to find that their methods of disciplining their children are considered wrong in the new country. If they do not find alternative ways of disciplining their children, they may begin to feel that they are losing control of their children, and losing authority in their own homes.

Another source of intergenerational conflict is the adult role that some children are required to play. Children often acquire English more quickly than their parents, and may sometimes be required to act as family negotiators and go-betweens. Teenage children may also have part-time jobs after school and on weekends. New responsibilities sometimes cause children to claim rights, privileges, and independence at an age that would be unthinkable in the home country.

Cultural conflict between home and school

Children may be exposed at school to many values that are in conflict with those of the home. It is relatively easy for immigrant children to change external aspects of culture such as style of clothing; but internal values and beliefs are more deeply ingrained and much more integral to the individual's identity. These intrinsic values are challenged daily by exposure to North American mainstream values. For instance, respect for elders may be less evident among North American children than in many immigrant families. Individual choice and self-determination is another North American value that is often in conflict with the emphasis many other cultures place on duty towards the family and the community. Older children are in contact with a teenage lifestyle that may be very different from the life of adolescents in their own cultures. Courses such as 'Sex Education', 'Sociology', 'Family Studies', and 'Personal Life Management' emphasize personal choice and autonomy, and relate to a lifestyle that is promoted in music videos and other media.

Some parents react with fear and suspicion when they feel that their children are being attracted to aspects of North American culture that the parents find disturbing. They may attempt to control exposure by refusing to allow their children to participate in certain activities such as field trips or co-educational sports.

It is sometimes very difficult for children to navigate between two cultures. If they attempt to integrate into the school culture, they may have feelings of disloyalty and dishonour towards their parents and community; if they choose to adhere wholly to their parents' values they remain isolated on the fringes of North American life and unable to participate in all that school has to offer.

As the children acquire English, they may become less proficient in the language of the home. When English becomes the dominant or preferred language of the children, poor communication between parents and their children can lead to serious conflict at home and negative interaction with the school (Yao, 1985; Wong Fillmore, 1991).

Parental involvement in the school

The active involvement of parents in their children's education is widely recognized to be a major factor in academic success. For several reasons, some parents who are recent immigrants may not become effectively involved in their children's education. One reason is that many immigrants find themselves doing more than one job, or doing shift work. Because of this, they have little time available to interact with their children and help with schoolwork or attend school events. Another reason for the low involvement of many immigrant parents is that they may feel handicapped by their lack of fluency in English, or their lack of knowledge about the educational system.

Also, in many countries, the involvement of parents in their children's schooling is neither expected nor desired. The role of the parent in many countries is to send the children to school, provide the books and uniforms, and exhort the children to work hard and bring credit on the family. The teacher and the school are entrusted with the rest. This is why, when teachers call immigrant parents about a concern over their child, the teachers are sometimes surprised and somewhat indignant when some parents seem to hand the problem back to the teacher. On the other hand, some immigrant parents wonder what kind of 'soft' system the schools are running if the teachers cannot take care of the children without advice from the parents.

'I give my whole child to you'
It is important not to interpret parental non-involvement as lack of concern. As one community representative explained:

The teacher wants parents to go to school. Maybe 20% go to talk to the teacher. They don't understand English. They're embarrassed. And they don't under-stand the idea of communication between teacher and parent. They resist having a relationship between teacher and parent. We don't have this in our country. It's non-existent. Parents and teachers meeting and communicating — not at all in our country. 'I have a child. OK. Teacher, I give my child to you. It's up to you to educate him. I give my whole child to you.' Parents ask, 'Why do they want me to go to school? What happens at school is the teacher's business. What happens at home is my business.' (Interview reported in Kaprielian-Churchill and Churchill, 1994: 87)

The 'risk factors' described above are not a 'profile' of the immigrant family or immigrant children. Few families or children experience all of these situations; indeed, some do not experience any of them. Nevertheless, it is important to be aware that experiences similar to these may be part of a student's background, and to be prepared to offer appropriate support when needed, as suggested in Chapter 4.

THE REFUGEE EXPERIENCE

In addition to the stresses that are normally associated with the immigrant experience, even for those immigrating under optimum conditions, those who arrive as refugees have often lived through traumatic experiences of oppression, war and flight.

Children of war and violence

Refugee children are often victims or witnesses of war and violence. Many have seen family members murdered, or do not know the whereabouts of some of them. Their family members may have been the victims of torture, and they may have been victims of violence themselves. Most have experienced some kind of family separation. For example, a study in Toronto showed that 'Virtually all Tamil students interviewed had personally experienced or witnessed such traumatic events as homes being bombed or burnt, property being confiscated, and close family members being drafted, arrested, attacked, tortured, or even killed' (Yau, 1995: 17).

By the time refugees arrive in their new country, some have spent many years in refugee camps, often in appalling conditions, waiting for official recognition of their status as bona fide refugees, and then waiting for one or another of the refugee sponsoring countries to accept them. This wait can be a period of extreme stress, and adults and children alike often become anxious and depressed. Previously good family relations may be worn down during this time, by squalor, noise, and despair; some adults retreat into silence and therefore are not providing the linguistic interaction their children need in order to develop proficiency in the first language. Kaprielian-Churchill and Churchill (1994) provide a graphic description of life in a Cambodian refugee camp along the Thai–Cambodian border in 1987, and emphasize that 'the impact of incarceration in a camp, no matter where or when, is dehumanizing. Life in a Salvadorean camp in Guatemala is as demoralizing as an Ethiopian camp. An Afghan camp in Pakistan is a debilitating as a Croation camp or a Somali camp. An Iraqi camp in Jordan is as unnerving as a Vietnamese camp' (Kaprielian-Churchill and Churchill 1994: 11).

Mental health experts have described typical phases in the refugee's adjustment to life in the new country (Canadian Task Force on Mental Health Issues Affecting Immigrants and Refugees, 1988; Freire, 1989). Initially there may be a phase of great elation and relief at having escaped from persecution or death at home and intolerable conditions in transit. However, it is not unusual for individuals to begin feeling very guilty about their own deliverance, when so many of their relatives and friends did not escape or even survive. For some, there is a stage of realization that their escape represents long-term exile, perhaps forever. This can be a period of great depression. For refugee claimants who are waiting for their claims to be heard, additional delays and insecurity of status may cause additional stress on families and individuals.

Many refugee children exhibit various symptoms of post-traumatic stress disorder: headaches, sleep problems, nightmares, feelings of fear, a tendency to cry frequently, and depressed or suicidal feelings (Carter and Mok, 1992). In the classroom, teachers may observe withdrawal, hyperactivity, aggression, difficulty with concentration, fearful behaviour, and reactions of intense anxiety to situations that recall some traumatic event, such as the sound of a car backfiring, the sight of a uniformed police or military officer, or a helicopter flying overhead. The artwork of many refugee children reveals some of their anxieties and preoccupation through their depiction of war and violence: planes, falling bombs, soldiers, and so on.

'I miss him so much'
The events described in this story are fairly representative of those experienced or witnessed by many refugees:

After the third period began I heard a lot of bomb sounds and gun shots. After a few minutes my principal announced, 'Please don't go outside, the forces are shooting the people.' I was afraid. My friend Ragu asked me to go home, so I decided to go to his home. While we were cycling along the road suddenly the armoured truck appeared and I knew something was going to happen. At that time I had forgotten myself and I started to run with my friend Ragu. He couldn't run with me, because he had a hole in his heart, so he ran very slowly but I dragged him. After a few minutes I heard some gun shots so I fell down to save my life. But Ragu didn't fall down. When I looked behind he was floating in a pool of blood. I ran to him and took him on my lap. That time he told me, 'Don't stay with me. If you stay with me the forces will arrest you. Please go! Don't care about me. I will be okay.' But I couldn't leave him alone so I stayed with him. Then the forces came beside me and kicked me and kicked Ragu also. Then I think he died, because I didn't see any changes in his face then. After that, the forces took me to the camp. I left my friend's body alone.

In the camp the forces gave me many kinds of punishments, but I didn't feel anything. I felt only one thing: that I had lost my friend. After two weeks, my school principal came to the camp and he released me, but I didn't feel happy then, because my best friend had died. Every day I think about him. I miss him so much. (Student from Sri Lanka)

A study of refugee students in Toronto showed that many students were still afraid of the government they had fled from, and were afraid of being spied on. There was also a sense of fear for relatives left behind. Several teachers commented that 'it was hard for these students to get their minds off the bad news from far-apart families, and to remain focused on their schoolwork with such lingering thoughts and images' (Yau, 1995: 25). The study found examples of a student who missed a term because of the death of his sister in the home country; a Somali student who had lost all his relatives; and a Nicaraguan student who had to leave school and return to Nicaragua.

Schools that receive refugee students need to be especially sensitive to the social and emotional needs of their students. For example, counselling programs need to be staffed by professionals trained in cross-cultural communications and knowledgeable about the experiences of refugees and the symptoms of post-traumatic stress syndrome. See Chapter 4 for more suggestions on providing psychological support for recently arrived immigrant and refugee students.

Case studies: refugee students in Toronto schools

These case studies are reprinted from a research study conducted in Toronto by Yau (1995: 17–21). The case studies describe some of the experiences of refugee families and children from different parts of the world.

Refugees from Sri Lanka
Pre-migration experiences
Most Tamil refugees interviewed in this study had undergone life-threatening conditions caused by the chronic civil war in Sri Lanka. As reported by some Tamil families, they were victims caught between the government troops on the one side and Tamil Tiger guerrillas on the other. Virtually all Tamil students interviewed had personally experienced or witnessed such traumatic events as homes being bombed or burnt, property being confiscated, and close family members being drafted, arrested, attacked, tortured, or even killed.

Because of the constant fighting between government troops and Tiger guerrillas, many school-age children sometimes had to stay away from school for one or two months, return to school for a week, and be interrupted again; in some instances, they had to stay at home for one or two years.

Migration experiences
Many Tamil refugees escaped from Sri Lanka by paying private agents, and stayed in a transit country for some time before landing in Canada where they declared their refugee status. But there were Tamils who had stayed in refugee camps, e.g. in India or in Colombo in Sri Lanka, for months until they were finally accepted by a host country.

Refugees from Central America
Pre-migration experiences
Many from Central America were political refugees fleeing for physical safety. Government corruption coupled with extreme poverty or social polarization had politicized people to rebel against existing régimes. For example, it was not uncommon to find those from poor or rural areas in El Salvador and Guatemala who had been involved in or were sympathetic to student movements or anti-government parties. As a result, they themselves, close family members or friends were subjected to government persecution – property being confiscated or destroyed, homes being bombed; or they were

under constant fear of being watched, arrested, detained, tortured or even executed.

Because of poverty, some did not have schooling at all. Two Guatemalan students we interviewed described how they had to drop in and out of school because their families were too large and poor to support them. Instead, both had to earn their living at an early age, doing all sorts of odd jobs – washing cars, shining shoes, delivering goods, selling newspapers, etc. Their stories were echoed in a newspaper article on Guatemala's street kids, who worked daily on the city streets to earn a few coins for themselves or their large families, while for them 'play and school are low priorities'. (Mansour, 1991, 8 July).

Some refugees from Nicaragua, however, were from middle-class backgrounds. They left after the rise of the Sandanista Government. Some parents had even participated in the revolution against the former government, but after the revolution they themselves were suspected, watched, or jailed by the new authority.

Migration experiences

Before Central American refugees found their way to Canada, many had gone through dangerous escapes and hard journeys, 'hiding by day and moving by night', and walking their way through forests to neighbouring countries (e.g., from Guatemala to Mexico, or from Nicaragua or El Salvador to Honduras), where they sometimes stayed in camps for at least a year, and where they often found themselves in poor living conditions and/or being discriminated against or harassed by local authorities or people.

A young Nicaraguan student left the country with his parents when he was four and stayed in Honduras for three years where he attended school. But as a Nicaraguan, he was harassed by local people and students in Honduras – for example, being pushed off stairs – an experience that was so traumatic that his parents thought their child needed professional help. On the other hand, three Nicaraguan sisters stayed in Costa Rica for two years where they enjoyed their school. These girls also reported that they had adapted to the school system in Canada, and were doing fine at school.

Refugees from Iran

Pre-migration experiences

Iranian students fled from homes mainly due to dissatisfaction and/or personal conflicts with the régime and its religious ideology. These refugees included those who were well-educated and/or from well-to-do families. For the school-age children, schooling was virtually uninterrupted until their escape from the country.

Migration experiences

While some Iranians left their country legally, many escaped with danger, sometimes after several attempts, to nearby countries where they stayed from a few months to a few years. Usually those who sojourned for a few months escaped to Canada via different routes and declared their refugee status upon landing. But there were also those who before landing in Canada stayed in a transit country (4 out of 14 interviewed), where they applied for Canadian immigration visas or declared their refugee status via the United Nations. These people waited for a year or up to several years until their applications were granted.

Refugees from China
Pre-migration experiences
Many refugees from China could perhaps be considered as economic refugees with the hope of providing better lives and future for their children. Indeed, some young Chinese students reported that they enjoyed their lives and schools in China, did not want to leave, or did not know why they had to leave their country. But in the wake of the June 1989 pro-democracy movement in China, there were Chinese refugees, including those who were well-educated or university students/graduates, who sought political asylum in Canada or other countries.

Migration experiences
Refugee claimants from China came to Canada through different routes. Some entered Canada on visitor's visas, some were travelling to South/Central America, and others had detoured through several countries, especially countries with few diplomatic ties with China, for several months before reaching Canada. Upon their arrival, some stayed in the country without official permits, while others applied for refugee status or permanent resident status. For a short period after the June 1989 Tienanmen Square Incident, a significant number of individuals in China as well as those in Canada who sought asylum were accepted by the Canadian government as political refugees.

Refugees from Vietnam
Pre-migration experiences
Those who risked their lives to leave Vietnam in the late 1980s and early 1990s came from different walks of life ranging from fishermen from the northern part of Vietnam to entrepreneurs from the south. Few were from professional backgrounds. The major push for their exodus was their deep discontent or frustration with the new Communist government: lack of freedom, discrimination and harassment of Chinese people by the government, fear of their sons being drafted to fight against neighbouring countries, poor future prospects for the young, and lack of good education for children.

In fact it was quite common to find children in Vietnam not attending school at all. In some cases, parents, mostly ethnic Chinese, did not want their children to receive Vietnamese education; those who could afford had their children taught at home by private tutors. In other cases, families were too poor to allow their children spend time in school; instead the children had to help out by working as street vendors. Of course, there were those who did attend schools in Vietnam, but their education was often disrupted by their families' constant travels to seek refuge.

Migration experiences
Many escaped from Vietnam via long difficult journeys (mostly by boat), which were fraught with danger from government troops, sea pirates, and natural disasters. Some students and parents had indeed escaped several times, and had been caught and jailed. Those who survived the dangerous journeys landed in one of the neighbouring countries — Cambodia, Thailand, Malaysia, Indonesia, Philippines or Hong Kong — and if they were lucky enough they were allowed to stay in refugee camps.

The second phase of their exodus experience began in the refugee camps, where they were confined in poor overcrowded conditions for an indefinite period of time, until the most fortunate ones were accepted by other countries. Aside from crowded, noisy and poor living conditions, these refugees were subjected to long periods of boredom and uncertainty – which often led to frustration and even violence. Most of the students and parents interviewed reported that they had stayed in refugee camps for at least a year, many for two or three years, and some even up to five years. The latter virtually grew up in camps.

In fact, at a secondary school, five out of six Vietnamese students we interviewed had only one or two years of schooling (the most up to primary grades) in their home country prior to their escape; they then spent a few years in refugee camps attending some classes learning English, math and/or Vietnamese.

Refugees from Ethiopia and Somalia
Pre-migration experiences
Students from Ethiopia and Somalia left their homeland due to the plight caused by internal political turmoil, military conflicts, and ongoing drought in their countries. Some Ethiopian students added that their own future was bleak under the political and economic pressure of the military régime. For the Somali students, it was estimated according to a local community that one-fifth of the Somali population has left the country as refugees to Europe, Africa (Ethiopia and Kenya), the United States, and Canada.

Migration experiences
Most moved from country to country, or stayed in a foreign country (e.g. in northern Africa, Europe, India) or refugee camps, from a few months to several years, before finally arriving in Canada either as refugee immigrants (for most Ethiopians) or refugee claimants (for most Somalis). (Reprinted by permission of the Toronto District School Board)

STRENGTHS OF IMMIGRANT LEARNERS AND FAMILIES

Although immigrant families and children face many difficulties in the transition from one country and one way of life to another, few would experience all of the difficulties described here, or experience them in equal degree. Also, far from being overwhelmed by their difficulties, most are astonishingly resilient and many are very successful in their new lives. Although teachers need to understand the experiences of newcomers and behave with compassion and sensitivity towards students and their parents, it is important also to recognize and value the attributes or strengths they have that may enable them to adjust successfully. It is possible that some strengths may be found among immigrants because only persons with those attributes would become immigrants in the first place; others may be developed as a result of their experiences.

As always, it is important not to overgeneralize. There are as many differences among immigrants as there are among the general population, and all of the attributes described later are also found among established residents of all cultural backgrounds. The following observations are not intended to paint a picture of immigrants as a group, but to highlight some of the attributes that many may possess and that may assist them to adapt well to their new lives and become successful students, employees, and citizens in their new land. Teachers may not always recognize these attributes among newcomers who may be in the early stages of adjustment. It is important to provide a welcoming and supportive environment for students of all backgrounds, as suggested in other chapters of this book, so that their strengths as well as their needs may begin to shine through.

Initiative

Many newcomers have taken dramatic action to improve their lives. For some this was a voluntary decision, and for others this was a decision taken under extreme duress, but in both situations a decision of this magnitude requires drive and determination. Initiative, drive, and determination are qualities highly valued in societies such as Canada, the United States, and other English-speaking countries.

A sense of community

Many immigrants are from cultures that have a strong collective orientation and a strong sense of community responsibility. Immigrants may be connected to each other through cultural groups maintained through their personal contributions and volunteer efforts, and are often very supportive of each other. Religion and religious institutions may also provide support to individuals and to families, and foster cultural cohesion.

Cultural awareness

People who have moved from one cultural environment to another often become much more aware of their own culture. This often leads to a strong sense of cultural identity. Some immigrant parents make special efforts to preserve important aspects of their culture by sending their children to language schools, by participating in cultural events, and by maintaining traditions in the home. At the same time, many immigrants value certain aspects of mainstream culture, and are able to make cultural adaptations in order to function in the mainstream.

Adaptability

Many immigrants are highly adaptable people, willing to change their whole way of life in order to achieve certain goals. Most are willing to learn a new language, and are not afraid to try new experiences. Many teachers find that newcomers who feel comfortable and well-accepted by their peers and their teachers display enthusiasm for new ideas, and a curiosity about their new school environment as well as about the subjects they study at school. This kind of mental flexibility is often highly valued by teachers.

Respect for education

Many parents indicate that improved educational opportunity for their children is one of the reasons for leaving their home country, and their greatest hope is that their children will succeed in school. Immigrant parents and children often have great respect for established institutions such as schools, and may value teachers in ways that some members of the established community may not. Many teachers find that their immigrant students are often highly motivated, respectful, and very hard-working. In the 15 to 24 age group, immigrants are more likely to be attending school or some other educational institution than their Canadian-born peers (Badets and Chui, 1994).

The extended family

Some families come from traditional cultures where the extended family is very important, and where children may be raised in multigenerational homes. Children may grow up with aunts, uncles, cousins, and grandparents as well as siblings and parents under the same roof, or in very close proximity. In extended families, grandparents and other elders usually have authority in the home, and institutions such as old people's homes are much less common than in more 'modern' societies. The adult members of the family may all be responsible for the welfare of each other and of each other's children.

The loss of the extended family network may be a major adjustment for some families. However, connections are usually maintained through regular letters and phone calls. Many adults send money home, and sponsor relatives to join them once they are established. Many who can do so make frequent visits back home. It is not uncommon for a family to send children overseas to stay with aunts and uncles, to protect the children from the dangers of war, or provide them with better educational opportunities. Young people of high school age who arrive alone or with other siblings as refugees often have, as a goal, the re-uniting of their families, and many adolescent students work and save, as well as going to school, to make this happen.

The extended family can be an important source of material and psychological support. Immigrant families may be much less accustomed to using institutionalized support such as social workers, psychologists, or school counsellors, or even teachers. The extended family may be able to help school personnel to solve problems that students have, at school or in relationships with the immediate family, without involving outside agencies.

Hard work

As we have seen, immigrants in Canada participate in the labour force at rates similar to, or in some age groups higher than, their Canadian-born peers, and many recent arrivals are willing to do jobs that others are unwilling to do. In their first few years many immigrants hold more than one job and may be attending language classes as well. Many immigrant teenagers work and contribute to the support of their families.

Newcomers often work hard in school too, and often spend more time studying than their native-born peers. This may be partly because everything takes longer for students who are working in a second language, but also because many students are keenly aware of their parents' aspirations for them, and feel that they must be successful in order to make their parents' sacrifices worth while. A Toronto study showed that immigrants do more hours of homework per week than their Canadian-born peers: an average of 11 hours per week compared to eight. The study also showed that refugees spend more hours on homework than the children of voluntary immigrants — an average of 14 hours — even though they often hold down jobs as well (Yau, 1995).

Citizenship

Many immigrants, especially refugees, are deeply grateful to their new country for extending to them an opportunity to re-create their lives. As we have seen, as a group they are more law-abiding than native-born residents, and most choose to become citizens. Many new citizens have a strong sense of their responsibilities, while some native-born residents may value their country but take the privileges of citizenship for granted.

'Canada is the home I have found at last'
These immigrant teenagers express a passionate commitment to their new country (Porter, 1991):

> *Being Canadian gives me a sense that I belong to a great land of opportuni-ties, that I am one of the many ethnic minorities who make up the cultural mosaic which is the fundamental character of this country. Most importantly, I feel that I am part of the Canadian family.*
>
> *I am proud to be a Canadian and I feel fortunate to live in one of the greatest countries in the word. Being a new Canadian does give me all the privileges a native-born Canadian enjoys. But there are also responsibilities which I must assume.* Chauncee Tang (Porter, 1991: 289)

> *When I arrived in Canada the first day, I decided to stay here permanently. You may ask me why I never wanted to return to my country. No, it is not my country. I never had a country. When I was a child, I knew only war which lasted so many years. Nowhere in my country can I live in peace. Peace had been the only thing I have searched for in a long time. Peace has been my passion since war revealed to to me its horror. I have lived through this horror and now, I just hope to live in a country where it is peaceful. Canada is the home I have found at last.* Thuy Van Luong (Porter, 1991: 280)

CONCLUSION

Immigrant students and the children of immigrants come from many different backgrounds and bring with them a great variety of experience. Newcomers face a period of adjustment on entry to their new schools; for some, this period is very stressful. During this period, they need the support of their teachers and the acceptance of their peers. The school can act as a stabilizing factor by providing a welcoming, safe, and predictable environment for newly arrived children. Mean-while, teachers skilled in cross-cultural communication, and knowledgeable about the experiences and expectations of different cultural groups in their communities, can offer support to parents who are raising children in a new cultural environment. Effective communication between home and school, and open discussion and negotiation of roles and responsibilities, are essential if the school is to be responsive to its multicultural community.

The next chapter suggests some ways to welcome newcomers and help them get off to a good start in their new educational environment. Chapter 4 provides advice on how to create an inclusive school environment where students of all cultural and linguistic backgrounds feel valued and supported, and Chapter 5 describes how teachers can create a welcoming and inclusive classroom community.

FURTHER READING

Clayton, J.B. (1996) *Your Land, My Land: Children in the Process of Acculturation.* Portsmouth, NH: Heinemann. This story of four recently arrived children in an American elementary school, told from the perspectives of the ESL teacher who is the author of the study, as well as the classroom teachers, the parents, and the children themselves.

Kaprielian-Churchill, I., and Churchill, S. (1994) *The Pulse of the World: Refugees in Our Schools*. Toronto: OISE Press. This study describes the experiences of refugee families and children, and analyzes the way various factors affect psychosocial adjustment and school performance. Contains recommendations for teachers, administrators, and government.

Opoku-Dapaah, E. (1995) *Somali Refugees in Toronto: a Profile*. North York, Ontario: York Lanes Press. This study examines the social, cultural, and linguistic backgrounds of Somalis in Canada, as well as their interaction with service organizations and mainstream society. Includes recommendations for government agencies, education, and social services.

Parker-Jenkins, M. (1995) *Children of Islam: A Teacher's Guide to Meeting the Needs of Muslim Pupils*. Stoke-on-Trent, England: Trentham Books. This book provides background information on the backgrounds and needs of many Muslim children in British schools. The book raises awareness of some traditional school practices that may be a source of difficulty for some children and their parents, and of some of the accommodations that schools can make.

Porter, J. (1991) *New Canadian Voices*. Toronto: Wall and Emerson. This collection of student writing about the immigrant experience contains personal stories and reflections that are moving, illuminating, and humorous. It can be used with students to stimulate their own talking and writing, or with teachers to raise awareness of the experiences and needs of their immigrant and refugee students.

Rutter, J. (1994) *Refugee Children in the Classroom*. Stoke-on-Trent, England: Trentham Books. Provides background information on refugees in Britain, and makes practical suggestions for welcoming and supporting refugee children in schools.

Yau, M. (1995) *Refugee Students in Toronto Schools: An Exploratory Study*. Toronto: Toronto Board of Education. This study provides background information on refugee students from different regions of the world, examines how schools have responded to their needs, and recommends several courses of action for educators.

CHAPTER 3

Getting Started in the Multicultural School

INTRODUCTION

A school that serves a multilingual, multicultural, and multiracial community can play an important role in helping all students and their families to feel welcome as new members of the school community. First impressions count for a lot; therefore, it is important to ensure that there is a procedure for receiving and welcoming newcomers, whether they are arriving at the beginning of the school year or at some other time, and whether they are arriving from a neighbouring school or from halfway around the world. To help students get off to a positive start in their new educational environment, it is also important to assess their educational needs, using procedures that are sensitive to their linguistic and cultural backgrounds, so that they may be placed in appropriate classroom programs. Some students may also need special support for second language acquisition.

This chapter begins by describing the kind of reception and orientation services that schools can provide for newly arrived students and their families. The next section suggests a process and specific strategies for initial assessment and placement. The third section describes some approaches to providing support for students who are learning the language of instruction. The chapter ends with a checklist that teachers and school administrators can use to assess the school as a welcoming and supportive environment for students from other countries and diverse cultural backgrounds.

RECEPTION AND ORIENTATION

A positive initial reception and helpful orientation services can have a very positive effect on the integration of new students into the academic program and the social life of the school. A positive first encounter also increases the likelihood that parents will want to continue a relationship with the school and become involved in their children's education.

The first impression that the new arrival receives is very important; from this first day the student will form expectations about the school and how well he or she will fit into it. Immigrant families, in particular, may arrive to register their children at any time during the school year, usually within days of their arrival in the country. Some older students may arrive at the high school without even the support of their parents. This may be because they have immigrated alone or because they know more English than their parents do. Sometimes the student arrives with a student who is already attending the school — a cousin, or the child of a neighbour — and who can play the role of interpreter.

If the school seems less than welcoming, or if routines seem to be disarranged and personnel put out by the arrival of a newcomer, the student and parents may be intimidated from the very beginning, and future efforts to involve parents may be futile. The following procedures will help to ensure a smooth transition for the student and the receiving teachers, and reassure parents about what is to happen to their children:

- **Create signs and notices** in the languages of the community and display them in prominent locations around the school. Include a 'Welcome' sign indicating where new registrants should go.
- **Establish a procedure for welcoming** students and parents the moment they arrive. Make sure that the staff in the school office, often the first contact with the new family, are trained to receive new students in a welcoming manner, and know what routines to follow.
- **Designate a team responsible for reception.** In a small school this may consist of the principal and the English as a Second Language (ESL) teacher. In a secondary school the team may include a counsellor and an ESL teacher. As soon as a new family or student arrives, a member of the team welcomes the family in a comfortable private space — perhaps a conference room or the principal's office. In secondary schools this may be a room in the school counselling area.
- **Use the home language** whenever possible. Communicate with students and their parents with the assistance of an interpreter, unless the student and parents are fluent in English. The interpreter might be a bilingual teacher or parent, a professional employed by the school district, or a senior secondary student trained for this role (see 'Multilingual services' in the next section). It is important that this individual have competence in both languages and a good understanding of both school systems. If none is immediately available, it is better to arrange the reception interview for a later time. It is not a good idea to use a student peer to interpret what may include some confidential or sensitive information.

Multilingual Welcome Poster: Reprinted with the permission of Communication Services, Peel District School Board, Ontario.

- **Allow plenty of time** for the reception interview. It takes more than twice as long to communicate through an interpreter; not only must the words be translated, but whole concepts must be explained, such as *field trip, home form, a brown bag lunch, a credit program, a six-day cycle,* etc. Even if the interview is conducted in English, these concepts must be explained so that parents have a clear understanding of what they mean.
- **Conduct an informal interview** to ask the necessary questions and complete the registration forms. Collect information about the child's previous school experience and physical health. Find out about the circumstances of immigration, but be prepared to back off if your questions appear to cause discomfort or distress. If necessary, you can get this information later, when the student has established a trusting relationship with you or another member of the staff.
- **Assess the student's linguistic and academic background and needs**, seeking relevant information from the parents and/or the student and using appropriate assessment instruments and procedures. Detailed suggestions on how to do this are provided in Chapter 9. Make a provisional placement into an appropriate classroom program and, for students who are learning English, a planned program of support for second language acquisition (see the section on 'Support for Second Language Acquisition' in this chapter). Explain the nature of the program to the student and the parents; emphasize that the placement is provisional and

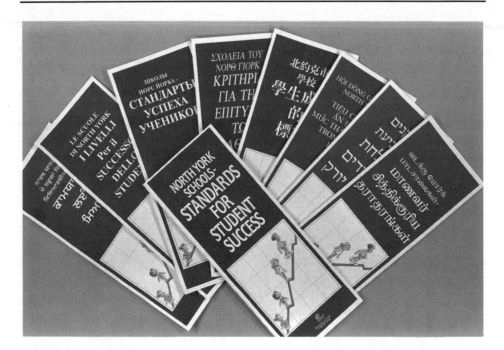

will be reviewed at the end of a specified period, or at any time that the student and/or the parents request this.

- **Provide basic information** about the length and structure of the school day, what the student needs to bring to school, and holidays. It is important not to overload the family with new information during this first encounter, but to establish a relationship so that orientation can continue during the weeks and months ahead.

Give the student or the parents a 'Welcome Booklet' in their own language that they can take home for reference. This booklet can give basic information about the school program, the structure of the school day and the school year, special activities and events, and the role parents are encouraged to take. Students could undertake this as a project, under the guidance of a teacher or an adult from the community. Include a page where you can provide personalized information: the name of the student's home room teacher and the ESL teacher, the principal's name, the school phone number, and what to do if the student is absent. Include the name and phone number of a bilingual contact person or interpreter, and the phone number of relevant community organizations. Update this booklet yearly and include a page of staff photos.

As an alternative or in addition to the booklet, create a video showing different aspects of the school program, with voice over in different languages. This could be developed by the school district rather than the individual school. Families can take these videos home, or you can use them in parent–teacher meetings.

- **Provide information about heritage or community language programs,** and indicate support for first-language maintenance. Encourage parents to use the first language at home to support the child's language development. Explain that bilingualism can positively affect academic performance, and a high level of development in the first language supports the acquisition of English (for an overview of the research in this area, see Cummins, 1996). The first language can also help to unite the family and maintain effective communication in the home during the period of adjustment, and is an important source of cultural pride and individual self-esteem. According to the authors of a Canadian study, 'A heritage language program can confirm identity, [enhance] self-respect, increase support from the home and capitalize on the first-language skills of immigrant and refugee children' (Canadian Teachers' Federation, 1990: 9).
- **Give the parents information** about English as a Second Language programs for adults that may be available in the local community.
- **Give the new student a basic 'starter kit'** of materials: pencils, coloured markers, a ruler, an eraser, a notebook, a picture dictionary. For older students who know some English, a monolingual English learner's dictionary might be more appropriate.

Basic supplies

Some families may have great difficulty in providing essential supplies and equipment for their children in the first year or two after arrival, especially if they have arrived as refugees. Set aside funds to assist in providing school supplies and clothing, such as gym shorts. Use this fund to subsidize field trips and other school activities.

Organize a school clothing exchange. Encourage families to send clothing (especially winter clothing and boots) to the school. Items such as ice skates or soccer boots can also be donated. To save students potential embarrassment, exchange the clothing with another school, so that the original owners of the clothes don't recognize them on the new owners. Organize a small 'clothing store' so that the clothing looks attractive. Home room or ESL teachers can bring individual students to the store to choose appropriate items.

- **Introduce a student ambassador** from the student's home room or English as a Second Language (ESL) class to the newcomer. This student escorts the new student and the family on a brief school tour, including a visit to the student's homeroom and the ESL room.

Student ambassadors

The role of ambassador could rotate so that many students have an opportunity to take this leadership role. Choose students to reflect the ethnic and racial make-up of the school. Some newcomers may be more comfortable with someone of their own gender. It is especially encouraging to newcomers if they meet others from their own background who have already successfully navigated the adjustment period and are comfortable in the school; however, it is not always necessary to assign an ambassador of the same background. Although bilingual student ambassadors can be especially helpful for students who are new to English, many newcomers will appreciate the help of a friendly English-speaking peer.

It is best to avoid the word 'buddy' because this implies that the students must become friends; this may not be realistic expectation. If friendship results, that is an additional benefit, but it is not the purpose of the program.

Give student ambassadors some training for their role. Include some discussion of how a recent arrival might feel during the first few days of school; some of the ambassadors will be able to draw on their own experiences and share them with others. The ambassadors could discuss what they would want an ambassador to do for them if they were in this situation, and generate a list of duties for which they agree to be responsible. This may include duties such as explaining classroom routines and sitting beside the newcomer for the first couple of weeks. In secondary schools, ambassadors may also be responsible for explaining how to read the timetable and escorting the new student to each class for the first full cycle, helping the student to get a locker and demonstrating how to use the combination lock, helping the newcomer to get a bus pass,

accompanying the newcomer to the cafeteria for the first few days, providing an orientation to the library, the computer lab, the counselling office, and other key locations and services in the school, and introducing the new student to one extracurricular activity.

Provide special recognition for ambassadors. This may consist of a button to identify their role, a letter home to parents (in the appropriate language) praising their child's helpfulness, addition of the student's name to a list on display in a prominent place, recognition in assemblies, a classroom visit and handshake by the principal, and so on.

INITIAL ASSESSMENT AND PLACEMENT

All students entering a new school need an accurate assessment of their needs. They may be native-born children entering kindergarten, students who are transferring from another school within the same city or country, or newly-arrived students who have started their education in other countries.

When the student's first language is not English, it is best to use the student's first or dominant language for at least part of the assessment, in order to gain an accurate perspective of a student's linguistic and cognitive development. At the same time, there is a need to find out how proficient the student is in the language of instruction. Informed by these assessments, teachers can make appropriate decisions about the student's academic and linguistic needs, and place the student in an appropriate program. Assessment begins with the reception interview, and may continue over a period of several days.

The reception interview

Some information can be gathered during the initial reception interview, with the help of an interpreter. Include these questions in the interview:

- Which language or languages did the child first learn in the home?
- What language is used in the home now?
- How many years has the student been in school?
- What was the language of instruction?
- Have there been any interruptions in schooling?
- Has the student developed any literacy skills in the first language? If so, at what age did the child began to read?
- What special aptitudes or interests has the child shown at school?
- Has the student experienced any learning difficulties or been provided with any specialized kind of education?
- What is the nature of the child's experience with English, if any, in the home country or since arrival?
- Are educational records available? (If so, you will need to get them translated and evaluated by a bilingual educator who is familiar with the system of education in the student's home country.)

It is important to explain the intent of these questions in order to get accurate information. For example, it is not uncommon for parents to report greater use or knowledge of English than is in fact the case, if they believe that the school values English more highly than other languages.

Having gained some general background information, you can use some of the following procedures to gain more detailed information about the student's linguistic and cognitive development. Elementary and secondary schools may use somewhat different procedures, because the school day and the academic program are organized differently, and more detailed information is required for placement at the secondary level.

Assessment procedures for elementary schools

The child at the elementary level is normally placed in a grade level program, and may also be placed in an English as a Second Language (ESL) class for some of the day. It is usually not necessary to do an in-depth assessment before placing children in the elementary grades; they are normally placed with their age peers. Although newly arrived students may be beginning learners of English, and even though they may have missed some schooling because of the circumstances surrounding immigration, it is not usually a good idea to place them with younger children. The apparent advantages of such a placement do not warrant the damage to self-esteem and motivation this can cause. Also, language learning takes place when children want and need to communicate; they are more motivated to do so when they are with their peers, involved in age-appropriate activities, and stimulated by learning new information and developing new skills.

Decisions about ESL placement depend on the organization of the ESL program. In some schools, students are withdrawn from the mainstream classroom with their age peers; in others, they come together as a mixed age grouping of students at a similar level of proficiency in English. If possible, it is preferable to design the ESL program so that children at the same grade level are grouped together. This enables the teacher to link the content of the program to the academic program of the mainstream class. It is best not to withdraw the children from their grade level classroom at times when they can benefit from involvement in the mainstream program: for example, when the class is involved in the arts or physical education program, or when the class is learning mathematics or science. The best time to withdraw children is during activities that require a great deal of linguistic or cultural knowledge, such as language arts or social studies. The ESL teacher can design lessons and activities related to the content of the grade level program, but delivered in a way that takes account of the children's present level of background knowledge as well as their level of linguistic development in English. In some schools, children are not withdrawn from their grade level classrooms; instead, the ESL teacher works within the mainstream classroom, team teaching with the grade level teacher and providing additional support to groups of second language learners.

Some children, especially those who have had limited experience of schooling, or who have had traumatic experiences en route to their new country, may benefit from staying in the ESL classroom for the first few days. Here they can develop some supportive relationships with other ESL learners and the teacher can assess the student's linguistic and educational needs in a low-pressure environment.

Assessment information can be gathered over several days or weeks as the child settles into the new school routine and becomes more comfortable with teachers and peers. The ESL teacher can work with students in the ESL classroom as well as with the classroom teacher and with bilingual educators to assess the student's needs. Initial assessment information is extremely important for tracking the child's progress in the months and years ahead. Assessment procedures may vary, depending on the age of the child, but it is not usually appropriate to use formal tests. Instead, you can use a variety of informal approaches to gather information about the child's level of educational attainment and knowledge of English.

Standardized tests are not appropriate, because they are usually normed on the performance of native-born, English-speaking students. For example, standardized reading tests are based on a curriculum that most newcomers have not been exposed to, and often contain items that are biased in favour of the dominant culture. Thus, reading tests used in North America may contain words such as 'nickel', 'sled', and 'travois', or refer to historical figures and events that only children raised in the United States could be expected to know. Only a test in the child's first language, based on content that would be familiar to children from the same cultural background, could provide a reliable indication of the child's performance in reading. Instead, use some of the following procedures:

Assess first language proficiency

Work with a bilingual colleague to collect some language samples, oral and written. For example, to assess the child's level of social language development, conduct an interview with the child to gather information about previous school experience, family, and interests. To assess experience with literature, read an age-appropriate story in the first language with the child, and engage in discussion with the child afterwards. If the child has developed some literacy skills in the first language, encourage the child to write a response to the story. To assess the child's skill in reading academic types of text, give the child a culturally appropriate piece of non-fiction text at a level that is appropriate for the child's age and level of schooling. Provide time for silent reading, and ask questions about the content.

Even if you have no immediate access to bilingual support, a writing sample can provide some useful information: for example, does the letter or character formation appear to be appropriately developed for the child's age? How long does it take for the child to produce the piece? Does the child check and edit the piece? How simple or complex does the writing appear?

Assess academic skills and knowledge

Provide some mathematics problems with all instructions and word problems in the child's first language. (Word problems, also known as story problems, are mathematical questions that consist of scenarios such as: 'Jane has ten cookies and four friends. How many does she give to each friend, and to herself, so that everyone has the same number of cookies?') Begin with very simple tasks and progress through major skills and concepts as they are sequenced in your curriculum. When the child begins to have difficulty, show some problems from further ahead and ask if anything looks familiar. The mathematics curriculum is sequenced differently in different countries and a concept or skill taught earlier in one country may be taught later in another.

With the help of a bilingual educator or assistant, find out what you can about the child's experiences in other areas of the curriculum such as science or geography.

Assess proficiency in English

- **Engage in personal conversation** in English with the student. Begin with questions such as 'What is your name?' If the student can respond with appropriate information (though not necessarily with correct grammar or pronunciation), continue with a simple interview. This will give you a sense of how well the students can perform in simple day-to-day social interaction in English.

- **Assess vocabulary knowledge** by using a set of pictures or picture cards showing different numbers, upper and lower case letters, colour samples, shapes, and pictures of items in different categories, such as 'animals'. Ask students to name the letters or numbers in English, or identify a specific item when you name it.
- **Assess the child's ability to follow simple oral instructions** in English: use some simple props and give some instructions such as 'Give me the yellow ball', 'Put the ball in the box', 'Show me the biggest one', 'Open the book at page ten', and so on.
- **Assess the child's aural comprehension** of literature by reading a simple story to the child, and ask simple questions about the story. Begin with questions based on factual comprehension and, if the child is able to respond, continue with questions about the child's personal responses, opinions, and inferences.
- **Assess reading comprehension:** give the child several illustrated story books to choose from. Talk about the book with the child, and read a page or two to the child before asking him or her to continue reading silently. Then ask questions about the story.
- **Collect a writing sample** by asking the child to write a response to the story, or by providing a choice of topics such as *My Best Friend* or *All About Me*. You can also use interesting magazine pictures to stimulate writing; have a set ready for students to choose from.
- **Use performance descriptors** relevant to children learning a second language. In many school districts, educators have developed performance indicators, assessment and observation forms, and checklists to help teachers assess and describe the development of students who are learning the language of instruction. For example, a curriculum document in Ontario includes 'ESL Program Interpretations' for use in assessing the performance of students as they progress through several stages in learning English as a second language (Ministry of Education and Training, 1995).
- **Observe how the child uses English in the classroom**, as suggested in the next section.

Observe the child in the classroom

You can learn a lot about the newcomer through classroom observation. For example:

- Does the child establish social relationships?
- Can the child follow oral directions in the classroom and follow classroom routines?
- Does the child use the first language effectively in the classroom?
- Does the child interact with peers in English as well as the first language?
- What strategies does the child use to gain meaning from English?
- Does the child make connections with concepts learned in the first language?
- How does the child approach learning tasks?

- How comfortable is the child with partner, small-group, whole class, and individualized activities?
- Does the child show a preference for specific kinds of learning activity, or particular classroom topics?
- What learning strategies does the child employ?
- Does the child retain key concepts from one day or week to the next?
- How does the child relate to the teacher: for example, does the child ask question or initiate interaction, or only respond to the teacher's questions or instructions? Does the child need frequent approval or reinforcement, or does the child show some independence in solving problems?

Start an assessment portfolio

Include in the portfolio a record of the initial interview, and all the assessment information you have gathered. During the year, add samples of work, observation checklists and forms, and information collected through conferences and journal responses. Date each item so you can see growth and development over time. Using assessment criteria that compare learners of English as a second language with each other, rather than comparing students with native speakers of English, describe the student's proficiency level in listening, speaking, reading and writing in English on entry and at regular intervals throughout the period of second language acquisition. This is estimated to be a period of five to ten years; for an overview of the research in this area, see Collier (1989) and Cummins (1996).

Take all factors into account

If your assessment indicates that a student may be functioning several grades behind his or her peers, do not assume that there is a learning disability. Low levels of first-language literacy skills or academic achievement can often be attributed to external conditions, such as disruptions in their schooling, or limited access to schooling in the country of origin. Students who have low levels of achievement because of *lack of opportunity to learn* have not *failed to learn*, and given appropriate support, including bilingual instruction and intensive peer tutoring, most have the potential to catch up to their peers (see 'Support Services' in Chapter 4). However, some students — about the same proportion as in the general school population — may have learning difficulties that are not associated with the fact that they are learning the language instruction or have gaps in their schooling. See 'Special needs' later in this chapter.

Assessment procedures for secondary schools

At the secondary level, it is important to gather as much information as possible about the newcomer's academic background and level of proficiency in English before choosing an appropriate program. This is because most secondary school programs are organized around subjects and levels of difficulty. Compulsory or 'core' subjects such as English, mathematics, science, history, and geography may be offered at several levels within each grade level, and students may also select from a variety of elective subjects. Also, students from other countries have a wide range of educational experiences that have to be taken into account when selecting the most appropriate academic program.

Secondary students may not be placed with their age peers for all their subjects. Placement will vary according to their experience with the subjects and knowledge of English. Newcomers may be placed in some subjects ahead of their peers — for example, if they have an advanced background in mathematics — or a grade or two behind — for example, at a beginning level in French or computer studies, if they have never had any experience with these subjects before. The school may also offer several ESL classes for students at different stages of proficiency in English, or special sections of content area courses offered to groups of ESL learners.

Newcomers need to be placed in programs that offer optimum chances of success as well as the potential to satisfy their aspirations. Therefore, each student needs to participate in an initial assessment; ideally, this is conducted by staff who are knowledgeable about the educational systems in the students' countries of origin, and who are trained in second language assessment techniques. The initial assessment may include several components and involve several different members of staff; it may take more than one day to co-ordinate all the procedures.

Reception and assessment centres

Some jurisdictions provide a specialized reception and assessment centre where all students who have recently arrived from other countries spend several days in an assessment process that includes first language assessment, assessment of proficiency in English, and a 'dynamic assessment' using a test–teach–test approach to find out not only what students know, but how they respond to teaching/learning situations and how they internalize or apply new learning (Parkin and Sidnell, 1992).

In a school district that receives large numbers of new students, the advantages of this approach are considerable. For example, scarce resources, including first-language resources, personnel with experience in second-language assessment, counsellors with cross-cultural training, and community resources can be more effectively used in a centralized location. Also, there is sufficient time to make a detailed, thorough assessment of the student's educational background and needs, in an informal classroom atmosphere where students are under less pressure than they might be during an in-school procedure where time and resources are limited.

This kind of reception and assessment centre is *not* an instructional program where students remain for an extended period of time; students are assessed, provided with some basic orientation information, and referred to their local schools with recommendations for placement.

Although it may seem practical to congregate all new students in a special school or program for several months or even a year or two, the disadvantages of such an approach far outweigh the perceived advantages for most students. For example, students may have no regular contact with their English-speaking peers, and therefore lack valuable opportunities for language learning. In addition, students who attend a program in a school other than their neighbourhood school will not have a chance to make friends with whom they can socialize out of school. Moreover, the 'school culture' of a separate instructional program is not the same as that of a mainstream school, and students will have to go through another major adjustment period when they are deemed ready to transfer to the neighbourhood school.

Even if the program is offered in their own school, segregating the students from the mainstream has the effect of marginalizing them, and allows the school to continue 'business as usual' without making the necessary adjustments to include them in the academic and social life of the school. Another problem is that, unless the curriculum closely parallels that of the mainstream program, many students and parents worry about 'falling behind' in their academic studies.

Intensive programs for language and literacy development

There are some students who would benefit from a concentrated program, offered within their own neighbourhood school if possible, to prepare them for the mainstream program of the school. Learners who have missed much schooling, because of conditions in their homeland or the circumstances of their immigration, and who would have difficulty relating to the mainstream program even if it were offered in their own language, would have a better chance of success if they initially received intensive and specialized support in a program designed specifically to meet their needs.

If possible, the students would receive bilingual instruction integrating language and literacy instruction with basic skills and concepts in mathematics, science, and social studies for a considerable period of time before being totally mainstreamed. During their time in this program, it is important to involve them in activities with English-speaking students; for example, in the arts or physical education, or through peer tutoring. It is important also to ensure that all teachers in the mainstream recognize that when they eventually receive the students, the task of second language acquisition is not 'finished' and they, too, need to act as language teachers and provide a supportive learning environment for these students.

In most cases, assessment is carried out at the receiving school, and there is a often a sense of urgency about getting the student into classes as quickly as possible. However, it is better to take a day or two and make an appropriate placement at the beginning than to make a rushed decision that may cause frustration to the student and the teachers, and cause the student to lose time until a more accurate assessment and placement can be carried out. Include in your procedures an assessment of the student's development in the first language, if possible, as well as an assessment of educational background, an assessment of skills in mathematics, and an assessment of the student's proficiency in speaking, reading, and writing in English.

Assess first language proficiency

If possible, work with a bilingual colleague to collect some language samples, oral and written. For example, to assess the student's level of social language development, a bilingual educator can conduct an interview to gather detailed information about previous school experience, family, and interests. An educator familiar with the education system of the home country can provide text in the student's home language and of a type that might be familiar to the student, and conduct a reading conference using the procedure described later in this chapter, but using the student's first language throughout.

If a bilingual educator is not immediately available, it may be possible to prepare a set of written instructions in the first language requiring the student to perform tasks such as 'Draw a _____', or to respond to some multiple choice questions. It is important to make sure that the tasks are relevant to the student's background knowledge and to teach the student how to answer multiple choice questions. A teacher with little or no knowledge of the student's first language could use the English version to determine at a glance whether the student was able to comprehend written instructions and questions in the first language. Preparing such multilingual assessment tasks might be better accomplished at the school district level, using all the available cultural and linguistic resources.

It is also helpful to collect a writing sample in the student's first language. Even if you have no immediate access to bilingual support, a writing sample can provide some useful information: for example, does the letter or character formation appear to be appropriately developed for the student's age? How long does it take for the student to produce the piece? Does the student check and edit the piece? How simple or complex does the writing appear?

Assess educational background

During the initial interview, find out as much as possible about the student's previous educational experience, with the assistance of an interpreter if necessary. If the student has educational documents, have them assessed by an educator who is familiar with the education system that issued them. Many students do not have documents, because they may have left the home country under conditions of extreme urgency. In this case, interview the student in some detail about his or her previous educational experience. Do not confine your questions to the subjects taught in your own school system; many students may have had experience of subjects such as philosophy, religion, or citizenship that may not be included in the curriculum in your school. Show the student some textbooks in subjects such as

science and geography, containing plenty of charts, graphs, diagrams, maps, and other visual material, and ask the student to identify items that seem familiar.

Some students may need a more detailed educational assessment conducted in the first language, especially in cases where there have been gaps in the student's education, or where school personnel are not familiar with the system of education in the country or countries where the student has received his or her previous education. It is best if the person carrying out this assessment is an educator who is familiar with the education system in the student's home country, as well as with the local curriculum, although this may be difficult to arrange in many schools. Arrange this assessment as soon as possible so that the student may be placed in an appropriate program and given the necessary support.

Assess skills in mathematics

Provide a mathematics assessment that focusses on key concepts and skills, beginning with simple computation and word problems from the elementary curriculum, before moving into the secondary curriculum. To reduce anxiety and allow the student some time to review, give the student a practice test to take home. Next day, the student can take a test that is almost identical, except that all the number values have been changed. Because the mathematics curriculum is sequenced differently from country to country, encourage students to skip over problems that seem unfamiliar and look ahead for others that they can do.

To assess mathematical skills and knowledge fairly

- Do not include problems that require the student to use a calculator. Many students come from countries where there is a strong emphasis on mental computation, and calculators are not allowed in the mathematics program.
- Do not expect students to use the same algorithms as those which are taught in your local curriculum. For example, students all over the world are taught different ways to regroup ('borrow' and 'carry') numbers, or do long division.
- Do not expect students to show every step in solving a problem. Many students have been taught not to do this, but to do as much mental computation as possible.
- Use metric measures unless the child is from a country that uses another system: for example, Imperial measures are still used in the English-speaking Caribbean.
- Avoid culturally-based problems such as those associated with sports, fruits and vegetables, or geographical knowledge.
- Provide the test in the student's own language. These tests must be translated by someone who is not only proficient in both languages, but is also familiar with mathematical terminology and the mathematics curriculum.

Assess oral proficiency in English

During the initial interview, find out if the student has had previous exposure to English. If the student has studied English as a foreign language in school, find out for how many years, and for how many hours a week. Some students may have received some English language training in a refugee camp. If the student has had no exposure to English, the student is a beginning level learner of English and there is no need to conduct any formal assessment. If the student has some knowledge of English, you can make an assessment of oral proficiency by conducting an informal interview in English.

Preliminary assessment of proficiency in English: listening and speaking

These interview questions will help you to assess how well the student understands oral English. Make sure to use performance criteria relevant to learners of English to describe the student's proficiency level.

Note: Do not expect the student to answer all the questions 1–7 in complete sentences; an answer that makes sense indicates comprehension, and it would be unnatural for native-speakers to answer in complete sentences.

1. *What is your name?*
2. *How old are you?*
3. *Where were you born?*
4. *On what date?*
5. *What language do you speak at home?*

6. *What is your address?*
7. *How many years did you go to school in your country?*

Proceed to question 8–13 only if the student was able to answer questions 1–7. Questions 8–13 are intended to elicit extended answers and you will be able to listen for grammatical features in the student's response such as the use of plurals, subject–verb agreement, or past tense. Sometimes you may need to use additional prompts such as *Can you tell me more about that?* or *Begin your answer like this . . . .*

8. *How did you get here today? Begin your answer like this: 'I . . . '*
9. *Why did you/your family come to _____?*
10. *Tell me about your last school.*
    How was it different from this one?
    Did you like it? Why? Why not?
    What subjects did you like?
11. *Finish these descriptions:*
    A good teacher is someone who . . .
    A good student is someone who . . .
12. *What are you going to do when you leave here today?*
13. *What are your hopes and wishes for the future?*
    Where do you think you will be five years from now?
    What do you think you will be doing five years from now?

Assess reading comprehension in English

If the student has formally studied English before, you can carry out an assessment of reading comprehension. The purpose of a reading assessment is to get some idea of how well students are able to deal with the language of instruction.

You can use tests adapted from standardized tests, use a reading inventory, or develop your own informal tests. Whatever procedure you use, interpret the results with extreme caution. Reading tests administered in the student's second language can give an estimate of *performance in reading in a second language*, but should never be assumed to measure the student's level of *achievement in reading*.

Tests adapted from standardized tests: It is not advisable to use standardized tests with linguistically and culturally diverse groups of students and compare their scores with norms developed for students who are native speakers of English and who have had long-term exposure to mainstream culture. Standardized tests are culturally biased in favour of the group for whom they were designed. The items on the test are selected according to certain assumptions about the body of knowledge or skills that children in a particular cultural and educational context could be expected to have acquired through exposure to the same set of experiences. In the diversity of social class, language, culture, and rural or urban background that constitutes society in North America, the United States, Great Britain, and Australia, no standardized test can be appropriate for all the children subjected to it.

Avoid the use of standardized tests unless you have access to cultural informants who can help you to eliminate bias as much as possible and interpret the results fairly. The use of standardized tests with linguistically and culturally different populations requires considerable adaptation of content, and the administration of the tests may also require revision. You will also need to develop your own norms based on the performance of second language learners, rather than on the performance of native speakers. Of course, once you have made these adaptations, the test is no longer standardized, and you will use them as informal tests only.

The most useful kind of standardized test is a reading comprehension test consisting of a series of short graded reading passages, each followed by a question on the content, usually in a multiple choice format. The student's raw score on the test is usually converted into a percentile, decile, standardized score, age-related norm, or grade level. These tests are often used when there are large numbers of students needing assessment, as they may be administered in a group setting and are quick to score. Reading comprehension tests can provide useful information on the student's proficiency in reading texts in the language of instruction, as long as some important adaptations are made. When you interpret the test results, remember that as soon as any aspect of the test is changed, it is no longer standardized.

How to adapt your own (non-standardized) test from a standardized test

- Remove culturally inappropriate content and vocabulary.
- Develop your own 'norms' or placement criteria related to the performance of second language learners and the placement options available for second language instruction.
- Teach the student how to take the test. Show the student how to mark the answer. Some students may be unfamiliar with the multiple choice format. Do not use tests that require the student to mark a separate answer sheet: this can be confusing.
- Provide some practice questions that are not scored. Give feedback on the practice questions.
- Do not give out the whole test at once. It is less intimidating if you give the student one page at a time, and you can monitor performance more closely.
- Do not time the test. End the test when three consecutive errors are made.
- If you want to measure growth, administer the same test again in six months to a year.

Informal reading inventories: An alternative to standardized test is the informal reading inventory. A reading inventory usually consists of graded word lists that are used to assess word recognition, and graded passages that can be used to assess oral reading strategies, silent reading comprehension, and listening comprehension. Not all of the components are appropriate for students who are not native speakers of

English; for example, the task of oral reading places too many demands on them, and many of their 'miscues' may be related to difficulties with pronunciation rather than difficulty in recognizing the words. However, using the graded passages for silent reading comprehension can reveal useful information about specific aspects of reading comprehension such as understanding the main idea, finding details, following sequence, relating cause and effect, or making inferences. Several versions of these have been designed; one that is relatively easy to administer is the *Burns/Roe Informal Reading Inventory* (Burns and Roe, 1993). As with standardized reading tests, it may be necessary to adapt some passages that contain culturally unfamiliar concepts.

Oral reading tests: why not use them?

There are two kinds of oral reading test. Word recognition tests consist of word lists, selected according to frequency in the language arts program or reading curriculum at specific grade levels. These tests are used to measure a student's sight vocabulary: the words that he/she can recognize and say on sight, with no supporting context.

There are some problems with this kind of assessment. Firstly, the words are selected on the basis of word frequency in the educational experiences of a particular cultural group. For example, in North America young readers encounter many stories about animals, and words for animals and baby animals appear early on the word lists. Children from cultures which do not attribute human qualities to animals, and do not value them as pets, cannot be assumed to have encountered these words with the same kind of frequency. At the same time, they may know other words which do not appear on the list, or appear much later in the list for the group on whose experience the test is normed. A second problem with word recognition tests is that this does not constitute reading. Reading single words in isolation is seldom required in real reading tasks. There are some one-word signs — street signs, signs in buildings, etc. — but these signs are never presented out of context: a sign on a door clearly labels the function of that room.

The second kind of oral reading test consists of prose passages which have been carefully graded and controlled for vocabulary and sentence complexity. The student reads the passage aloud, and the tester notes hesitations and miscues. These tests can provide helpful information about pronunciation patterns and the analysis of miscues may indicate some of the reader's strategies for dealing with text, such as self-correction, re-reading, or making meaningful substitutions. However, oral reading tests do not provide a true assessment of reading comprehension. Reading aloud is unnatural behaviour, except for performance purposes such as reading a speech or a newscast — in which case, it has been rehearsed. Students reading aloud in a second language are often concentrating more on pronunciation than on comprehension and may get little or no meaning from what they read. It is not unusual for a student to perform well in oral reading but then be unable to answer comprehension questions on the text, or to stumble and falter through a reading passage that they are able to comprehend when they read it silently.

Informal teacher-designed tests: As an alternative to formal tests, informal assessment procedures can be used. An important advantage of informal, locally-designed assessment procedures is that they can be designed to match the local curriculum, and tailored to individual students. Another advantage is that they are much less intimidating to students than formal tests.

The reading conference and the cloze test are both useful instruments for assessing reading comprehension. The reading conference is more time consuming; when time is limited, a cloze test might be a better choice. If you are doing an in-depth assessment over a period of several days, you could use both.

How to conduct a reading conference

- Collect a variety of real texts. These may consist of fiction, or you may choose texts related to an area of the curriculum. For example, you could choose a page from a book on world geography, or the geography of the student's home country. Choose texts at several levels of difficulty, beginning with children's picture books and working up to texts at the secondary level.
- Choose a text that is appropriate for the student's present level of second language acquisition. If you are not sure, begin with the easiest text and work up, or ask the student to choose a text.
- Give the student a few minutes to survey the entire text silently for a minute or two, to get an idea of what kind of text it is.
- Ask the student what kind of text this is: for example, is it fiction or non-fiction? What is it about? Ask what cues were helpful: e.g., headings, subheadings, graphic material, key words, etc.
- Indicate a section for the student to read silently.
- When the student appears to be ready, ask the student to retell the main idea or story line.
- Ask questions that encourage the student to refer back to the text in order to find details or examples, relate cause and effect, and make predictions, inferences, and judgments.
- If the student performs the task with ease, repeat the procedure with a more difficult text.

How to construct and use a cloze test

- To create a cloze test, first choose a short passage of expository text from a grade-level textbook. Select passages from a variety of texts at several different grade levels, so you can develop tests at different levels of difficulty. Make sure that the passages you choose do not assume prior knowledge that the newcomer may not have.

- Construct the cloze passage by typing out a section of text, deleting every seventh word. Some will be content words (nouns, verbs, etc.) and some will be function words (prepositions, articles, conjunctions, etc.). Leave the first sentence or two intact, or provide a short introduction to support comprehension of the cloze passage that follows.
- Choose a passage that you think the student will be able to read. If you are not sure, begin with the easiest text and work up.
- Ask the student to fill in the missing words, using any words that make sense. Encourage the student to supply a word in the first language if he or she can't think of the word in English. If the student is able to get meaning from the text, he/she will insert words that make sense within the context of the passage.
- In scoring this test, **accept all meaningful words**; students are not expected to predict the exact words used in the original piece. A response that is *semantically correct* but *grammatically incorrect* is correct for the purposes of the test: it indicates that the student is able to follow the meaning of the passage. If at least 75% of a student's responses are appropriate, he or she is able independently to read and get meaning from text at this level. Students who insert responses that are between 60% and 75% correct will need some instructional support (Law and Eckes, 1990).
- If the student performs the task with ease, repeat the procedure with a more difficult text.

Interpreting and sharing the information: Whether you use the conference and cloze procedure or an informal reading inventory, or prefer to adapt your own test from a standardized text, you will need to establish some criteria for placement. To do this, try the procedure on groups of second language learners who are already placed in various aspects of the school program. If you correlate their performance on the reading assessment to the teacher's assessment of their performance in the subject, you will be able to identify specific levels of performance that are a 'required minimum' for success in particular subjects or grade levels.

Be cautious about sharing the results of the initial assessment with other teachers. For example, do not give a grade-level equivalency; this can be very misleading when describing second language learners, whose actual reading proficiency (in their first language) is usually much greater than the level of performance they can show in their second language. Teachers who are not aware of this may make negative assumptions about the student's intellectual capabilities, and hold low expectations for the student's performance (for more on the importance of teachers' expectations, see Chapter 6). In fact, the knowledge students may bring to a subject will often help to compensate for the difficulties they may have in reading English. Also, supportive teaching can help students deal with material that is beyond their independent comprehension level and help them develop as readers. Several of the resource books listed at the end of this chapter provide excellent practical advice to classroom teachers on how to support students who are learning the language of instruction.

Describing performance

Instead of using grade-level equivalency to compare second language learners with native speakers of English, describe what kind of reading task the student is able to accomplish in English. For example, it would be helpful for teachers to know that a student in the early stages of learning English may be able to:

- recognize the Roman alphabet in upper and lower case print
- recognize common signs, symbols and other environmental print
- comprehend simple sentences with common vocabulary in material that deals with familiar concepts and is supported by visual material
- understand common grammatical structures in highly supported contexts: e.g., simple verb tenses, negatives, questions, plurals, pronouns, common adjectives and basic prepositions
- demonstrate comprehension by:
    drawing or pointing to a picture
    pointing to, reading aloud or writing down a key word or phrase
    responding to simple Yes/No questions
    expressing personal responses through patterned statements
    completing a simple cloze passage
    completing a graphic organizer
- follow short direct written instructions related to familiar topics and tasks
- apply reading strategies such as sight recognition, simple phonics, familiar syntactic patterns, context, and background knowledge in order to gain meaning from print material that is appropriate to the student's level of proficiency in English
- choose appropriate material in English for independent reading and personal enjoyment

Assess the student's writing in English

If the student was able to participate in the reading assessment, go on to collect a writing sample. Students with limited proficiency can respond to a picture by listing what they see. Others may construct a more detailed description or write a story. With more advanced students, it would be helpful to collect more than one writing sample of different kinds: for example, a piece of personal writing, a narrative, a letter, a descriptive piece, or some expository writing.

Topics for Writing

Give students a choice of topics. Students who have had several years of English as a foreign language in their own countries, or who have already been in an ESL program in another school, may be able to respond to one of the following topics:

Write a letter to a friend in your own country. Tell your friend about your life in Canada.

Write a letter to introduce yourself to your new teachers.
Describe your favourite teacher in your old school.
Describe a holiday that you celebrate in your country.
Do you think boys and girls should go to separate schools? Why, or why not?
hat are your wishes and hopes for the future?

Many new students will bring a bilingual dictionary with them; allow them to use these during the writing assessment. It would also be a good idea to have bilingual dictionaries in the students' languages available in the classroom. The purpose of the assessment is to find out how the student handles a writing task, using all the resources available. You might want them to identify which words they looked up. If a student asks you for a word — for example, the word for an object in a picture — write it down so that the student can copy it and continue with the writing task.

When you assess the writing sample, use a holistic approach, looking at the student's communicative intent before focussing on the surface errors which second language learners make. Consider the relevance of the information, and how it is organized, before you consider word choice, sentence structure, spelling, and punctuation.

Start an assessment portfolio

Keep all the assessment information and a copy of the information you have gathered through the initial interview in a file or portfolio. During the year, work with the student's subject teachers to add samples of work and other information to the portfolio. This portfolio may be maintained by the ESL teacher or by a counsellor with special responsibility for monitoring the progress of the second language learners in the school. It can also be shared with parents during parent–teacher interviews and student-led parent–teacher conferences.

Make a provisional placement

The decisions that are made about a student's placement can colour the student's whole school experience. Unfortunately, newcomers are sometimes placed in classrooms where the only likely outcome is failure, either because the students are not adequately prepared for the subject, or because the teachers are not adequately prepared for the students. To minimize errors of this kind, it is important to review the initial placement after a couple of weeks, and at regular intervals after that. See 'Support Services' in Chapter 4 for suggestions on how to monitor the progress of individual students and groups of students.

Most secondary school students will need to be placed in an ESL class, and perhaps one or two content courses designed specifically to meet the needs of ESL learners (if these are available). Most students, including beginning level learners of English, will benefit from being placed in at least one mainstream subject where they can interact with their English-speaking peers. Most students can participate successfully in the mainstream mathematics program, even if they are new to English, as long as they have the necessary background in mathematics. For beginning learners of English, the visual or kinetic aspects of subjects such as Physical Education, Family Studies, Visual Art, or Music will support comprehension and foster second language acquisition.

Some students need a lot more support than others. Students whose education has been interrupted, and who have limited literacy in their own language, will benefit from being placed in one classroom with a trained ESL teacher for at least half of the day. Here they can concentrate on basic literacy and numeracy skills. Their program may be supplemented with bilingual support and intensive peer tutoring (see 'Support Services' in Chapter 4). They may be starting several grades behind their peers, but most are anxious to learn and, given time and the right kind of support, many can reach the same goals in the end. Hamayan (1994) provides guidance for teachers on how to design the instructional program for students with low levels of literacy in their own language.

Once students have been placed in a program designed to meet their needs, it is important to monitor their progress and provide academic and social support, as suggested in Chapter Four. All students feel more secure if there is somebody in the building who understands their needs, especially if they are newcomers, second language learners, or members of a cultural minority in the school.

Special needs

Some newly arrived and culturally diverse students — about the same percentage as in the overall school population — have special learning needs. However, it is important to be extremely cautious in making this judgment. When considering a student for psychological assessment, or in interpreting the results of such an assessment, it is essential to take into account the fact that the student may still be learning English and may be unfamiliar with some of the cultural knowledge and experiences that may be taken for granted in curriculum and assessment. In this case poor performance on curriculum-based assessment tasks or on standardized IQ and achievement tests may be attributed to the fact that the tests are administered in the child's second language, and performance on such tests is interpreted from the perspective of the majority culture.

It takes a lot longer than is commonly recognized to become academically proficient in a second language. According to Cummins, many students achieve 'Basic Interpersonal Communication Skills', with an emphasis on oral language, within two or three years. However, a period of five years or more may be required for second language learners to acquire 'Cognitive Academic Language Proficiency' (Cummins, 1984, 1996). Other research has shown that teachers tend to overestimate the proficiency of students learning English as their second language, basing their assessment on the students' surface communication skills: teachers rate the students as native-like in performance after a year or two, whereas formal assessment indicates that the students do not achieve native-like proficiency even after six years in an English-speaking environment (Klesmer, 1994).

Most students receive direct bilingual or second language instruction for a much shorter period. According to McKeon (1994), almost 25% of the students who are learning the language of instruction in US schools do not receive specialized ESL or bilingual instruction. Most students are fully integrated into mainstream classes within a year or two, although they are still in the process of acquiring the language of instruction. If teachers assume that the language acquisition process is complete once students demonstrate competence in Basic Interpersonal Communication Skills, they may assume that students who perform below expectations on academic tasks or formal assessments are learning disabled. The students may be referred for assessment by educational psychologists who also assume that the students have already completed the process of second language acquisition and that the assessment instruments are therefore valid (Cummins, 1984, 1996). One result is that second language learners often end up over-represented in special education programs. In many such cases, the problem may lie in the program of instruction rather than the student's cognitive development. (See also 'Opportunity to Learn' in Chapter 9.)

This does not mean that no student who is learning English as a second language can be identified as having special needs– even if they are very recent arrivals. Some special needs may become evident during the initial reception interview, especially if these needs have been identified in the home country, or if they relate to a physical disability such as hearing impairment. Some students may have special education needs that have not previously been identified, especially if they are from countries where special education services do not exist or are very limited.

It is important to identify students with special needs as soon as possible so that they can receive the special support they need, in addition to ESL and other support that is provided for newcomers and students who are learning the language of instruction. Teachers may identify these needs through observation of the student's learning rate and strategies, and through assessment of the student's growth in English. Before making any referral for further assessment — for example, by an educational psychologist — adopt an 'ecological' approach that takes into all the variables within the learner and within the teaching–learning context (Cloud, 1994). This will help teachers to distinguish between low levels of academic achievement that are a result of limited schooling, or linguistic or social behaviour that are a normal part of the students' adjustment towards the new culture and language, and problems that may indicate a learning disability. If a student is to be formally assessed, it is important to do so before the first language has begun to lose ground. It is also important to involve a bilingual educator in any additional assessment, such as psychological tests, so that the tests can be conducted in the first language, and culturally biased items can be identified and eliminated or interpreted with caution. Make sure that parents are informed and involved in the process.

The initial assessment of a student's educational needs may indicate a need for second language support. The next section describes some approaches for supporting students who are learning English as a second language.

SUPPORT FOR SECOND LANGUAGE ACQUISITION

There are three fundamental principles to consider in designing a program for students who are learning the language of instruction:

(1) Students who are learners of English as a second language need *a planned program of support for several years*. Students who are fully 'mainstreamed' too soon into grade level classes without language support are at risk of failure; in a Canadian study of secondary school students, even students who entered the school with an 'advanced' knowledge of English, compared with other newly arrived ESL learners, had a dropout rate of 50% (i.e., 50% of the students left school without graduating); among students who arrived at secondary school as beginning learners of English, the dropout rate was 95.5% (Watt and Roessingh, 1994). Many students left school when they were integrated into the mainstream program with little or no continued support for second language acquisition. Other studies have shown that it takes five to ten years to become proficient in using English for academic purposes (for an overview of the research, see Collier, 1987; Cummins, 1996).

At the secondary level, schools and school districts may need to rethink some common practices. For example, in school districts where there is an age limit on enrolment, many immigrant students reach the age limit before they are able to reach the level of proficiency in English that is required for graduation. This was the case in Alberta, where the high dropout rate among ESL students might be more accurately described as push out (Watt and Roessingh, 1994). An age limit for high school completion discriminates against immigrant students who are learning the language of instruction. An examination or other kind of assessment that sets standards for performance in English based on the performance of native English speakers constitutes another barrier for second language learners, who have not had the opportunity to learn the required skills (see Chapter 9 for more on assessment and opportunity to learn).

(2) Although they continue to need support for several years, second language learners also need *opportunities for involvement in the mainstream program of the school*. Even beginning learners of English need to interact on a regular basis with fluent or more proficient users of English; therefore, it is not appropriate to keep them entirely apart from the mainstream program. Second language learners may be able to function very well in some areas of the curriculum, as long as their teachers are aware of their needs and provide an appropriate learning environment where they can learn new content and skills, and develop their knowledge of English at the same time. Therefore, all teachers need to be proficient in adjusting instruction to the needs of different groups of students in

the class, and in using instructional strategies that integrate language and content. Although it is beyond the scope of this book to discuss second language acquisition and instruction in detail, some of the resources listed at the end of this chapter provide valuable advice on these and related topics.

(3) Students' first languages continue to be important in their linguistic, social, and cognitive development (see Cummins, 1996, for a thorough discussion). Therefore, it is important that the school *promote the maintenance and continued development of students' first languages*, and set them alongside English as languages of the school and classroom. Chapters 4 and 5 include some suggestions on how to do this.

There is no single model for the delivery of second language instruction that is appropriate for all schools or all students. The language program may vary from school to school and from student to student, depending on factors such as the demographic composition of the school, the local resources that are available, and each student's individual needs. Many schools in Canada, the United States, Britain, and Australia have a teacher or a group of teachers who are responsible for teaching English as a Second Language (ESL) to students who arrive at the school with limited experience in the language. However, this is not the only model, and many schools develop a program based on one or more of the models described below.

Reception centres

These are intended, as the name implies, to receive newly arrived students. Many provide assessment and referral services, as described earlier in this chapter. Others provide an instructional program to help newcomers adjust to their new academic and social environment and begin to learn English. In some school districts there may be only one or two centres, and students from across the district attend the school where the centre is instead of attending their local school. In others, every school may have such a centre.

Reception centres that provide instructional programs as well as assessment services have the advantage of concentrating resources, and providing a program specifically designed for ESL learners. However, there are significant disadvantages associated with removing students from neighbourhood schools and mainstream classrooms. For example, the teachers in the reception centre are often the only English speakers available to the students; if students have no regular contact with their English-speaking peers, they are denied valuable opportunities for language learning. In addition, students who attend a centre in a school other than their neighbourhood school may not have a chance to make friends with whom they can socialize out of school. Moreover, the 'school culture' of a reception centre is not the same as that of a mainstream school, and students will have to go through another major adjustment period when they are deemed ready to transfer to the neighbourhood school. Even if the centre is in their own school, segregating the students from the mainstream has the effect of marginalizing them, and allows the school to continue 'business as usual' without making the necessary adjustments to include them in the academic and social life of the school. Another problem is that, unless the curriculum closely parallels that of the mainstream program, many students and parents worry about 'falling behind' in their academic studies.

In spite of the disadvantages, there may be some students who would benefit from a concentrated program such as a reception centre can offer. Learners who have missed much schooling, because of conditions in their homeland or the circumstances of their immigration, and who would have difficulty relating to the mainstream program even if it were offered in their own language, would have a better chance of success if they initially received intensive and specialized support in a program designed specifically to meet their needs. If possible, the students would receive bilingual instruction integrating language and literacy instruction with basic skills and concepts in mathematics, science, and social studies for a considerable period of time before being totally mainstreamed. During their time in the reception centre, it is important to involve them in activities with English-speaking students; for example, in the arts or physical education, or through peer tutoring. It is important also to ensure that all teachers in the mainstream recognize that when they eventually receive the students, the task of second language acquisition is not "finished" and they, too, need to act as language teachers and provide a supportive learning environment for the students.

Withdrawal programs

In some school districts, these are referred to as 'pull-out' programs. Students at all grade levels may be withdrawn from the regular classroom for part of the day, to work with the ESL teacher. In secondary schools, this program is often offered as an alternative to the English program. Secondary schools may also offer parallel programs in core subjects such as History, Geography, or Science, so that students can continue to make academic progress in an ESL environment. The ESL setting provides a low-risk setting for learners to begin speaking English, learn about their new environment, and make friends. The ESL teacher also has opportunities to assess the learners' needs and strengths, and to select content and resources that are directly related to the learners' needs and backgrounds. As far as possible, the content is related to the mainstream curriculum, and the ESL teacher maintains close contact with classroom teachers.

Methods of withdrawal vary. Some programs withdraw all the students at the beginning level at the same time, to create more or less homogeneous groupings in terms of language proficiency. This means the ESL teacher can plan instruction for the whole group. However, it means that students at different grade levels are in the same group, and that makes it difficult to appeal to the maturity level of all the learners, or to relate the program to what is going on in their mainstream classrooms. Other programs withdraw all the ESL learners at the same grade level. This means the teacher works with students of varying levels of proficiency in English. This is more demanding for the teacher, who has to provide several different tasks related to a particular topic, at different levels of linguistic difficulty, rather than one task for all the students. On the other hand, heterogeneous groupings are more supportive of language acquisition; the less proficient students have opportunities to interact with more proficient peers who act as language models and informants, while the more proficient students increase their metalinguistic awareness as they rephrase, explain, and provide examples for their peers. Also, it is easier to design a program that parallels the mainstream program if the teacher is working with students from only one or two grade levels.

It is usually best to withdraw students from the mainstream when the other students are involved in subjects such as language arts or social studies, that are linguistically and culturally very demanding. This has implications for timetabling in the school. To facilitate grade-level groupings, it would be helpful if these subjects were 'blocked in' at the same time. In some schools, the best approach might be to create an 'ESL core' class for students at each grade level, where the students receive instruction from the ESL teacher in core subjects such as mathematics, science, social studies, and language arts, and are involved in the mainstream program for the rest of the day.

The program needs to be flexible. As soon as students demonstrate a level of proficiency that will allow them to be successful in an area of the curriculum, they can benefit from participation in the mainstream program. For example, many students arrive from other countries with a level of proficiency in mathematics that is similar to or above that of their age peers, and it would be best not to withdraw them during the mathematics period. A mathematics program delivered by a teacher sensitive to the needs of second language learners can be an ideal language learning environment even for students at the beginning level of second language acquisition, especially if there is plenty of opportunity to 'talk mathematics' through involvement in group activities (see 'Co-operative Learning Groups' in Chapter 5).

A well-planned withdrawal program can reduce the demands on grade-level teachers and on second language learners by providing alternative curriculum and instruction for the most linguistically and culturally demanding aspects of the curriculum. Withdrawal is appropriate for students in the first two years of second language acquisition. Meanwhile, grade-level and subject teachers are responsible for continuing to support language acquisition at times when the second language learners are integrated into the mainstream program, and after the students 'graduate' from the withdrawal program.

Supported integration

An integrated program of language instruction occurs in the mainstream classroom, where the language learners are integrated with fluent speakers for some or all of the day. It would be counterproductive to keep ESL learners apart from the mainstream program while they learn English; a language is best acquired by using it to do something meaningful, such as learning how to play baseball, solving a mathematics word problem, creating a dramatic retelling of a story, planning a class outing, or working on a group project. Therefore, even beginning learners of English need to spend part of the day in the mainstream classroom, interacting with peers and teachers on content-based tasks. The mainstream classroom offers opportunities for second language acquisition, social integration, and academic growth that the ESL classroom alone cannot offer. A well-planned integrated model also fosters positive intercultural attitudes among all the learners. For these reasons, the mainstream program is an important component of the ESL program.

Integration does not occur simply by giving a student a desk in the classroom. The classroom teacher and the ESL teacher need to work collaboratively to develop an effective integration program. This may be a new way of working for both teachers. It is important to delineate roles and expectations. For example, neither teacher is a teaching assistant, although there may be times when one teacher may assume more of a support role. Before starting, it is advisable for the teachers to establish what each other's strengths are, and build on those. Teachers working together need to communicate openly and value each other's point of view; it would be helpful to agree on a process for addressing disagreements before starting to work together.

Supported integration allows teachers to work from their own strengths and talents, and provides a model for students as they develop their own collaborative skills. Integration in the mainstream provides language learners with more opportunities for interaction with their peers in the mainstream classroom, as well as the extra support they need to enable them to participate in classroom activities and follow the same curriculum as their peers. In addition, the presence of another teacher in the room provides an extra pair of eyes and ears for observing the participation of the second language learners in classroom activities, or the interaction patterns between the second language learners and native speakers of English in the classroom. This is important in evaluating the effectiveness of the program or of specific activities.

It is beyond the scope of this book to provide detailed suggestions on how to integrate language and content instruction; however, many of the resource books listed at the end of this chapter provide excellent advice.

Bilingual education

While ESL programs and teachers can provide immensely valuable support to second language learners and their teachers, it has to be acknowledged that learning in a second language, no matter how supportive the program, is less effective than learning in the first. This is not a new concept: according to a UNESCO report published in 1953, 'it is axiomatic that the best medium for teaching' is a child's first language (UNESCO, 1953; cited in Corson, 1993: 71). Therefore, one of the functions of the ESL program is to compensate for the fact that the students are learning in a language other than their own.

A potential problem of monolingual (English-only) programs for second language instruction is that many students are in danger of losing their first language, with negative social and academic consequences (see Wong Fillmore, 1991; Cummins, 1996). On the other hand, providing instruction in the first language only does not meet the students' needs for academic and social integration, not only within the school, but in the wider society beyond. In order to have equal opportunities for success, all students have to learn the dominant language.

Bilingual education is available in some areas of the United States, where many schools and school districts have large populations of specific language groups such as Spanish. Bilingual education involves the use of both the target language and the first language of the students as languages of instruction. Some bilingual programs are designed to be transitional, providing support for linguistic and conceptual development only until the students have acquired enough English to enable them to function in English only. Others are designed to maintain first language development and support the students in becoming fully bilingual. Some programs that include second language learners and native speakers have the aim of promoting bilingualism in all the learners, including speakers of the dominant language.

What does 'bilingual' mean?

There is some disagreement about what the term 'bilingual' means. The *Nelson Canadian Dictionary of the English Language* (1997) defines 'bilingual' as 'using or able to use two languages, esp. with nearly equal fluency'. However, the term has different connotations in different contexts. For example, although Canada is officially a bilingual country, this is a legal and constitutional definition; most anglophones are functionally monolingual.

Some school districts use the term 'bilingual' to describe students who arrive at school speaking a language other than the dominant language, and are learning the language of instruction at school. Gregory (1996) observes that such students are far from bilingual, in the sense of being competent in two languages, and prefers the term 'emergent bilinguals'.

Many 'bilingual' programs are not intended to develop full bilingual capabilities in the children. Some school districts use the term for programs that are provided to students who are designated 'bilingual', even when the program itself is offered in English only. Cummins (1996) points out that some 'bilingual' programs offered to such students promote 'subtractive bilingualism' which entails the loss of the first language — often with negative academic consequences. Cummins contrasts this approach with 'additive bilingualism' which promotes the development of the child's first and second languages, and suggests that 'the evidence points clearly in the direction of metalinguistic, academic, and intellectual benefits for bilingual children who continue to develop both their languages' (Cummins, 1996: 109).

It should be noted that, in spite of the common use of the term 'bilingual' to describe students and programs, the dominant approach in Canada, the United

States, Britain, and Australia is the ESL model, where English is the only language of instruction.

Bilingual programs — especially those designed to promote full bilingualism — offer the best opportunities for students to meet *all* the learning outcomes for the particular grade or subject they are enrolled in. In addition, continued development of the first language supports cognitive and affective development. In the best of all possible worlds, all second language learners would be involved in rich, content-based bilingual programs. However, this is an option only in contexts where there are enough students in a school of a specific language group. Also, in some educational jurisdictions, especially where an official language or languages are enshrined in law, it is not permissible to offer academic instruction in any language other than the official language(s). For example, in Ontario, in Canada, the academic curriculum may be taught only in French and English, the two official languages.

Resource teachers

In some schools and school districts, resource teachers support classroom teachers and students in a variety of ways, usually in settings where there are too few ESL students to create ESL classes, or where they are scattered across grade levels in ways that make class groupings impractical. ESL resource teachers may work in one school, or in several schools on an itinerant basis, and they usually work with teachers as well as directly with students. For example, an ESL teacher in a school, or an itinerant teacher working in several schools, can support teachers by finding or developing alternative resource material, or leading staff discussion groups related to the needs of ESL learners. The ESL resource teacher may provide direct assistance to individual students or small groups on a limited withdrawal basis. The ESL teacher can also provide support for students by setting up and monitoring volunteer and peer tutoring programs.

ESL resource assistance may be available within a school as one component of a larger ESL program. For example, an 'ESL Resource Centre' may serve as a drop-in centre where students who have 'graduated' from the formal ESL program can come for occasional assistance and advice. This may be offered outside the regular school day, at lunch time or after school, so that students do not have to leave the mainstream program in order to receive assistance.

Learning Standard English

Many children speak varieties of English that differ markedly from standard English. For example, many children in the United States speak Black English Vernacular (also known as African American Vernacular English and, in popular usage, 'Ebonics'). Many children of Caribbean background speak an English-related creole language that is so different from English that many linguists classify it as a distinct language. However, most of these children consider themselves to be English speakers, and typically they have had much more exposure to standard English than their peers from other language backgrounds such as Spanish or Vietnamese.

Most speakers of Black English Vernacular and other varieties of English, and speakers of English-related creole languages, are able to switch between the variety they use at home and a variety that is closer to standard English. However, some students may not have full control of certain features of standard English, such as the marking of the past tense or plurals, because they are unconsciously applying the grammar rules of another linguistic system. Students who produce approximations of standard English are often able to get their meaning across, and can follow most of what goes on in class, but their language use is often viewed as deficient, and there are occasional misinterpretations — sometimes serious — when both parties to an interaction use the same words or phrases with different meanings. The students often receive the message that their own language is 'wrong' or 'bad English' , and this can have negative effects on self-esteem. Also, teachers who lack information about language and language variety often regard these students not as learners of standard English, but as English speakers who are careless, lazy, or of limited intellectual capacity.

It is important to recognize and validate the linguistic systems that students bring to school, and all languages and varieties of languages should be viewed as equally valid forms of communication.

At the same time, it is the function of the school to help all students to develop proficiency in standard English. Children need an awareness of the pragmatic value of standard English, not as a language that is superior to their own, but as a language that is associated with success in the wider society. A Language Awareness program for all students can help promote positive attitudes towards language diversity and language variety (Hawkins, 1987).

Speakers of varieties of English other than Standard English and speakers of English-related creole languages need focussed instruction, and a raised awareness of language, in order to become fully proficient in the standard or prestige variety (Coelho, 1991a). Because these learners have had a lot of exposure to English and know most of the basic vocabulary, it is not appropriate to provide them with an instructional program designed for children who are learning English as a new language. Instead, they need teachers who will explain and provide practice in specific areas of difference between standard English and the variety that the children speak. In this way, teachers can help their students to 'move on to the next step — the step vital to success in America — the appropriation of the oral and written forms demanded by the mainstream' (Delpit 1986: 383).

What is Standard English?

Standard English is one of many varieties or dialects of English. The standard dialect is the one which is spoken by those in authority and those with education, and is usually the most widely accepted and understood in the society at large.

The term 'standard' is often used as if it were synonymous with 'correct'; in fact, all varieties are equally 'correct', and standard English owes its status more to might than to right. A famous saying among linguists, commonly attributed to Max Weinreich, is that 'a language is a dialect with an army and a navy' (McArthur, 1995: 291). Standard English has no *intrinsic* value that makes it superior to any other, although it does have *pragmatic* value as the language of education and the language of power.

Corson, discussing Bourdieu's metaphor of 'cultural capital,' representing the advantages that accrue to individuals whose cultural resources are held in high esteem, describes 'linguistic capital' as facility in producing the right kind of language at the right time for the right audience (Corson, 1993). It is this kind of facility in standard English that all students need if they are to take advantage of educational opportunity and have full access to employment, community involvement, and participation in the democratic process.

CONCLUSION

Schools in multicultural communities can help all students get off to a positive start by providing a warm reception and helpful orientation services, an initial assessment that is sensitive to each student's linguistic and cultural background, and a program to support students who are learning the language of instruction.

Although most of the recommendations in this chapter are in practice somewhere, not all are being implemented in the same place or at the same time. Therefore, instead of trying to implement every suggestion at once, choose those that seem feasible in your own school at the present time, and adapt them to your circumstances. For example, you may not have the personnel to implement a reception and orientation program as elaborate as that described in this chapter — but every school can provide some kind of welcome for newcomers. If your first initiatives are successful, you will be able to build on them and develop new initiatives in future years. It is also important to recognize that some initiatives are best implemented at the district level: for example, the development of multilingual orientation videos and other multilingual resources.

As schools begin implementing some of the strategies suggested in this chapter, it is important to take the time to assess what the school is doing, to reflect on the results, and focus on aspects of the program that may need improvement. Teachers and school administrators can use the checklist below to help assess the school as a welcoming and supportive environment for culturally diverse groups of students and parents.

CHECKLIST: GETTING STARTED IN THE MULTICULTURAL SCHOOL

This checklist can be used by teachers, students, parents, and school and district administrators. The checklist is organized as a series of indicators under the three broad topic areas discussed in this chapter: 'Reception and Orientation', 'Initial Assessment and Placement', and 'Support for Second Language Acquisition'. The rating system can be used and interpreted as follows:

yes = whenever appropriate
not yet = this is an area that may need special attention
n/a = not applicable, or not available at this time

Reception and orientation

yes not n/a
    yet

❑ ❑ ❑ There is a planned program of reception and orientation for students and parents.

❑ ❑ ❑ There is a team responsible for reception and orientation.

❑ ❑ ❑ A member of the reception team welcomes the family in a comfortable private space.

❑ ❑ ❑ Orientation materials are available in the languages of the community.

❑ ❑ ❑ Interpreters and translators are available.

❑ ❑ ❑ Multilingual signs and notices welcome newcomers and provide direction.

❑ ❑ ❑ There is a classroom ambassador program.

❑ ❑ ❑ School staff communicate support for the maintenance of heritage languages.

❑ ❑ ❑ Parents receive information about the availability of heritage language programs.

❑ ❑ ❑ Students receive appropriate assessment of their educational background.

❑ ❑ ❑ Initial placement is reviewed at regular intervals and/or at the request of students or parents.

❑ ❑ ❑ Parents receive information about English as a Second Language programs for adults.

❑ ❑ ❑ New students receive a 'starter kit' when they enter the school.

❑ ❑ ❑ There is a special fund to support students in need: e.g., for school equipment and field trips.

Initial assessment and placement

yes not n/a
    yet

❏ ❏ ❏   The school has a planned procedure for the assessment of each student who arrives at the school.

❏ ❏ ❏   Interpreters are available for the initial reception interview.

❏ ❏ ❏   There is a procedure to assess the student's level of proficiency in the first language.

❏ ❏ ❏   Academic assessment is conducted in the student's first language, using tasks and materials that are likely to be familiar.

❏ ❏ ❏   Assessment of proficiency in English includes listening, speaking, reading, and writing.

❏ ❏ ❏   Proficiency in English is assessed using criteria relevant to students who are learning English.

❏ ❏ ❏   An assessment portfolio is maintained for each student from the day of arrival.

❏ ❏ ❏   Opportunity to learn is considered in all assessments.

❏ ❏ ❏   Students who may have special needs are assessed in consultation with a bilingual educator who is familiar with the student's cultural and educational background.

❏ ❏ ❏   Appropriate support is available for students who have had limited access to schooling.

❏ ❏ ❏   Each student's progress is reviewed on a regular basis.

Support for second language acquisition

yes not n/a
    yet

❏ ❏ ❏   All students receive a planned program of support for second language acquisition.

❏ ❏ ❏   All second language learners, including beginners, are involved in an educational program that assists them to continue their academic development as the same time as they learn the language of instruction.

❏ ❏ ❏   Long-term support is available for second language learners.

❏ ❏ ❏   All second language learners, including beginners, have opportunities for interaction with English-speaking peers.

❏ ❏ ❏   Students' first languages are viewed as linguistic, academic and cultural assets.

❏ ❏ ❏   All teachers consider the needs of second language learners in planning lessons and choosing resources.

❏ ❏ ❏   All teachers have access to a skilled ESL professional who can assist with lesson planning and curriculum design.

FURTHER READING AND RESOURCES FOR TEACHERS

Chamot, A. and O'Malley, M. (1994) *The CALLA Handbook: Implementing the Cognitive Academic Language Learning Approach.* Reading, MA: Addison-Wesley. A practical guide on how to integrate language and content instruction in grade-level and subject classrooms.

Clegg, J.(ed.) (1996) *Mainstreaming ESL: Case studies in integrating ESL students into the mainstream curriculum.* Clevedon, England: Multilingual Matters. A collection of articles from Britain, Canada, Australia, and the United States, providing practical classroom strategies for integrating language and content instruction in mainstream classrooms as well as suggestions on school policy.

Cloud, N. (1994) Special Education Needs of Second Language Students. In Genesee, F. (ed.) *Educating Second Language Children: The Whole Child, the Whole Curriculum, the Whole Community.* Cambridge: Cambridge University Press. Cloud provides helpful and detailed advice on an issue that could be only briefly mentioned in this chapter.

Cummins, J. (1996) *Negotiating Identities: Education for Empowerment in a Diverse Society.* Ontario, CA: California Association for Bilingual Education. Cummins surveys recent research and makes recommendations for school policy and classroom practice in culturally and linguistically diverse schools.

Enright, S. and McCloskey, M. L. (1988) *Integrating English: Developing English Language and Literacy in the Multilingual Classroom.* Reading, MA: Addison-Wesley. A rich source of ideas for integrating elementary-level ESL learners through interactive, content-based activities.

Esling, J. (ed.) (1989) *Multicultural Education and Policy: ESL in the 1990s.* Toronto: Ontario Institute for Studies in Education. Contains articles on ESL integration and content-based language instruction.

Freeman, Y. S. and Freeman, D. E. (1991) Portsmouth, NH: Heinemann.*Whole Language for Second Language Learners.* This book emphasizes the importance of involving students in meaningful language activities and provides many practical examples for teachers.

Genesee, F. (ed.) (1994b) *Educating Second-Language Children: The Whole Child, The Whole Curriculum, the Whole Community.* New York, NY: Cambridge University Press. This volume includes chapters on classroom practice for language teachers, grade level teachers, and subject teachers.

Gibbons, P. (1993) *Learning to Learn in a Second Language.* Portsmouth, NH: Heinemann.This book is filled with practical suggestions for teachers of elementary school children.

Gregory, E. (1996) *Making Sense of a New World: Learning to read in a second language.* London: Paul Chapman. The author provides helpful practical advice, embedded in a theoretical framework, to teachers of young children who begin learning English when they arrive at school.

Law, B. and Eckes, M. (1990) *The More Than Just Surviving! Handbook: ESL for Every Classroom Teacher.* Winnipeg: Peguis. Useful book for classroom teachers integrating second language learners into the classroom program.

Met, M. (1994) Teaching content through a second language. In Genesee, F. (ed.) (1994b) *Educating Second-Language Children: The Whole Child, The Whole Curriculum, the Whole Community.* New York, NY: Cambridge University Press. This chapter provides useful guidelines and practical examples of language and content integration.

Richard-Amato, P., and Snow, M. (eds) (1992) *The Multicultural Classroom: Readings for Content-Area Teachers.* White Plains, NY: Longman. Very useful collection of readings on theoretical background and practical classroom strategies for the integrated classroom.

Rigg, P. and Enright, S. (eds) (1986) *Children and ESL: Integrating Perspectives.* Washington, D.C.: TESOL. A helpful book for teachers at the elementary level.

Rigg, P. and Allen, V.D. (eds) (1989) *When They Don't All Speak English: Integrating the ESL Student into the Regular Classroom.* Urbana, IL: National Council of Teachers of English. Collection of articles on topics such as program design, creating an effective language learning environment, language variation, language experience, and content-based language instruction.

Scarcella, R. (1990) *Teaching Language Minority Students in the Multicultural Classroom.* Englewood Cliffs, NJ: Prentice Hall. This book provides important background information on second language learning and learners, and develops some principles for the provision of culturally responsive education in multicultural schools.

Spangenberg-Urbschat K. and Pritchard, R. (eds) (1994) *Kids Come in all Languages: Reading Instruction for ESL Students.* Newark, Delaware: International Reading Association. This excellent collection of articles provides practical advice on language learning and literacy development in all classrooms.

CHAPTER 4

An Inclusive School Environment

INTRODUCTION

Immigrant children, the children of immigrants, and children who are not of the dominant culture have particular needs as they navigate two cultures and establish their identities as bicultural, bilingual individuals in a multicultural environment. They have to learn the dominant language and culture in order to be academically successful and become integrated into the social life of the school and the wider community; at the same time, they need the security and sense of identity that the home language and culture can provide. A school that serves a multilingual, multicultural, and multiracial community has a responsibility for ensuring that everyone in the school values cultural diversity, and for helping all students and their families to feel included and valued in the school community without giving up aspects of their culture that are important to them.

   This chapter describes how teachers and school administrators can provide a physical and social environment that is inclusive of all the learners and all the cultures represented in it. The chapter also describes important services that need to be in place to support students from other countries and diverse cultural backgrounds who may have to make major adjustments to a new cultural, social, and educational environment. The third section of the chapter suggests some ways of involving parents of all cultural backgrounds in the education of their children. A checklist is provided at the end of the chapter; this can be used to assess the school as an inclusive and supportive environment, and as an institution that has strong connections with the community it serves.

AN INCLUSIVE PHYSICAL AND SOCIAL ENVIRONMENT

Important messages are communicated by the physical and social environment of the school. This environment includes the learning resources in classrooms and libraries, the visual environment, the oral language environment, the extracurricular program, and the special events that are celebrated in the school.

An inclusive school proclaims with pride its multilingual, multicultural, multiracial orientation to anyone walking into or through the building, and reflects in a matter-of-fact and unselfconscious way the presence of all the groups represented in the school population.

The visual environment

The visual impressions that students receive from display material in classroom and hallways, as well as from the signs and notices that are posted around the school, can communicate messages about which languages and cultures are valued in the school community. Make sure that the visual images presented to students, parents and teachers as they move around the school equitably and positively represent the presence and the experience of all the groups in the school, and reflect a variety of cultural perspectives.

- **Display a graph or chart** near the main entrance of the school, showing the linguistic and cultural backgrounds of the students in the school. Update this chart regularly. This task could be rotated from class to class, as part of the mathematics program of the school.
- **Post signs and notices** around the school in the languages of the school population. Many schools have some kind of 'Welcome' sign, and perhaps a sign indicating the main office, in several languages. This is a good start, but unless the practice is extended to other areas of the school, and until it becomes usual and matter-of-fact to post multilingual signs, it remains a token only. Signs can be made by students and parents (see also 'Parental involvement' in this chapter). In addition to the signs that direct people around the building, the Multilingual Resources for Schools Project suggests many other ways that students' languages can be used in the school and in the classroom (Multilingual Resources for Children Project, 1995).
- **Include photographs of students of many different racial and cultural backgrounds** in hallway displays, showing students of both genders engaged in a wide variety of activities in addition to athletic activities. Although these are important, achievement in athletics may not be equally valued by all members of the school community. Some students invest their out-of-class time in other, less celebrated activities. For example, the photo displays could show students involved in the peer tutoring program, the chess club, or a cultural organization within the school.

  The displays can also show what students are doing within the classroom. In addition to providing students and parents with a visual depiction of the wide

range of subjects and activities that constitute the curriculum, these displays can help to raise expectations about who participates and succeeds in different kinds of programs. For example, some photos could show 'visible minority' and female students engaged in mathematics and science activities, male students in traditionally female activities such as cooking, sewing, and working with younger children, or females in Industrial Arts and other traditionally male subjects.

- **Create theme displays that are inclusive in orientation.** In special displays about 'famous authors' or 'great inventors', include the contributions of people of many different cultures and both genders — many of whom are unnamed and unknown. For example, modern achievements in science and technology were developed within a continuum that began thousands of years ago, in Asia and Africa, with the invention of the first tools, the first use of fire and the first attempts to cultivate nature. The concept of zero, fundamental to binary processing and thus all computer technology, is non-European in origin. Inclusive theme displays acknowledge the interdependence of knowledge so that students see themselves and their world within the continuum of human knowledge and experience.

- **Feature the work of artists from many different cultural traditions** in visual art displays. In displays of student artwork, include pieces that reflect the traditions of the students' own cultures as well as pieces that involve them in experimentation with new forms of expression. The aesthetic development of all students is enriched by opportunities to explore art forms from their own or other

cultures: for example, Islamic design, Rangoli patterns, Chinese brush painting and calligraphy, Aboriginal styles of painting and carving, African styles of sculpture, and masks, dolls, puppets, textile designs, jewellery and ceramics of many different styles and cultural origins.

• **Choose classroom and library material** that provides realistic and positive images of different cultural and racial groups, that reflects many types of family structure, different socioeconomic status, and different cultural values, but also communicates the fundamental similarities among cultures and peoples. Establish a procedure for evaluating new material, using criteria such as those suggested in 'Learning Resources' in Chapter 8. Involve parents and students in choosing new resources.

The oral language environment

The inclusive school is multilingual not only in the backgrounds of its students, but in actual language use around the school. For example, important announcements are made over the public address system or in school assemblies in the major languages of the school. Multilingual announcements not only ensure that all the students in the school understand what is going on; they also communicate important messages about the value of all languages as media of communication. The students selected to make the announcements will gain in stature as well.

Whenever possible, use the languages of the students and their parents during home visits, to welcome parents to school events, in parent–teacher interviews, and in artistic and cultural performances.

In interaction with students or their parents, ensure that you pronounce their names correctly. Ask students to model the pronunciation of their names for you, and give you feedback on your pronunciation. It is helpful to know something about some of the conventions that apply when a language that uses a non-Roman alphabet or set of characters is transliterated into English; students can often provide this information. Make sure also that you know which is the given name and which is the family name; assumptions about 'first' and 'last' names are not universal. People of some backgrounds also have religious names, generational names, and gender markers such as the equivalent of 'Miss'; find out which names are appropriate for you to use.

In their social interaction around the school, encourage students to use the language that seems most appropriate for the context. For example, it would be unnatural for a group of Cantonese speakers to use English with each other, unless a non-Cantonese speaker is involved in the group interaction. It is important to support students' first languages in order to promote second language acquisition and self esteem. Hearing a variety of languages in their daily lives and seeing them accorded equal worth by teachers helps all students, including monolingual speakers of the dominant language, to expand their awareness of language, and to view all languages as equally valid forms of communication. Students' languages also have value as tools for learning: for example, in exploratory talk and group activities, in drama activities, and in peer tutoring (see 'A Multilingual Classroom Environment' in Chapter 5).

The school has enormous power to promote or inhibit the use of languages other than the language of the school, and to influence attitudes towards students' languages. Language is of profound importance in the psychological health of individuals and communities. For example, in previous generations, Aboriginal children attending schools in North America were punished for using their own languages. The impact of the loss of language and cultural identity has been devastating, and indigenous languages need special support from educational institutions today if they are to survive. As Chartrand points out, 'If an Aboriginal language dies, it dies absolutely. Unlike immigrants to this land, who can get spiritual consolation from knowing their language, though locally gone, survives elsewhere, Aboriginal peoples can only say goodbye to their cultural legacy when, with a particular generation, their language goes' (Chartrand, 1992).

Extracurricular activities

Different cultural groups may have different expectations about what should be available to students through the extracurricular program of the school. Some time-honoured activities may no longer be relevant in all communities — at least, not in their traditional formats. For example, North American high school institutions such as football and cheerleaders, the school yearbook, and semi-formal or formal dances and proms relate only to the experiences of the dominant group, and often another era. In many communities they are also economically unrealistic. In elementary schools, the Christmas concert is not inclusive of all cultures and faiths and may no longer be appropriate in the multicultural school. This does not mean that there will no longer be activities and events that bring students together for recreational and social activities — these are essential in creating a community in the school — but it is important that the activities relate to students' interests and lifestyles. A winter concert that is secular in nature and includes a variety of cultural forms of expression may be more suitable. Here are some other ideas to consider:

- **Provide recreational or non-competitive sports programs** in addition to intermural and intramural competition. Many students are interested in recreational sports as a social activity, but not in organized team competition.
- **Find out what sports students are interested in.** Some students may be interested in sports that may not have a long history in the school, such as soccer and cricket in North American schools.
- **Promote a variety of extracurricular activities.** Some students are interested in activities that have not traditionally had a high profile in the school, such as debating clubs, choral groups, chess tournaments, language clubs, and badminton competitions. Promote these and other events as vigorously as activities and as spectator events, and post photographs of these events as prominently as photos of the various athletic teams.
- **Be flexible about the commitment students have to make**. Many high school students work after school or have family responsibilities and therefore cannot make the commitment to regular practices before or after school, but they may still enjoy learning to play an instrument or joining a fitness group during their lunch hours.
- **Make sure that school dances are planned by a representative group of students,** include many different types of music, and are economically within the reach of all students.
- **Make sure that the food served in school cafeterias and at school events** includes items that meet the cultural and religious dietary needs of all students. For example, many elementary schools in North America have 'Hot Dog Days;' it would be more appropriate to make a greater variety of food available so that all students can participate, and choose a more appropriate name for the event. Ensure that activities involving food are held outside periods of fasting that some students may be observing: for example, Muslim students fast from dawn to dusk during Ramadan.

Food for thought
School cafeterias in Toronto schools have changed their menus over the last few years. There are now more vegetarian dishes, and students buy fewer than half as many hamburgers as they used to. Chinese food, falafels, rice dishes, and

Reprinted with the permission of the Toronto District School Board

Jamaican patties are increasingly common. Trends are similar across the country, if not as dramatic.

From an interview with students at Parkdale Public School in Toronto:

Ashley Ramnarine, an eight-year-old Hindu in Grade 2, won't eat any meat during lunch, instead choosing from the vegetarian pizza, salad and vegetable patties the school offers . . . she has other friends who can eat only some lunches . . . . Farwah Rubab, 13, and her sister Mamoona, 10, are Muslims who came to Canada from Pakistan two years ago. They say it's important to them that the school provides food they can eat because the lunch menu can sometimes isolate them from other children. 'If they're eating something we can't eat, we just go away because we feel so different,' Farwah said. (Skelton, 1997: from an article in the *Globe and Mail,* Monday 23 June)

- **When you plan a field trip,** remember that students educated in other countries, and their parents, may not understand their value as part of the instructional program. Field trips that involve overnight stays are especially difficult for families whose values include the isolation of females from interaction with males outside the family. Some groups of parents may need special assurances about chaperones before allowing their daughters to attend dances, field trips, and other activities.
- **Support student clubs and activities that are organized by specific linguistic or cultural groups.** These can be a very important source of support to students. At the same time, they provide a way for students to affirm their culture and invite other students to participate as well. Students can plan the activities with the help of a staff adviser. This is a leadership opportunity for students who might otherwise not have the experience. Typical activities that students choose include homework clubs, music, chess or other games, debating, storytelling, political discussion, drama, dance, and simple informal socializing.
- **Maintain extremely good contact with parents** in order to reassure them that the events you are sponsoring are organized in consultation with staff, and properly chaperoned. There is a special role for teachers and parents of the same cultural backgrounds in helping students to plan an event and giving parents the information and reassurance they need.
- **Consider offering some activities to males and females separately,** especially if you have Muslim students. For example, dancing or recreational swimming in mixed groups might prevent some girls from participating.
- **Consult students and parents about the content of music, drama and dance programs.** Whose music will the students play? What instruments will be included? Whose music and in what languages will the students sing? Whose drama or dance will be performed?

When a 'traditional' play is chosen, non-traditional casting is in order; this opens up opportunities for everyone, and makes a strong antiracist statement at the same time. Other events that would interest students of many different backgrounds include oral performance such as storytelling, debating, poetry reading and choral recitation.

- **Recognize a wide range of talents and contributions** through school awards, trophies, and scholarships. For instance, there could be an award for the student, the teacher, or the class that has done outstanding work in antiracist education; the students who participated in the chess tournament, the choral concert, or the storytelling festival; the student who has made a contribution to his or her cultural community; the student who has performed excellent work as a peer tutor; or the new arrival who has made impressive progress in learning the language of the school. Awards need not recognize only 'the best' or 'the winners', but may also recognize participation and commitment.

Scholarships promote harmony

A group working to promote racial and cultural harmony is offering high school graduates $500 scholarships toward their post-secondary education.

The new scholarships, offered by the Harmony Movement, are devised to reward graduates in the Greater Toronto Area who have done work to promote harmony within their school and community, says Sharon Ho, project co-ordinator for the four-year-old group . . . Ho says the 20 scholarships will help establish a larger presence for the movement in high schools. (Toronto Star, 24 June 1997: E2)

- **Organize an antiracism group** that offers interesting activities and has a high profile in the school. Students interested in antiracist action need opportunities to be involved in activities that promote fun and fellowship as well as philosophy. For example, they might design and paint a mural in one of the hallways of the school to celebrate the theme of cultural diversity and unity. Students and teachers who have had some training in antiracist education can provide leadership to this group. A popular name for this kind of group is STAR: Students and Teachers Against Racism.

Special events

In addition to regular activities that students participate in after school or during the lunch hour, schools organize special events during the year. For example, the traditional school year in North America includes celebrations and special events in honour of Christmas, Valentine's Day, Easter, and Hallowe'en. These events give strong messages about the relative importance of the different racial and cultural groups in the school.

Festivals and special days that are celebrated or ignored tell everyone who is important in the school and in the society. The length of time spent preparing for a specific event also communicates something about how important it is: if the whole of December is given to Christmas, and Diwali, Hanukkah, and the Chinese New

Year receive brief mention, one culture has been accorded greater importance in the eyes of everybody.

It is important to celebrate the major holidays of all the cultural groups in the school, and to accord them equal importance in the life of the school, whether these are public holidays or not. Explore underlying values, as well as superficial aspects of culture such as food and dance. Stress commonalities: for instance, Hanukkah, Christmas, Diwali, and other holidays can be explored and celebrated as 'Festivals of Light' related to the anticipation of the new growing season. Students, and perhaps parents too, can take part in official announcements on those days. Explain to parents the philosophy of this approach: the intent is not to discourage students from their own religious convictions and observances, but to promote harmony and understanding among all the groups in the school by emphasizing underlying commonalities.

Schools often invite artists into the schools to give musical and dramatic perform-ances, or to involve students in particular forms of artistic expression. Over the course of the year, make sure that these events involve artists of a variety of backgrounds and demonstrate different cultural sources and traditions in their work. For example, storytellers could tell several stories from different cultures related to a common theme.

Special events such as African Heritage Month (celebrated in February in many American and Canadian schools), or South Asian History Month (celebrated in May in some schools in Canada) are 'emergency measures' intended to counteract curriculum bias. Like all emergency measures, they are useful until a general cure or preventive can be developed, but as permanent solutions they are not satisfactory. For example, many students of African or South Asian heritage may feel further marginalized by an approach that seems to present their experience as an 'add-on' rather than integral to the curriculum in every classroom; what about the other eleven months, and what about the cultures that don't have a special month? In the long term, the entire school program has to change and become inclusive of many different cultures and perspectives (see Chapters 7 and 8).

Multicultural events that focus on food and festivals can be a lot of fun, as long as everyone is included. For example, people of British and European ancestry whose roots in Canada, the United States, and Australia go back several generations can also explore and display their cultural heritage, alongside Aboriginal, Sri Lankan, or Iranian students. It is important to keep in mind that if this kind of festival is the only opportunity that some groups have for cultural expression, their cultures are trivialized by such a one-dimensional representation. Indeed, an emphasis on the superficial or exotic differences of clothing and traditional customs — an emphasis on the 'otherness' of other groups — can even reinforce stereotypes. In contrast, antiracist education advocates 'a critical stance toward the way our society is organized, the values on which it is based, and the ways in which power is exercised and restricted' (Hodson, 1993: 688). For more on this topic, see 'Approaches to Antiracist Education' in Chapter 7.

In addition to celebrating food and festivals, the whole school could be involved in a special 'Antiracism Week.' Using a cross-curricular, integrative approach, every class could do some work on antiracism. For example, students could make posters in the art class, create plays in the drama class, collect and present surveys and statistical data in the mathematics class, write personal responses and opinion pieces, poems, and stories in the English class, study the work of human rights activists from around the world in history or social studies classes, help to organize special assemblies and displays, and honour the antiracist work of individuals and groups in the school. Parents and community members could be invited to partici-pate.

Adopting some of the ideas described in this section will help students of all cultures to feel included as members of the school community, and to value linguistic and cultural diversity. It is also important to pay special attention to the needs of individual students and specific groups within the school, as suggested in the next section.

SUPPORT SERVICES

Effective schools monitor the progress of all students, and provide academic and social support to those who may need such support. All students feel more secure if there is somebody in the building who understands their needs, especially if they are newcomers, second language learners, or members of a cultural minority in the school. In elementary schools, the classroom teacher provides guidance and emotional support to individual students, and the ESL teacher may take on the role of counsellor and advocate for newcomers. Middle and secondary schools often have guidance counsellors who support students outside the classroom. School administrators also provide guidance and support to students and their families.

In multicultural and multilingual schools, staff who can be most effective in a counselling role are knowledgeable and non-judgmental about the students' cultural backgrounds, willing to intervene or mediate on behalf of students when conflicts or difficulties arise with other students or teachers in the school, and able to organize specific kinds of support for students. Support services include monitoring and counselling individual students and specific groups, peer tutoring and bilingual tutoring programs, study groups, peer mediation, multilingual services, role models and mentors, and antiracism training.

Monitoring

Every school needs to have an effective means of monitoring the progress of individual students and specific groups.

Monitoring individual students

It is important to monitor the academic progress and social integration of all students who are new to the school — whether they have come from another country, another school district, a local school, or as new kindergarten entrants — especially those from homes where English is not the primary language. Immigrant students, in particular, may arrive at any time during the school year and often miss the regular induction procedures; and even if they do arrive at the beginning of the school year with an age cohort that is also new to the school, they may not have the linguistic or cultural knowledge to understand what is going on.

A new student's progress needs to be monitored on a regular ongoing basis. In an elementary school this might be undertaken by the principal, in consultation with the ESL teacher. In secondary schools the counselling staff and ESL staff could work together to track progress in psychosocial adjustment, language learning, and academic continuity.

Monitoring begins with the record of the initial interview and the other material in the student's assessment portfolio. It is important to make sure that the student's new teacher or teachers receive some general information about the new student. In an elementary school, the ESL teacher or counsellor probably has to contact only one or two teachers, and this can be done fairly informally — for example, by sitting down together with the contents of the assessment file. In secondary schools, where the student may have several teachers, the counsellor may send a short note to each teacher giving basic information about the new student's country of origin, first language, and length of time in the country, as well as the name of the student ambassador who is guiding the student through the first few days in the school. Include an invitation to see the assessment information and discuss it with the counsellor or ESL teacher.

After the student has been in classes for two or three weeks, hold a team meeting with the teachers involved. Ask teachers to bring work samples, observation checklists, and other material that is informative about the student's progress. A secondary purpose of this meeting is to reassure teachers who may have limited experience of working with second language learners, and share with them the insights and experience of the ESL teacher and others who have a repertoire of strategies for teaching and assessing these students.

Continue to consult teachers periodically, and request that they provide you with work samples, observation checklists, and other assessment information so that you can keep the assessment file current. This is extremely important in tracking students' academic and linguistic development. If monitoring reveals problems of an academic or personal nature, the staff involved will need to coordinate an appropriate response to assist and support the student. For example, increased support may be offered through bilingual peer tutoring. It may be a good idea to invite parents to a meeting, with the assistance of an interpreter. Bilingual educators or personnel from community agencies may be able to assist staff in helping the student and the family.

A common problem is that after the first year in a new school system, the student progresses to the next grade and the new teachers may be unaware that the student is a recent arrival — especially when the student is transferring from one school to another. Some immigrants, especially refugees, move several times in the first few years as they seek to establish themselves in their new country. It is extremely important to pass on information to the new teachers or the new school, so that teachers are aware of the need to adapt the instructional program and assess the performance of second language learners appropriately. Also, although students may leave formal ESL classes and become completely integrated into the main-stream program within two or three years, it is important to continue monitoring their progress throughout the period required for language acquisition: at least the first five years.

Monitoring groups of students

Another aspect of monitoring is the tracking of specific groups of students, such as students from a specific ethnocultural group, especially if this is a relatively new group in the school. The purpose is to monitor equity in the school, and discern patterns that might indicate that some kind of intervention is in order: for example, if students of a specific cultural group are disproportionately represented in certain subject areas, or over-represented in less academically challenging programs; if some groups of students do not participate in extracurricular activities; if a particular group experiences conflict with authority more than other groups in the school; or if a group of students is over-represented among the dropout statistics. This kind of monitoring helps a school to become more accountable to its community, to identify what seems to be working well, and to identify where changes are required in order to better meet the needs of all the students in the school. According to McKenna:

> Schools should be fountains of information, even embarrassing information. We should be able to open our information, and our strategies, and our successes to everyone . . . not just to the individual parent but in a collective way. How many of our students are failing, how many are dropping out and those kinds of things — so we can monitor it before it happens, and try to improve upon it. (McKenna, 1989: 20)

The purpose of group monitoring is not to label, stereotype, or blame specific ethnocultural groups of students who may be experiencing social or academic difficulty in the school. If a specific group is doing less wall or has more problems than others, this is an indicator of a systemic problem: the school program is not meeting their needs. Schools that do not know how well they are serving all their students are not able to evaluate their effectiveness or engage in quality assurance in order to be accountable to their communities.

Counselling

Staff who have a particular interest in immigrant students and who have appropriate training in cross-cultural counselling — if such individuals are available — can provide effective counselling services to recently arrived and culturally diverse students. Cross-cultural counsellors need a good knowledge of the cultural backgrounds and experiences of the cultural groups they work with, as well as the ability to view each student or parent as an individual rather than as a stereotypical member of a group. Some counsellors are bicultural, working with a specific cultural group; other counsellors work with diverse groups. Counsellors may sometimes adapt some of their own behaviours to help people of other backgrounds feel more at ease: for example, it may be appropriate to provide gender-specific counselling. Counsellors may be bilingual, or they may work with interpreters, in which case they phrase their remarks carefully and allow sufficient time for effective interpretation. Counsellors are also knowledgeable about community resources and agencies that provide specific services or serve specific cultural groups.

In some school districts, counsellors are members of staff with that job title. In others, teachers and administrators serve as counsellors or student advisors. English as a Second Language teachers and bilingual teachers often fill these roles on a day-to-day basis. Very close supportive relationships are fostered in most ESL classrooms; indeed, the content of the ESL program includes issues involved in immigration and adjustment. Other counsellors will need to develop ways of reaching out to students, perhaps by visiting the ESL class, in order to explain the role of the counsellor. Most immigrant students have no experience of such programs; they need information about the services that are available, and reassurances about the confidentiality of the counselling relationship.

Even if everything is going smoothly, it is important to establish contact and provide reassurance that there is support available. For example, counsellors or other staff serving in this role can meet with the new students on a regular basis, either individually or with small groups.

Counselling may be of an academic nature. Find out where the students feel comfortable and where they may be experiencing difficulty, and review students' assessment portfolios and report cards with them. It is especially important at secondary school to assist students to understand the programs and courses they need to complete high school graduation requirements and enter the work force or the post-secondary institution of their choice.

Counselling may also be of a personal nature and assist students in their adjustment to a new culture by organizing peer support programs or putting students and their families in touch with personnel and agencies that are able to provide culturally sensitive services. In many cases, counselling will need to be provided in the student's first language. Group counselling for specific linguistic and cultural groups conducted by bilingual teaching staff or by community groups are very helpful. Group counselling sessions that focus on specific aspects of culture shock and adjustment help to generate a sense of solidarity and commonality of experience that can be very supportive for newcomers, and provide them with helpful coping strategies (Edelson and Roskin, 1985).

Counsellors need to keep in touch with various community groups and public agencies that offer services designed to meet the needs of specific cultural groups. It may be more appropriate to refer some students to these organizations for support if there is no member of the school staff who is familiar with the student's cultural background. It may be possible to contract with such groups to provide some staff development for counsellors and teachers. However, it not appropriate for schools to rely totally on community-based services and resources for *all* culturally sensitive services. Many community organizations depend on volunteers and do not have the resources to give schools the kind of time that would be required. The onus is on the school to learn from these organizations in order to become more responsive to the needs of the community.

Another counselling role is conflict mediation: counsellors ensure that all students, teachers, and parents are aware of procedures to be followed in cases of ethnocultural or sexual harassment, and that everyone in the building knows how to initiate a complaint or seek support from counsellors or other support people in the school.

Peer and cross-grade tutoring

Peer tutors are an important resource in every classroom (see 'Partners and Peer Tutors' in Chapter 5 for more information on how to provide peer tutoring in the

classroom). It may also be possible to organize a program to train older students to act as tutors to their age peers and to younger children in the same school or in the local elementary school. See Samway *et al.* (1995) for practical suggestions on how to use cross-grade tutoring in elementary schools.

To make tutoring attractive to secondary students, and to honour its importance, the program may carry academic credit — for example, in Co-operative Education, Community Service, or Life Skills, depending on what is available under local curriculum guidelines. This program would be especially valuable to senior students who may be interested in a teaching career, and could encourage students to consider becoming teachers. The experience will provide them with an opportunity to find out if teaching would be attractive to them, as well as evidence of leadership and teaching-related experience that will be valuable in developing a portfolio for entrance to teacher education programs.

It is important to make sure that students of all ethnocultural backgrounds are involved. This program may help in improving the representation of teacher candidates at Faculties of Education and eventually improve ethnocultural representation in the teaching profession. Participation in this program can be honoured in the awards and recognition systems of the school.

Bilingual tutoring

Some students arrive from other countries having missed several or even many years of schooling. In many cases, their limited educational background would make it difficult for them to relate to the classroom program even if it were delivered in their first language. These students will need special support, because they have not had opportunities to develop concepts that might be taken for granted in students who have been in school full-time. The most appropriate instruction for these students is bilingual. Concepts are introduced and developed in the first language; then the concepts are used as a vehicle for second language instruction. For example, it is best if children learn basic concepts about shape, colour, and number in the first language before transferring to the language of instruction. Similarly, basic skills in literacy and numeracy can be introduced in the first language; as students learn the second language, these skills will be transferred to the new language.

Secondary school students who are fluent in both languages can be involved in tutoring as part of a credit program in International or Modern Languages, as part of a co-operative education program, or as volunteers (see 'Multilingual Services' in this chapter). In some school districts, paid or volunteer tutors may visit the school several times a week to work one-on-one or in small groups with the students. Local teacher training programs may also be a good source of bilingual tutors.

Tutors need training in teaching techniques, second-language instruction, and cross-cultural communication. It is essential that a staff member undertake the training and monitoring of tutors in the school.

Study groups

Educators in multilingual contexts often express concern about the low levels of academic achievement, and the low rates of participation in advanced mathematics and sciences, of some ethnocultural groups: for example, African Americans in the United States. At the same time, other groups of students, such as students of Chinese, Japanese, and Korean background, are doing very well in mathematics and science, even though some are recent arrivals who are learning the language of instruction. While many factors are involved, including cultural and socioeconomic background, parental involvement, previous educational experience, teacher expectations, and self-esteem, there is one teachable learning strategy that many of the high achievers use, and that others can be taught: group study and practice (Fullilove and Treisman, 1990).

Study groups are usually informal, student-organized support systems that rely on collaboration and peer tutoring to help all group members. Students at law school and medical school use study groups as a strategy for dealing with the sheer volume of material to be learned. Some groups of students adopt study groups outside class in order to help each other review the day's material, often using a shared first language to help each other to understand. Study groups that are more formally organized as an adjunct to the academic program constitute an important intervention to enhance academic achievement among some groups of students and redress existing academic inequity.

Student to student: the power of the study group

This intervention program on behalf of minority students was implemented and documented at the University of California at Berkeley (Fullilove and Treisman, 1990).

A survey of the achievement of several racial/ethnic groups in first-year calculus at the university revealed that Chinese American students were over-represented among the high achievers. An interesting ethnographic survey also revealed that they studied for more hours per week than other students, and they usually studied in groups. These informal study groups not only contributed to academic success; they also provided very important social support as students adjusted to university life. The situation for African American and Hispanic students was very different. In spite of high motivation, high SAT scores (Scholastic Aptitude Test), good high school background and strong parental support, they were not doing well; for example, African American students taking first year calculus — a prerequisite for science, mathematics and engineering programs — were over-represented among the low achievers, and 40% of those who remained in the course failed at the end of the semester. These students tended to separate their social lives from their studies; they went to to class alone and studied alone. When they encountered difficulties, they did not seek assistance from peers. Socially and academically isolated, they were competing in a difficult course with those who were supporting each other.

Learning from the effective study methods of the Chinese American students, the staff at Berkeley developed a 'Mathematics Workshop Program' that organized the 'at risk' students into small study groups. Participants pledged to work for high grades and to keep ahead of assignments. This was not a remedial program. Students did not receive additional instruction drill, or practice. Instead they were assigned very challenging problems to work on. They were taught how to work co-operatively, helping each other to test solutions and find alternative approaches. The results were impressive: since the implementation of the program, the number of African American students participating in the study group who earned grades of D+ or lower has been reduced to an average of 5%. In some years not one student in this group failed. Also, African American students who participated in the program were two to three times more likely to receive a grade of B- or higher than those who were not involved in the program.

The Berkeley approach has been implemented in several universities and in several disciplines: medicine, science and technology. It can be implemented in schools too. For example, the study group approach was adapted and implemented at Albany High School in California. This school, like countless others in North America, had a problem of racial imbalance in the mathematics program: too few African American and Hispanic students in advanced math programs, and far too many in the remedial math program. Staff involved in the program report that since the program was initiated, twice as many African American students pass advanced math courses, and more minority students are going on to university (Marlow and Culler, 1987).

Studying with others is easier, more fun, and often more effective, and the groups provide social support for academic success that many students otherwise lack. Study groups help students to develop the spirit of intellectual inquiry and the sense of academic fellowship that are essential elements of true scholarship. The power of the study group is a student-centred resource that can be available in every school. Schools promoting academic equity among different sociocultural groups might consider the formal implementation and supervision of study groups outside of regular class time, especially in the core subjects, such as mathematics or English, that are gatekeepers to success in the rest of the academic program.

How to implement study groups

- Identify students of all racial and cultural backgrounds who are having difficulty in a specific subject area such as mathematics or English, but whose teachers feel that they are capable of better performance.
- Communicating with students and parents in their own languages, share information about the importance of success in the subject area, about the students' present level of achievement, and about the kind and amount of study that is required for excellence. Invite students and parents to participate in study groups.
- Interview students and parents who decide to opt for the study group. Students and parents may sign a contract specifying the student's commitment in terms of time, effort, and willingness to help others. At Albany High School the students accepted for the program received a congratulatory letter, and so did their parents (Marlow and Culler, 1987).
- Provide study space at lunch time, after school, and on weekends.
- Provide teacher supervision. The teachers do not need to be experts in the subject so much as facilitators who can show students how to study and how to work together.

Peer mediation

Peer support is important in non-academic areas as well. Peer mediation is especially helpful in culturally diverse settings. Peer mediation programs are in effect in many middle and secondary schools in North America, and are intended to help students with a wide range of problems: truancy, conflict with teachers, conflict with parents, cultural conflict, racist incidents, aggressive behaviour, feelings of alienation, financial difficulties, conflicting demands of school and work, difficulties with personal relationships, and any other problem that may be contributing to poor performance or to constant conflict with authority or with peers, within and beyond the school.

How to implement a peer mediation program

This model is in effect in schools in North York, Ontario (Geddis, 1995). The program can be adapted to the particular social and cultural context of any school.

- The program involves students identified as leaders by students and teachers. 'Leader' in this context means any student who has an influence on others, whether that influence is viewed as positive or negative. The important factor is that the students are high-profile and respected by many of their peers. Even 'negative' leaders can become engaged in school, perhaps for the first time, through their involvement in a program that recognizes their strengths.
- The students are interviewed for placement as peer mediators.
- Students accepted into the program are organized into gender-specific groups of about 10 per group. Each group is culturally and racially representative of the student population in the school, and has a balance of 'positive' and 'negative' leaders.
- The groups meet in a regularly scheduled period with a teacher who serves as the group leader.
- Student mediators receive academic credit for their work, — for example, in Co-operative Education, Community Service, or Life Skills, depending on what is available under local curriculum guidelines.
- The training consists of exploring one's own strengths and values, learning how to identify and solve problems, identifying and practising cross-cultural communication skills, learning mediation and counselling skills, and understanding ethical issues such as confidentiality.
- Students in difficulty are referred to the peer mediation program by administration, by staff, or by themselves, or may be invited to participate by a peer mediator.
- The peer mediators usually meet one-on-one with the students seeking help. Students meet with peers of their own gender, and often of their own cultural and/or linguistic background. The peer mediator provides non-judgmental support by listening, encouraging the student to identify the problem, and offering suggestions. The peer mediator student reports back to and seeks support from other members of the peer mediation group and the teacher. Sometimes the group and /or the teacher make a referral to an appropriate source of help, sometimes to an agency outside the school.
- An important feature of the program is public relations: the program needs to have a high profile in the school and enhance the status of the students involved in it. The program should not be perceived as a 'policing program' or a co-opted group working for the administration of the school; this would

compromise its ability to create trust among the students. The point of the program is peers helping peers, in a relationship in which both groups benefit: the students in difficulty receive support and help, and the students providing support learn to use their leadership skills in positive ways to help others and enhance their own status. At the same time, 'school tone' is improved by the presence of this program.

Multilingual services

The multilingual school needs to provide services in the languages of the school. However, this can be difficult to arrange if there are few bilingual teachers on staff. Community members do not have the necessary training, and may not have the time, while students may lack the training, the maturity, and the linguistic sophistication required. Professional translation and interpretation services are costly, and professionals do not always have the necessary cultural and educational knowledge to be helpful in school settings.

You may be able to locate develop bilingual resources that often exist in the school and in the community. For example, there may be students in the senior grades, as well as community volunteers, with the necessary bilingual skills. These individuals can be trained to provide multilingual services in the school. In addition to providing an important service to schools, students and volunteers involved in translation and interpretation services receive recognition for their bilingual and multilingual talents — talents that often go unrecognized. In addition, working bilingually promotes development in both languages and affirms the value of bilingualism. Also, participation in this program may help to encourage students of diverse linguistic and cultural backgrounds to aspire to a career in education.

Develop your bilingual resources

Multilingual school districts can develop and capitalize on the bilingual talents of their students. For example, students in senior grades at the secondary school can be trained as bilingual translators, interpreters, tutors, peer counsellors, and classroom assistants. Teachers in the Modern Languages or International Languages program could offer a course that trains a multilingual group of students for these roles. Schools that have co-operative education programs could incorporate this course into the program.

The course should carry academic credit, and students should be required to demonstrate adequate oral and written skills in both languages as a prerequisite for enrolment. Course content might include the ethics as well as the practicalities of translation and interpretation, and include some cross-cultural training. In addition, students need to receive specific training for the role of tutor, peer counsellor, or classroom assistant. The students need to be supervised by the teacher in practicum assignments, and eventually they may be required to spend a specific number of hours of service in their own school or in local elementary schools.

Duties might include:

- assisting with initial reception and orientation;
- development of the school's 'Welcome Booklet' or video for new students and parents;
- interpreting at parent–teacher interviews or meetings;
- making multilingual announcements on the school's public address system, or in school assemblies;
- assisting teachers to make telephone contact with parents;
- translating school newsletters, forms, and other written communication with parents;
- writing letters and invitations to community groups;
- making multilingual signs, posters, and notices for the school;
- helping teachers and librarians to find and evaluate text and audiovisual material in languages other than English;
- providing bilingual tutoring to students who need to develop concepts in the first language before transferring to English;
- serving as bilingual classroom assistants in classrooms where there are beginning learners of English;
- providing bilingual peer counselling services to recently arrived students;
- developing bilingual resources for use in bilingual tutoring programs;
- acting as classroom assistants or discussion group leaders in International or Heritage Languages classes.

Role models and mentors

The need to provide young people with positive role models and mentors is a constant theme in minority education. Role models present students with examples of achievement among a wide variety of people, including some of their own ethnocultural background. Mentors develop a one-on-one relationship with a student, sometimes of the same ethnocultural group, to provide individual support and advice.

Role models in the school

Students of all ethnocultural backgrounds need to be presented with role models with whom they can identify. The multicultural and antiracist school has to make special efforts to provide all students with images of, and direct interaction with, models of competence and excellence of many ethnocultural backgrounds, of both genders, and in a variety of roles. According to Pine and Hilliard:

> There are at least two reasons to ensure cultural, racial, and ethnic diversity in America's teaching force. First, the existence of differences among teachers is itself an equity lesson for students, who must be taught respect for and understanding of people from groups other than their own. Second, children of all

racial and cultural groups must have access to attractive role models. (Pine and Hilliard, 1990: 597)

Ideally, the ethnic composition of the school staff is representative of the linguistic, cultural, and racial diversity of the student population and the local community. In such schools, students are presented daily with models of authority and success with whom they can identify. However, this is seldom the case, since most teachers, like other professionals, are members of the dominant cultural group. In fact, there is evidence that the proportion of minority teachers is declining in the United States, even as the proportion of minority students is increasing (Graham, 1987; Zapata, 1988; Whitaker, 1989).

Some schools attempt to compensate for a lack of cultural and racial diversity among teachers and administrators by encouraging parents to volunteer in the school and by hiring bilingual classroom assistants. These individuals can be very helpful, but cultural diversity needs to be represented at every level of the school hierarchy; otherwise, damaging messages about the relative status of different groups are communicated to everyone in the school and the community.

In spite of these difficulties, role models are available within the school, though often unrecognized. An alternative resource exists among the students themselves, and schools can organize a program to develop students as role models for their peers. For example, a counsellor or other staff member could work with teachers in the middle and secondary grades to identify a group of students representing the ethnocultural diversity of the school and a variety of achievements, talents, and leadership skills.

How to develop students as role models

A counsellor or other staff member could meet several times with a culturally and racially diverse group of students who have been identified as leaders and models of success in the school. The purpose is to discuss the importance of role models, encourage the students to share their own experiences, especially with regard to living and studying in a multicultural environment, and help them to develop their presentation skills. Questions for discussion might include:

- What is your proudest accomplishment?
- What are your aspirations for the future?
- Where do you find help, support, or encouragement?
- How do you help others?
- Who are your role models? Why?
- What are some of the difficulties you have had to overcome?
- How do you deal with problems?
- How do you deal with prejudiced or racist comments attitudes and comments, whether they are directed at you or someone else?
- What choices have you made about language and culture?
- What advice would you give to younger students?

Meanwhile, a teacher could work with a class of younger students, in the same school or in the local elementary school, on the theme of 'People We Admire'. In addition to finding out about famous people of many backgrounds whose lives provide inspiration to everyone, students are invited to talk and write about real and ordinary people in their own lives whom they admire. To support the theme, the group of older students could be invited to the class to make a panel presentation, or to be interviewed by pairs or small groups of younger students.

Involvement in a program of this kind enhances the prestige of senior students of diverse cultural backgrounds and recognizes a variety of talents and aptitudes that may not be recognized in the traditional awards system. At the same time, the younger students are exposed to models of excellence and leadership of their own and other cultural backgrounds.

Role models in the community

Role models are also available in the community. For example, schools can invite members of specific ethnocultural groups into the school to interact with students as positive role models. Choose people who represent a variety of cultural back-grounds and both genders, and who can make effective presentations to groups of students about their own learning experiences and strategies for success in a variety of fields.

A day or a series of presentations can be organized, so that students choose several different presentations. Teachers act as moderators in the discussions, and supervise the students. Parents can be invited to participate as well, especially if some of the sessions are held in the evenings or on weekends. In small, informal group sessions, the presenters describe their lives and their jobs, and describe their experiences in working towards their present positions. Presenters who are immigrants, women, or members of a racial or cultural minority discuss the effects their backgrounds have had on their lives and their work, describe the strategies they adopted for countering difficulties, and offer students some of the insights they have gained from their experience.

Mentors

Mentors are role models too, but their involvement with students is more personal, usually one-on-one, and usually of longer duration. Mentors may be older students, university students, teachers, or members of the community. Mentors and students are usually of the same gender. Cultural mentorship, providing students with mentors of their own background, is especially important for some students. For example, co-operative education programs can place students with cultural mentors for the workplace component of the program.

How to organize a mentorship program

Organizing a mentorship program entails the following responsibilities:

- surveying staff, students and the community to identify suitable individuals of a variety of ethnocultural backgrounds who may be interested in undertaking this role;
- screening potential mentors;
- surveying staff, students, and parents to identify students who would benefit from regular contact with mentors;
- meeting with mentors to define their role, suggest activities and approaches, and provide advice;
- meeting with students to describe the program and invite participation;
- informing parents about the program and seeking parental consent;
- promoting the program through school newsletters, announcements, and bulletin board displays;
- organizing special events for groups of students and mentors: for example, guest speakers, or end-of-year banquets and recognition and awards ceremonies to honour participants;
- honouring participation in this program in the awards program of the school.

Antiracism training

Many schools and school districts have clearly stated policies to address and eliminate racism. However, as Pine and Hilliard point out:

> To augment clearly stated policies, intervention programs must be established to challenge prejudice, discrimination, and racism. The study of the history, purpose, and dynamics of racism must be recognized as a valid endeavour. An examination of stereotyping in the media, in textbooks, and in the popular culture ought to be included in the curriculum. Every controversial issue associated with racism needs to be studied, discussed, debated and critically confronted (Pine and Hilliard, 1990: 594).

All students need some training in recognizing and countering bias and discrimination through their involvement with an inclusive curriculum (see Chapters 7 and 8). All teachers need to develop their awareness and receive training in antiracist education through their involvement in staff development activities. It is important that all staff development programs, no matter what their focus or content, include antiracism as a fundamental principle.

In addition, some groups of students and teachers who show special interest or leadership can be given opportunities to develop their role as antiracist leaders and advocates in the school. Intensive programs can be designed to build cross-cultural sensitivity among group members from a variety of backgrounds, and to develop critical thinking and leadership skills. For example, students can learn how to recognize prejudiced or racist words and actions among students and teachers, and learn how to respond by following the appropriate procedure for making a complaint — or, if there is no procedure in place, by developing one and presenting it to the school administration and the student body for approval and implementation. Students can also be involved developing antiracist criteria to be used in reviewing and selecting curriculum materials, as well as in the actual review process.

Students Against Racism

Students are able to organize themselves to combat racism, as this example shows. In Ann Arbor, Michigan, students designed and administered a survey to every high school student in the district, compiled and analyzed the results, and made a series of recommendations to the school board. The recommendations included student-led workshops and discussions in all the high schools, re-evaluation of the policy on 'tracking' that had the effect of segregating students by their socioeconomic status and race, the development of a multicultural curriculum, and guidelines for dealing with 'racial incidents' between students and staff.

For more information on this initiative, see Polakow-Suransky and Ulaby (1990).

Some school districts organize antiracism leadership camps, where teams of students and teachers from several schools come together for a week of in-depth exploration of the issues involved in antiracist education and develop their leadership roles in the school and in the wider community (North York Board of Education, 1987). The experience includes some time for school teams to meet and develop a plan of action to be implemented when they return to school.

In addition to supporting students in the school, an inclusive school finds ways of reaching out to and supporting parents, as suggested in the next section.

PARENTAL INVOLVEMENT

Parental involvement is a key factor in school success, and a key component in building effective schools in low-income and ethnic minority neighbourhoods (Edmonds, 1979). At the same time, many educators identify parental involvement as one of their biggest challenges. The kind of involvement that teachers have traditionally valued is manifested by parents who attend parent-teacher meetings and interviews, Open Houses, and school concerts, work in the Parent–Teacher Association, and volunteer time to help teachers in the school or to accompany their children's classes on field trips. However, as Finders and Lewis point out, 'our interpretations of parents who care may simply be parents who are like us, parents who feel comfortable in the teacher's domain' (Finders, and Lewis, 1994: 54). In a culturally diverse community, all families may not find this model for parental involvement to be relevant to their needs or expectations.

Low income, immigrant, and minority parents tend to participate less than white middle class parents of the dominant culture in formal activities organized to promote communication between the school and the home (Delgado-Gaitan, 1991). This does not necessarily indicate a lack of interest in the education of their children; on the contrary, poor, immigrant and minority parents often have great expectations that the school system will enable their children to overcome the economic difficulties and social alienation that they have experienced themselves. Parents who are not members of the dominant culture often do not feel comfortable in the school or talking to teachers, especially if they do not feel confident in using English. Also, the pressures of resettlement in a new country, and of difficult hours of work, often make it impossible for parents to attend at times that are convenient for teachers (see also 'Parental involvement' in Chapter 2).

Many immigrant and minority parents do, in fact, participate in the education of their children, in ways that are not always visible to the teachers in the school. Many parents prefer a role that they can carry out in the home, in their own domain. Research has shown that this role can have a significant effect on their children's education, and that parents do not have to be well-educated themselves to play this role. For example, Clark's (1983) ethnographic study of low-income African-American families in Chicago showed that, in addition to visiting the school regularly, the parents of the high-achieving students supported their children at home in several important ways. They talked to their children often, provided encouragement and assistance, established clear and consistent expectations regarding behaviour, monitored how their children spent their time, had high expectations for school success, and expected their children to continue to post-secondary education (Clark, 1983).

Instead of expecting parents to support the school in ways that may conflict with their lifestyles, schedules, and values, or place them in situations where they feel uncomfortable or inadequate because of their own lack of education, limited proficiency in English, or unfamiliarity with the school system, schools serving a socioeconomically and culturally diverse community can reach out to parents in two ways:

- Find appropriate ways to invite parents into the school building, to encourage direct contact with teachers, and to establish genuine two-way dialogue;
- Support parents by sharing with them some of the strategies that can be used at home to promote school success.

Parents and community in the schools

Traditionally, schools have invited parents into the school as an audience. Parents are invited to come and see their children perform or to look at their work, or to hear from teachers about their children's progress at school. This is essentially a one-way relationship, one in which many parents may be physically present, but have little real involvement in what happens at school. Also, as we have seen, low-income and minority parents tend not to visit the school as often as middle class parents of the dominant culture.The school serving a socioeconomically and culturally diverse community can improve attendance and involvement by implementing some important changes. For example:

- **Announce meetings in the parents' own languages.** Written notices sent home with children often do not reach the parents — especially notices sent home with secondary school students. Personal telephone calls in the home language, usually in the evenings, are often the most effective way of communicating with parents and inviting them to meetings.
- **Survey parents,** through their children, at the beginning of the school year, to find out the most convenient times to hold meetings. It may be necessary to repeat meetings at different times, or hold them on weekends, so that parents have more flexibility in attending.
- **Hold meetings with specific groups of parents,** using interpreters and school-community workers to communicate with the parents in their native languages. Meetings can focus specific topics such as 'Parenting in a New Culture' or 'Dealing with Cultural Conflict.' Representatives of community groups can be invited to act as resource persons for such meetings. Make sure to allow enough time for interpretation and explanation, and leave part of the agenda open for parents to raise issues and ask questions.

   You can use these meetings to establish parent networks to help you communicate with parents through a telephone fan-out system. The parent network can also be a source of support to newly arrived families, or to families experiencing difficulty. For example, the parents of children who are successful and happy in school can share with other parents their knowledge about 'how I help my children to succeed at school,' or 'how I help my children to balance two cultures.'
- **Be specific about the purpose of all meetings**. Some parents may assume that the child is in some kind of trouble unless the purpose of the telephone call or the meeting is very clearly explained.
- **Avoid professional jargon** in parent-teacher meetings and interviews. Terms such as 'outcomes', 'benchmarks', or 'credits' may be mystifying to non-professionals, especially those who are unfamiliar with the system.
- **Arrange to have interpreters** with the necessary educational expertise as well as bilingual proficiency. These may be specially trained high school students (see 'Multilingual services' in this chapter). It is especially important to use properly trained interpreters if you are going to be discussing sensitive or confidential issues, or dealing with problems or situations of conflict.
- **Involve students in student-led conferences.** For example, instead of a parent–teacher interview, have a three-way conference involving the student, the parent, and the teacher. Spend some time in class preparing students for their role. The student-led conference works best if each student maintains a portfolio of work. A few days before the event, in consultation with the teacher, the student selects several pieces of work done during the term. During the conference, the teacher explains the purpose of the particular learning activity or assignment and the student shows the work, comments on performance, and explains what he or

she has learned from the activity. Remember to include an interpreter unless the parent is comfortable in English, or the student has both the maturity and the English proficiency to act as interpreter.

The student also shows the parent around the classroom, explains the purpose of different learning centres or materials, and explains the material displayed on the bulletin board.

- **Arrange to have all the students present** (or as many as possible) during a parent–teacher evening, and teach a demonstration 'mini-lesson' for the parents. Parents may like to sit with their own children, and may want to participate with the children in a group activity. Include several different kinds of learning activity and provide commentary, with interpretation in the languages of the parents. Alternatively, you could make a video of your classroom, with voice-over provided by students in different languages. Encourage parents to ask questions.

- **Improve communication and establish trust** by ensuring that there is a two-way flow of information and advice between parents and teachers. Parents must see that there is some follow-up if they are to invest their time in this kind of involvement. For example, if parents have a specific concern or make a specific request for change in the school routines or classroom program, the school must be seen to pay attention to these requests and be prepared to negotiate some compromise.

  Engage in dialogue and reach consensus with individual parents and parent groups about the roles of parents and teachers: for example, who is responsible for monitoring specific aspects of student behaviour or performance? How much homework, and of what kind, should be assigned at specific grade levels? How can parents intervene on behalf of their children when problems of conflicts arise? What are the rights and responsibilities of parents, teachers, and children? What constitutes appropriate discipline in the home?

- **Make sure that all written communication with the home is comprehensible.** Parents may have difficulty with written communication in English: school handbooks, report cards, newsletters, information about field trips, and so on. Even if the parents understand English, such communication often assumes prior knowledge of the school system. Ensure that all documents are written in plain English and available in the major languages of the school as well.

- **Establish an English as a Second Language program for adult learners** in the school, and encourage parents to attend. The content of the program may include, as well as general orientation and survival information and skills, information about the school program in which the learners' children are in-volved. The teacher of this class can organize classroom visits so that parents can see first-hand what their children are doing.

  It is to the children's as well as the parents' advantage if they are able to access services (such as education) in English. Parents who continue to rely on inter-preters are less likely to initiate or respond to interaction with the school or other institutions.

- **Invite parents to help the school.** For example, parents can help to provide multilingual signs and notices for the school, or make tape recordings of books in their own languages. Some parents may enjoy telling stories in their own language, participating in the family studies program when students are cooking, or demonstrating a technique or style in visual arts.

    Parents can participate in content areas such as social studies as well. For example, a class studying World Religions can find out first-hand from parents or religious leaders about the beliefs and practices of different religions, or explore a theme such as 'Coming of Age' or 'Families'. In elementary schools, a class can be involved in a literature-based unit about 'Grandparents and Elders', and a special 'Grandparents' and Elders' Day' can be organized. Each child brings as a guest a grandparent or an elder from the extended family or the community. Students are involved in planning the event, sending invitations in the appropriate languages, and acting as hosts. To enhance the profile of this event and acknowledge the status that elders enjoy in many communities, involve the school principal in a formal welcome.

    Parents and community members can also help the school to find and select multilingual material for school and classroom libraries. Teachers can share with parents the criteria they use in selecting books, including antiracist and antisexist criteria. This provides an opportunity for parents and teachers to discuss the values promoted in the school, and to explore the potential for cultural conflict between home and school.

- **Invite organized community groups to play a role in the school.** For example, there are many cultural and religious organizations which can provide a source of information, assistance or referral to both teachers and students. These organizations represent a group that includes potential role models for students: educated, informed, professional, assertive, and altruistic. Boards of education could contract with some of these organizations to provide services such as culturally sensitive counselling services, family referral, culturally relevant curriculum development projects, outreach to parents, and staff development.
- **Share information about the school system** during parent meetings and interviews. Explain the philosophy and goals of the education system to parents who were educated in other countries. For example, the goals of education in many North American, British, and Australian schools include, in addition to academic skills and knowledge, the development of important social skills. Activities which some parents and students may regard as frivolous (for example, field trips, projects, or group work) have a sound pedagogical basis, rooted in a more student-centred, activity-oriented approach to education. Emphasize that social skills are as important in academic success, in the community, and in the workplace as academic and technical expertise.
- **Share with parents insights from research** on what counts in improving student performance. For example, most students don't do enough homework. They may complete all the *required* assignments, but that is insufficient for academic excellence. The students who do well are those who do more than the required homework, and who have a regular program of review. School achievement can be directly related to the amount of time students spend studying and watching television, and parents need to know this (Kunjufu, 1988).

  A school could survey its own students and parents about homework and television watching, and correlate those results to achievement. Share the information with students and parents: they all need to know what works. Then the parents and teachers can decide what to do about it. For example, you might decide to organize peer tutoring programs and homework study groups (see 'Peer tutoring' and 'Study groups' in the previous section of this chapter).
- **Make expectations explicit.** Parents need to know exactly what is expected in terms of behaviour and routines such as completion of assigned homework, arriving on time, being prepared for class, and so on. Negotiate with parents some agreement on appropriate consequences for failing to to meet these expectations, make sure that all students and parents understand them. Give examples, or invite students to provide examples, of specific kinds of behaviour. For example, what does 'Teachers and students will show respect to each other' look like or sound like?
- **Encourage community groups to use the school** for cultural events, organizational meetings, and religious observation. Information about the availability of the school can be circulated to the community in the school's multilingual newsletter. Community use of the school can foster a sense of belonging and ownership, and parents who have been in the building for events that are

organized by themselves or their community representatives are much more likely to feel at ease visiting the school for matters to do with their children's education. When inviting the community to use the school, it is a good idea to suggest that when it seems appropriate to the group concerned, the school administration and staff would appreciate being invited to attend special events or meetings organized by the group. The attendance of members of the school staff at such events demonstrates support of the group and its values, and further strengthens school–community relations.

Parents helping children at home

The school can be an important source of help and advice to parents who want to help their children at home. Parents do not have to be educated or even able to speak English to do this.

Supporting academic achievement at home

In the United States, a study of Vietnamese children found that these students were performing exceptionally well in mathematics and science, and very close to the national average in language and reading tests (Caplan *et al.*, 1992). Their families had been in the United States for an average three and a half years, and parents and children had arrived with little or no knowledge of English. The children had missed months or years of schooling and experienced the trauma of the refugee experience. All attended school in low-income urban districts, All of these are factors that normally might be expected to have a negative impact on school achievement.

The study found that it is what happens in the home that supports the children's success in school (Caplan *et al.*, 1992). For example:

- Homework is a major component of family life and dominates week nights after dinner.
- Children spend about twice as much time doing homework as the general American student population.
- The parents' lack of education and limited knowledge of English prevents them from direct involvement with their children's studies; instead, they undertake most of the chores so that children can concentrate on their studies, and establish standards and goals for the evening's studies.
- Children in the family study together, with older siblings helping younger ones. The older children seem to learn as much as they teach, and younger children learn not only the academic content or skills, but important strategies for learning.
- Learning is regarded as intrinsically satisfying; children experience satisfaction from their own learning and from their sense of increasing competence as well as from helping each other to learn.

- Effort is regarded as more important than ability in accomplishing goals, and success in school is regarded as the key to social acceptance and economic success.
- There is an emphasis on interdependence and a family-based orientation to achievement, in contrast to the emphasis on independence and individual achievement that characterizes 'mainstream' culture in the United States.
- Children whose families value their cultural heritage and regard the past and the future as equally important do better than children whose parents more readily accept 'American' values such as fun and excitement, or material possessions.
- Larger families actually give children an advantage.
- Children whose parents share household responsibilities and have a more egalitarian relationship achieve better school results than those whose parents had a more strictly traditional relationship.
- Children whose parents value education equally for boys and girls, and require them to be equally responsible for chores in the home, do better in school.
- Children whose parents read aloud to them — whether in English or in their home language — achieve better results in school.

A famous British study in a low-income, multiracial and multilingual community in Haringey, London, showed that parents do not have to be literate in either their first or the second language in order to be involved in their children's education at home (Tizard *et al.*,1982). In the United States, the Pajaro Valley Family Literacy project involved Spanish-speaking parents in reading and discussing books in Spanish with their children, including books written by the children (Ada, 1988). The project had positive effects on the children's motivation to write as well as the amount of reading in the home and the parents' sense of efficacy.

The Haringey Project
Methodology:
Over a period of two years, researchers compared the growth in reading of three groups of young children. Many of the children were from homes where English was not the primary language, and where parents had limited knowledge of English. Some parents were not literate in any language.

- One group took books home to read to their parents, who received relatively little instruction on how to conduct the reading sessions.
- Another group received extra help from a specialist reading teacher in the school, who met the children four out of five days every week for reading instruction in small groups and individually.
- A control group received no intervention at all.

Findings:

- The children who read to their parents made significant gains in comparison with both control groups.

- No comparable improvement was made by children who received extra help at school.
- The gains were greatest among children who were initially having difficulty with reading.

Implications:

- Parents do not need to be literate, or proficient in the language of instruction, to support their children's literacy development.
- The home reading program may be one of the most effective ways of supporting literacy development in a multilingual community.
- The role of reading teachers and consultants may need to change, so that they are working more with parents than with children and other teachers.

Children who read with or to their parents engage in more than the simple act of reading or listening to a story. They may retell the story or parts of it, and parents may engage in discussion that encourages children to make predictions about the story, to relate it to their own experience, or to elaborate on the story. It does not matter what language is used for this discussion, as long as it is one that the parent and child can use to communicate effectively with each other; the cognitive activity is the same in any language, and language development stimulated by this kind of activity in the first language will transfer to one that the child is learning. Undoubtedly, shared reading experiences encourage children to associate reading with emotional security and love.

Book Time: A Home Reading Program
This program is based on the Haringey experience. Parents opt into the program by agreeing to read at least five books a week to or with their children. Each week the child takes home a new set of books in a specially-designed book bag. Some of the books are selected because they will assist children to develop the background knowledge and vocabulary; others are chosen to represent a multi-racial, multicultural community in positive ways.

There is a videotape of teachers modelling several strategies for helping children to get meaning from pictures and print, and expand on the information in the stories. Many of the parents see their own children in these videotapes, which are available for parents to view in the school at any time; several copies are available for loan as well. When teachers have conferences with parents, these strategies are discussed. (Davies *el al.*, 1990)

Clearly there are many ways that parents can support their children at home, even if they have limited education or limited knowledge of English themselves. Teachers can help parents to undertake this role by sharing specific strategies, and explaining the rationale and behind them. For example, many parents assume that speaking English at home is the best way to support their children's acquisition of English. Teachers can inform them about the value of their continuing to use the native language at home, and reassure them that if they speak to their children in the first language, and provide reading material at increasing levels of sophistication in that language, the children will continue their acquisition of formulaic, rhetorical forms of the language as well as the language of day-to-day interaction.

It is also helpful to discuss with parents and students the value of becoming bicultural as well as bilingual. Children need to adopt behaviours appropriate to both home and school; it is less stressful if their parents approve of new behaviours and learning styles which they adopt in their new school.

Schools can also provide workshops for parents to demonstrate aspects of the curriculum and teaching methodology, and provide parents with material and techniques they can use at home to support their children's development. For example, *Family Math* is a program designed to improve performance and participation in mathematics, especially female and minority students, through activities that parents or older siblings and children can do together (Stenmark *et al.*, 1986).

How to help your children at home

Provide this advice to parents in the language in which they are most comfortable:

- Talk to your children often. Tell them about your day, and ask them about theirs. Take an interest in their problems, and give them examples of how you solve yours.
- Limit the amount of TV your children watch, and make sure you know what they are watching.
- Make sure your children do at least an hour of homework every night in the elementary grades, an hour and a half in middle school, and two to three hours in secondary school. If the children have no homework from school, get them to show you what they did during the day, and encourage them to review the day's lessons. You can also give them something to read, or a puzzle to work on, or you can play a game that involves talking and thinking.
- Establish a regular time for homework every week night, and ask your children to explain what they are going to do. Ask your children to show you the work when it is finished.
- Set up a regular place for homework. This does not have to be a separate room. It's best if you can be in the same room or nearby so you can supervise what your children are doing. Make sure the children are not distracted by TV or other noise.
- Encourage your children to help each other, or to study together with other students from their class or grade.
- Read to your children, or get them to read to you, in English or in your own language. Stop a few times and ask questions: 'What does this make you

think of?' 'What do you think will happen next?' 'Do you remember when . . . ?' 'What do you like best about this story?'
- Take your children to the library and get them library cards. Make sure they go to the library regularly to get books of their choice, in English and in your own language. Always have reading material in your home — books, newspapers, magazines — in both languages.
- Use your first language at home with your children.
- Have high expectations for your children and help them to imagine themselves training for a satisfying job or studying at college or university in the future.

CONCLUSION

Schools are important social institutions as well as places of academic learning. Students need to learn how to live and work in an increasingly diverse community and world, how to recognize inequity in a variety of contexts, and how to act as responsible citizens who have the right and the duty to work for social justice. Schools serving multicultural, multiracial, and multilingual communities have an especially important role in promoting cultural harmony while recognizing important cultural differences. Schools can do this by providing a school environment where students of many different backgrounds feel valued and included, and where all students learn to respect each other and value linguistic and cultural diversity. Multicultural schools also need to provide some special services, or adapt some existing ones, to support individual students and groups of students in the school. In addition, it is essential to find effective ways of involving parents of all linguistic and cultural backgrounds in the education of their children.

Teachers and school administrators can use the following checklist to assess the school as an inclusive and supportive environment, and as an institution that has strong connections with the community it serves.

CHECKLIST: AN INCLUSIVE SCHOOL ENVIRONMENT

This checklist can be used by teachers, students, parents, and school and district administrators to assess the school environment.The checklist is organized as a series of indicators under broad topic areas that correspond with the recommendations and suggestions in this chapter.

The rating system can be used and interpreted as follows:

yes = whenever appropriate
not yet = this is an area that may need special attention
n/a = not applicable, or not available at this time

An inclusive physical and social environment

yes not n/a
      yet

❑ ❑ ❑   Display material is carefully selected to provide realistic and positive images of different cultural and racial groups.

❑ ❑ ❑   There is a process for evaluating textbooks and other resource material.

❑ ❑ ❑   Guidelines for the selection of resources include criteria related to cultural diversity.

❑ ❑ ❑   Students and parents are involving in selecting resource material.

❑ ❑ ❑   Signs, notices, and displays in the school building are multilingual, and reflect a variety of cultural perspectives.

❑ ❑ ❑   Students' home language are used in school announcements, parents' meetings and interviews, cultural events and performances, etc.

❑ ❑ ❑   All teachers in the school know something about the naming practices and forms of address that are usual in the various school communities, and can pronounce the names of all their students.

❑ ❑ ❑   Students are encouraged to make natural language choices in social interaction around the school.

❑ ❑ ❑   There is a variety of extracurricular activities.

❑ ❑ ❑   Students and parents are consulted about their preferences and interests in extracurricular activities.

❑ ❑ ❑   The school awards program recognizes a wide range of talents and contributions, including those that may be especially valued or promoted in some of the cultural groups in the school.

❑ ❑ ❑   There is an active student /teacher antiracism group in the school.

❑ ❑ ❑   Special events are planned to be as inclusive as possible of all the cultures in the school.

❑ ❑ ❑   Equal treatment is given to important festivals and special days of all the cultures in the school.

Support services

yes not n/a
      yet

❑ ❑ ❑   Each student's individual progress is carefully monitored.

❑ ❑ ❑   When an individual student appears to be having difficulties, there is a planned program of intervention and support.

❑ ❑ ❑   The school monitors the progress of specific groups of students.

❑ ❑ ❑   The school takes appropriate action when a specific group of students appears to be having social or academic difficulty.

❑ ❑ ❑   The school provides individual and group counselling services related to students' academic and social needs.

yes not n/a
    yet

❏ ❏ ❏   Counsellors and teachers serving in that capacity have the knowledge and skills required for effective cross-cultural counselling.

❏ ❏ ❏   There is a procedure for conflict mediation when students experience ethnocultural harassment in the school or beyond.

❏ ❏ ❏   The school has established mutually supportive relationships with community groups and agencies.

❏ ❏ ❏   There is an organized peer tutoring program which includes training and supervision.

❏ ❏ ❏   Bilingual tutors are trained to work with students who arrive with limited educational background.

❏ ❏ ❏   There are organized study groups in the school.

❏ ❏ ❏   There is a peer mediation program in the school.

❏ ❏ ❏   Multilingual services are provided by trained interpreters and translators.

❏ ❏ ❏   All students have opportunities to meet role models and mentors of diverse cultural backgrounds.

❏ ❏ ❏   All staff development programs include antiracism as a fundamental principle.

❏ ❏ ❏   There are opportunities for teachers and students to be involved in antiracism training.

Parental Involvement

yes not n/a
    yet

❏ ❏ ❏   The school is creative and flexible in finding ways to invite parents into the school.

❏ ❏ ❏   Written communication with parents is in a language they understand.

❏ ❏ ❏   Parents' meetings are held with specific linguistic and cultural groups.

❏ ❏ ❏   Parent networks are established as a means of communication and support.

❏ ❏ ❏   Students are trained to lead their own conferences involving the teacher and their parents.

❏ ❏ ❏   Parent–teacher communication consists of a two-way flow of information and advice.

❏ ❏ ❏   Expectations regarding student attendance and behaviour, homework, parental involvement, etc. are negotiated, realistic, and explicit.

❏ ❏ ❏   The school has an English as a second language program for adults.

❏ ❏ ❏   Parents are invited to help the school in ways that are appropriate.

yes not n/a
    yet

❏   ❏   ❏   Organized community groups play a role in the school.
❏   ❏   ❏   Community groups use the school for meetings and special events.
❏   ❏   ❏   Parents receive helpful practical advice on how to help their children at home.

FURTHER READING AND RESOURCES FOR TEACHERS

Alladina, S. (1995) *Being Bilingual: A Guide for Parents, Teachers and Young People on Mother Tongue, Heritage Language and Bilingual Education.* Stoke-on-Trent, England: Trentham Books. The author speaks directly to bilingual parents and children, as well as to teachers. The book could provide the foundation for discussion at parent-teacher interviews and meetings, and could be a course text for students in secondary school English classes.

Baker, C. (1995) *A Parents' and Teachers' Guide to Bilingualism.* Clevedon, England: Multilingual Matters. In a very readable question-and-answer format, this book provides helpful advice to parents and teachers on raising and teaching bilingual children.

Bilingual Education Office (1986) *Beyond Language: Social and Cultural Factors in Schooling Language Minority Students.* Los Angeles, CA: Evaluation, Dissemination and Assessment Center, California State University, Los Angeles. This book includes chapters by well-known writers and researchers in multilingual and antiracist education.

Blackledge, A. (1994) *Teaching Bilingual Children.* Stoke-on-Trent, England: Trentham Books. A collection of articles from several international contexts on how schools can bring student's languages into the school and strengthen the links between home and community.

Cummins, J. (1996) *Negotiating Identities: Education for Empowerment in a Diverse Society.* Ontario, CA: California Association for Bilingual Education. This book is about how to reverse patterns of school failure among culturally diverse students — for example, by promoting among students a sense of pride in their own language and culture, and a belief in their ability to learn, and by involving minority parents in the education of their children.

Genesee, F. (ed.) (1994) *Educating Second-Language Children: The Whole Child, The Whole Curriculum, the Whole Community.* New York, NY: Cambridge University Press. Several chapters in this book are about the interaction between school and community, and between majority and minority languages.

Multilingual Resources for Children Project. (1995) *Building Bridges: Multilingual Resources for Children.* Clevedon, England: Multilingual Matters. This book is filled with interesting ideas for bringing community languages into the school.

Page, N. (1995) *Sing and Shine On! The Teacher's Guide to Multicultural Song Leading.* Portsmouth, NH: Heinemann. An inspiring book about the power of song to create a community in the classroom and in the school, and to enhance self-esteem and motivation to learn in all students. Very useful for teachers planning school concerts and other performance events.

Reading and Language Information Centre. Located at the University of Reading, Bulmershe Court, Ealey, Reading, UK 2G6 1HY. Publications include books on working with parents, a database of multicultural resources, and books on multilingual schools and classrooms.Website address: http://www.rdg.ac.uk/AcaDepts/eh/ReadLang/home.html

Samway, K. D., Whang, G., and Pippitt, M. (1995) *Buddy Reading: Cross-Age Tutoring in a Multicultural School.* Portsmouth, NH: Heinemann.The authors share their experiences with cross-grade tutoring in an elementary setting; their suggestions on how to set up the program and train the tutors are helpful to teachers at all grade levels.

Stenmark, J.K., Thompson, V., and Cossey, R. (1986) *Family Math.* Berkeley, CA: Regents, University of California. Intended to help parents of diverse cultural backgrounds become involved in their children's' education, the material in this book is intended for use with parents and children in a series of workshop sessions that focus on problem-solving skills and the use of concrete and manipulative materials. Also available in Spanish as *Matemática para la Familia.*

CHAPTER 5

An Inclusive Classroom Community

INTRODUCTION

In inclusive classrooms, teachers work with their students to create a classroom community that welcomes newcomers, whether they arrive from other schools in the same district or from countries around the world, and whether they speak the language of the school or are beginning learners of the language. In addition, students learn about each others' linguistic and cultural backgrounds, and have many opportunities for positive interaction with each other. Through these experiences they learn to respect each other and to value linguistic and cultural diversity.

This chapter describes some strategies that teachers can use to create an inclusive and orderly classroom where students of all backgrounds feel valued as members of the classroom community, and where there are routines to keep the classroom running smoothly. At the end of the chapter is a checklist that teachers can use to assess the classroom as a welcoming, inclusive, safe, and supportive learning environment for all students.

BUILDING AN INCLUSIVE CLASSROOM COMMUNITY

Teachers can use some of the strategies described here to build a sense of community and belonging that supports all the students in the classroom. The strategies are organized into eight subtopics:

- Introductions
- Class surveys
- Inclusive displays
- Partners and peer tutors
- Co-operative learning
- Support for language learning

- A multilingual classroom environment
- Classroom routines

Introductions

Teachers can use some of the following strategies to help everyone to feel welcome in the classroom, and ease the transition for newcomers:

- **Introduce newcomers** as speakers of Cantonese, Spanish, Farsi, etc. who are also learning English. Avoid referring to a student as someone who 'doesn't speak English'; nobody likes being described in terms of what he/she cannot (yet) do. Each student arrives in the classroom with at least one language already established, and it is important to acknowledge this.
- **Learn how to pronounce** the new student's name, and write it on the board as you say it, so that all the students learn the name.
- **Seat newcomers** or beginning learners of English beside someone who speaks his or her first language for the first few weeks. Make time for personal contact with new students at least once during each lesson.
- Use **structured group interviews** to help students introduce themselves to each other at the beginning of the year, or at any time that classroom groupings change.

WHO'S IN OUR GROUP?

(1) **Interview your partner**:
   What is your name?
   How do you spell it?
   Where were you born?
   How long have you/your family been in this country?
   What language(s) do you speak?

(2) **Can you think of other questions** to ask your partner?

(3) **Introduce your partner to the group**. For example: This is _____. He/she was born in _____. He/she speaks _____.

(4) **Be ready** to introduce your group to the class.

Note: Beginning learners of English can be involved in this activity with the assistance of a bilingual peer.

GROUP INTRODUCTIONS: ALL ABOUT NAMES

(1) **Interview your partner**:
   What's your given name? How do you pronounce it? How do you spell it?
   What's your family name? How do you pronounce it? How do you spell it?
   In your culture, is your given name your first name, or is it the last?
   Does your given name have a meaning?
   Do any of your names show if you are male or female?
   Who gave you your given name?
   Do you like your name?

Would you ever change your name?

Does your family name have any religious significance?

Does your family name tell something about where your ancestors came from?

Does your family name tell what occupation your ancestors had?

Does any part of your name show which generation of your family you belong to?

Does any part of your name show what clan or kinship group your family belongs to?

In your culture, do women usually keep their own family name after they marry?

Whose family name do children have in your culture?

In your culture, how do people give names to their children?

In your culture, is it usual to be named after someone else, living or dead?

Can you tell me anything else about your name, or about names in your culture?

(2) Introduce your partner to the other members of the group so that everyone can pronounce and spell your partner's name, and knows at least one interesting fact about your partner's name.

(3) After you have finished the introductions, everyone in your group must be ready to introduce all the members of the group to the whole class, and tell us something interesting about each person's name.

Note: Students may need to take the questions home to consult family members in preparation for the interview. The interview can be shortened, simplified, or conducted in several languages in order to meet the needs of the students. As a follow-up activity, students can write a journal entry about their own names, or write about their partners and display the information, together with photographs, on the class bulletin board.

Class surveys

If you survey the class during the first days of the year or semester, you will learn a lot about the linguistic and cultural backgrounds of the students, and perhaps lay the groundwork for dialogue with the students on an individual basis.

- **Begin by sharing information about yourself,** orally or in writing; students will be more willing to share information about themselves if you have already revealed something about yourself to them. Adapt your use of language to the age and proficiency level of the students; with young children and beginning learners of English, use several photographs of key events in your life to provide additional support for comprehension.

Welcome to our class!

My name is Ms. Nguyen and I will be your teacher for Mathematics this year. I hope we will get to know each other well during the time we spend together; to start us off I'll tell you a few things about myself and about this class, and ask you some questions about yourself.

I came to Canada from Vietnam when I was fifteen years old. I could already read and write Vietnamese and some Chinese when I came but I didn't know much English and I didn't know how to speak it at all. I was very shy and I felt very embarrassed in most of my classes, but I was good at mathematics and I had a teacher who helped me to learn the English words for mathematics. We did a lot of group work, and I learned from listening to other students explaining the problems. Soon I began to understand what people were saying, and I even began helping other students with their math problems.

I have been teaching since 1990. I believe education is important because it gives you more choices in life. Being successful in mathematics is important because we all need to use math in our daily lives, and it is your 'passport' to many other fields in science and technology. Also, mathematics can be fun when you feel confident in the subject.

My idea of a good classroom is one where everyone participates, everyone learns, and everyone has fun at the same time. In this class, we will do a lot of problem solving in small groups so that everyone gets plenty of opportunity to talk and work together. I will also give mini-lessons on important skills for students who need it.

If you want to know more about me or about this class, write some questions here:

_____

_____

_____

_____

_____

- **Conduct a language survey.** You can work with students to generate questions about language knowledge and use. Students may respond individually, or they may interview each other. Encourage students to go beyond 'what language do you speak' by talking about the various contexts in which they choose to use one or another of their languages (Edwards, 1996).

  In addition to gathering information on each student, involve the students in collating and charting the information for display in the classroom and for sharing with others in the school. If every class is involved, the information can be collated into a chart for display in the front entrance of the school and for sharing with parents in school newsletters.

- **Design a questionnaire or interview** to gather information on the cultural backgrounds of all the students, as well as other relevant information. Don't forget to interview or survey new students who arrive later in the term.

STUDENT QUESTIONNAIRE

What's your name?
Where were you born?
If you were born outside Canada, when did you come to Canada?
What language do you usually speak at home?
What language do you usually speak with your friends?
What languages can you read?
Which language do you read best?
If your first language is not English, which language do you feel most comfortable in for expressing complicated thoughts and ideas?
Have you been to school in any other country?
What do you like most about school?
What do you dislike the most about school?
Do you feel confident about (subject), or do you feel that you have difficulty in this subject?
Are you involved in school activities and/or sports teams?
What are your interests outside school?
What else would you like me to know about you?

Note: Learners who are new to English will need the help of a bilingual peer to complete the questionnaire. If you are working with younger children, shorten and simplify the questionnaire. If you are a grade level or core teacher working with the same group of students every day, for most of the day, you could conduct the survey by oral interview over a period of several days.

Inclusive displays

The visual environment of the classroom can give important messages to students about their membership in the classroom community. Make sure to include everyone in the material you display in the classroom. For example:

- **Trace the students' roots on a political world map** that is permanently displayed in the classroom or homeroom. For each student, make a small name tag (or have the students make their own) and pin it on their county of origin or ancestry. Add newcomers to the map as they arrive. Students can point out their own countries on the map, and perhaps tell you or the class something about it if they already know some English.
- **Take a photograph of every student in the class.** Students write a sentence or two about themselves. Some students may be able to do this in two languages; others may be able to do it only in their own language, and you or another student can write the English version for them. Keep this as a permanent display and encourage students to add to the information about themselves at any time. Include yourself in the display, and remember to add newcomers as they arrive.
- **Involve the students in creating classroom displays.** Students from specific groups might like to prepare a display featuring a special day or holiday, or you

might invite all the students to contribute to displays related to a general classroom theme, such as 'food an nutrition', 'men and women who made a difference', 'great artists', 'mathematics in architecture' and so on (see Chapters 7 and 8).

Partners and peer tutors

Peer tutors in the classroom can help all teachers meet the needs of diverse groups of learners. Peer tutors can be especially helpful in providing extra help and support to newcomers and second language learners.

- **Organize classroom partners and peer tutors for newcomers.** Students who are just beginning to learn English will benefit from the support of a bilingual partner for the first few weeks in your class. Students who have some English already will appreciate the support of a friendly English speaker. Social skills are more important than academic skills in selecting students to act as partners for second language learners.
- **Give peer tutors specific responsibilities.** For example, you can assign a student to work with a second language learner on a mathematics problem. When the language learner can verbalize aloud each step in English, both students have succeeded in their assigned tasks.

- **Give recognition to partners and tutors** for undertaking their responsibilities. 'Recognition' sometimes means 'marks', especially in secondary school, but you may use any form of recognition that boosts the self-esteem of the students and enhances their status in the classroom or the school. A letter of commendation (in a language that the parents understand), a visit and a handshake from a school administrator, or recognition in a school assembly are alternative ways of highlighting the value of peer tutors in the school community. Let students know what they stand to gain by acting as peer tutors: 'Those who teach learn the most'.

Co-operative learning

School may be the only place where students have opportunities for daily contact with people of different racial and cultural backgrounds. However, students will not unlearn prejudice simply by going to the same school or sitting in the same class as those of other racial or cultural backgrounds. Indeed, students in multicultural schools often seem to become increasingly polarized as they get older, so that by the time they reach secondary schools their social segregation becomes obvious to anyone walking through the school cafeteria or watching groups of students moving around the school. In the classroom, too, students tend to choose to work with others of similar background or with similar interests to their own. Thus it is possible, and even usual, for students in multicultural schools and classrooms to have very limited contact with students of other backgrounds. Tensions arise among different groups, based on stereotyped perceptions of 'the other' and a lack of rapport.

Allport (1954), writing about desegregation in the United States, warned that specific measures must be taken to equalize the status of different groups within the school and within the classroom. Involving students in activities in mixed co-operative learning groups may be one of the best ways of doing this. The shared goals of the group members result in a common sense of identity and purpose and help to promote positive interpersonal interaction. The frequent, meaningful, and mutually supportive contact involved in co-operative learning assists students to view each other in non-stereotypical ways. By assigning students to work in heterogeneous groups, teachers communicate their expectations that students can and will work effectively and co-operatively with people of different backgrounds.

More may be achieved by this kind of organizational change in the classroom than by any amount of reading, writing, and talking overtly about race relations. Many studies have revealed that intergroup relations improve dramatically after co-operative learning experiences in heterogeneous groups, *whatever the content of those learning experiences,* and that the improvement in race relations has long-term effects (Kagan, 1986; Slavin, 1983, 1990).

Co-operative learning activities may be very simple or very complex, as the following examples show.

Interviews

Interviews are especially useful at the beginning of the year or when students are working in new groups. You can use interviews to help students introduce themselves to each other and 'break the ice', or to share knowledge, viewpoints, or questions on a new topic that the class is going to study. You can also use interviews at the end of a lesson or instructional unit to help students reflect on a learning experience.

Follow this procedure for interviews:

(1) Assign students to learning teams of four.
(2) Within these groups of four, students divide into pairs to interview each other.
(3) Students take turns reporting on the interview to the other members of the group.
(4) Call on students at random to present a report for the group.

Adaptations:

- Beginning learners of English may need to be partnered with bilingual peers,
- In a group of three: #1 interviews #2, #2 interviews #3, and #3 interviews #1; skip step 3.
- In a group of five: in step 2, two students interview each other, while the other three follow the procedure for groups of 3.

Topics for interviews

These topics can be used when students are just getting to know each other:

- What is your favourite place (movie, book, music, subject, etc.)? Why?
- Tell me about a famous writer (musician, artist, actor, leader, scientist, etc.) in your culture.
- Tell me about someone you admire, and tell me why.
- Have you ever studied this topic before? What do you know about it?
- Have you ever studied this subject before? How do you feel about it?
- Tell me how you like to spend your time when you are not at school.
- What do you hope to be doing in five years?
- Tell me about your most exciting day.
- Tell me about your favourite game.
- What was the best thing that ever happened to you at school?
- If you could change one thing about this school, what would it be?

More topics for interviews

Topics for interview may be related to the content of a lesson:

- How do you feel about the poem we just read?
- Did this story remind you of anything in your own life or in the life of someone you know?

- How do you feel about the activity we just finished? What did you learn?
- What were the most important points in this chapter or this lesson?
- Explain to me how you worked out this mathematics problem.
- What important new words did you learn in this lesson or this chapter?
- Tell me what you think is going to happen next in the story.
- Tell me who you liked the best or least in the story.
- Why you think this character behaved this way? What you would do in this situation?
- How do you think this problem should be solved?

Group brainstorming

Use group brainstorming to generate ideas. Group discussion gives all students an opportunity to take risks in a way that they may be reluctant to do in front of the class — especially those who may be intimidated by the prospect of speaking English in front of the whole class. Group brainstorming can be used as a prereading strategy, or after reading to encourage students to speculate about alternatives (what if . . .). Group brainstorming is also useful in generating ideas for projects.

Follow this procedure for group brainstorming:

(1) Assign the discussion task and specify exactly what the students are to accomplish. This is usually some kind of list.
(2) Establish a time limit. This helps to keep the groups focused on the task.
(3) Take up the ideas that have been generated, making sure to acknowledge each group's work. For example, you can take one idea at a time from each group until all the ideas are listed on the chalkboard or chart. Another time, you might let the groups share with each other by sending representatives to look at the work of other groups and bring back useful ideas, or double up the groups so that they can present their ideas to each other. Another approach is the 'gallery walk': each group creates a chart, list, or mind map categorizing their ideas, and posts it on the classroom wall. Students walk around the room, looking at the charts developed by other groups. When all the students have finished the walk, they return to their own groups and revise their charts or visuals to include new ideas.

Learning teams

Learning teams are groups of students working together on a common task. It is especially important for the second language learners to hear other students using the language of the subject, and to have a non-judgmental forum in which to ask questions.

Use learning teams to help students review, internalize, or apply new concepts and information. For example, after a classroom presentation of new material, pose a review or extension question to the whole class and instruct students to discuss

the question in small groups. You can use learning teams for practice tests or assignments, in preparation for a similar test or assignment that each student performs individually. Learning teams are also effective in problem-solving activities, such as in mathematics, because students have to verbalize each step in a process in order to make sure everyone understands.

For group problem-solving in mathematics, group students so that strengths in mathematics and proficiency in English are evenly distributed. Give one copy of the problem to each group, or display it on an overhead projector. This encourages the group to solve the problem together. Circulate to support the group process. If some groups finish quickly, or become frustrated, encourage intergroup visits by 'ambassadors' to offer or seek help, or to share alternative strategies.

What are these house numbers?

(1) Review what you know about how houses are usually numbered in North American cities. Use the words *odd, even,* and ***consecutive*** in your discussion.
(2) Make sure everyone in your group knows what ***product*** means in mathematics.
(3) Discuss this problem together, and make sure everyone in your group can explain how to solve it. There may be more than one way!

Problem:

The product of these house numbers is 2915. What are the numbers?

Note: For homework, students could write similar problems involving the product of two adjacent page numbers in a book. Next day, students solve each other's problems.

To encourage everyone to participate, to stay on task, and to support each other, let students know that when you take up the task, you may call on anyone in a group to report for the team. Give a time limit for the task.

Jigsaw activities

This method of small-group organization and instruction was developed more than 15 years ago as a strategy to counter racial polarization in desegregated schools in the United States (Aronson *et al.*, 1978). In Jigsaw, students in a heterogeneous group are each responsible for learning a different part of the material, and then sharing the information with each other. Jigsaw activities help to develop higher-level cognitive skills such as evaluation and synthesis of facts and opinions, especially if the task involves problem-solving as well as knowledge of facts.

An element of conflict or controversy makes the task more engaging and intellectually challenging than simply collecting and sharing facts (Coelho, 1992, 1994). For example, in a simulation of 'urban planning' each student might be assigned a role such as environmentalist, property developer, town planner, or local resident, and prepare to present information and opinions from that point of view. (For more examples, see the student materials in Coelho, 1991b; Coelho and Winer, 1991; Coelho *et al.*, 1989.)

Follow this procedure for Jigsaw activities

(1) Group students in heterogeneous 'home groups' that have already spent some time working together. Give each student in the group a different learning task that will be a component part of a larger task or topic. Each home group has the same topic and sub-topics.

(2) Regroup students in 'expert groups' to work on the assigned task. Provide the resource material, or help the students to find it. Provide some guiding questions and instructions. Encourage students to work together and help each other to understand, learn and rehearse the material. Circulate from

group to group to help learners with their learning task and to observe the group process. In their expert groups, learners may take a quiz, or prepare one, or complete an assignment on their component of material. Depending on the task assigned and the organization of your timetable, students may spend several hours or several days working in their expert groups.

(3) When you feel everyone is ready, direct students back to their home groups, where they will share their information with each other. Students synthesize the information through discussion. They are accountable for knowing their own material or role, sharing it effectively with members of the home group, and learning from members of the group.

(4) Assign a task or a problem that requires understanding or knowledge of all four pieces of information. Each student produces an assignment, or contributes to a group project, or takes a test, to demonstrate synthesis of all the information presented by all group members.

It is sometimes useful to create expert groups that are more homogeneous than the home groups. For example, you could group the students who need the most support in the same expert group, provide materials and activities that are tailored to meet the needs of this group, and spend more time giving direct instruction and assistance to this group. Meanwhile, another group may be doing independent research through library research and interviews.

Co-operative projects

Co-operative projects provide the most open-ended, student-directed, and democratic learning experiences. Groups work on topics and resources selected by the group members rather than by the teacher, and discover new information as a result of their own questions about it. This method places greater emphasis on individualization and students' interests, and is useful for end-of-year assignments and independent study projects. Students need plenty of experience with projects and with more teacher-directed group work before attempting this.

Group Investigation, a method for involving students in planning and co-ordinating group projects, has had very positive results in conceptual development, language acquisition, and intergroup relations in multiethnic schools in Israel and the United States (Sharan, 1990).

Follow this procedure for co-operative projects:

(1) With the students, choose a general topic or problem for investigation. For example, if the class has been doing some work on 'The Sea' you might outline some criteria for choosing a related topic that they would like to investigate in depth. Students could brainstorm a list of topics and then vote on one, such as 'Whales'.

(2) In informal groups, students brainstorm questions about the topic which they then share with the whole class. Write a combined list of student-gen-

erated questions on the board. Work with the class to decide which questions to use, and then group the questions in categories and create general subtopics.

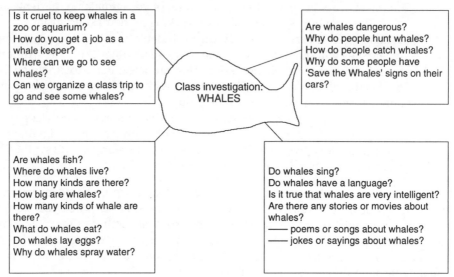

Is it cruel to keep whales in a zoo or aquarium?
How do you get a job as a whale keeper?
Where can we go to see whales?
Can we organize a class trip to go and see some whales?

Are whales dangerous?
Why do people hunt whales?
How do people catch whales?
Why do some people have 'Save the Whales' signs on their cars?

Class investigation:
WHALES

Are whales fish?
Where do whales live?
How many kinds are there?
How big are whales?
How many kinds of whale are there?
What do whales eat?
Do whales lay eggs?
Why do whales spray water?

Do whales sing?
Do whales have a language?
Is it true that whales are very intelligent?
Are there any stories or movies about whales?
—— poems or songs about whales?
—— jokes or sayings about whales?

(3) Instead of assigning students to specific groups, encourage students to form groups on the basis of their interest in the topic. If some groups are too large, the students can discuss how to subdivide the topic further and make smaller groups.

(4) Organize a steering committee with a representative from each group. This group meets with you at the beginning and end of each work session to coordinate tasks and time lines.

(5) Students meet in their groups to identify subtopics and tasks for each group member, or for partners. They may need to do some preliminary research to find out what is involved in their topics.

(6) Students research the information, using library reference, interviews and surveys, visual media, etc., with teacher assistance as required.

(7) Students synthesize their information for a group presentation. Students decide how they will present their information.

(8) Each group presents to the whole class.

This approach can be used to investigate a problem that has occurred in the school, such as 'Should we have a Christmas play this year?' Teams of students can gather information on different aspects of the problem and make recommendations. For example, one team could interview parents, while another interviews students, another interviews teachers, and another interviews the school administrators. See also 'Guided projects' in the next chapter.

Support for language learning

You can help students who are learning the language of instruction by giving public support for their endeavours.

- **Explain to all students** at the beginning of the year that your classroom is a language classroom as well as a place for learning mathematics, social studies, or other subject matter. Explain the importance of a supportive environment, where language learners feel comfortable speaking English, without fear of ridicule or criticism from classmates.
- **Suggest some ways that your English-speaking students can actively help** their classmates who are learning English — for example, by repeating or rephrasing, by using gesture and drawings to help explain something, by writing a word down, and by employing effective strategies for seeking clarification and confirming comprehension.
- **Communicate positive attitudes towards the task of language learning.** The task is not overwhelming, given the appropriate language learning environment and positive motivation. Anyone who has acquired one language can acquire another. Point out role models who have been successful in the task: other students, teachers, and public figures.
- **Communicate positive attitudes towards second language learners.** Students who are learning English are not 'having language difficulties'; they are linguistically enriched, and bilingualism is an admirable goal. Individuals who become fully bilingual are an asset to their communities and to the nation.

A multilingual classroom environment

Students in multilingual classrooms need teachers who demonstrate positive attitudes towards language and linguistic diversity. The communication of these attitudes is often implicit, and occurs when the teacher adopts a multilingual perspective and establishes a multilingual climate in the classroom. Some of the approaches suggested here may require a shift of attitude on your part. Talk about them with your colleagues, your students, and their parents, and begin by adopting those that are most comfortable for you.

- **Learn some simple expressions in the students' languages.** The students will greatly appreciate your efforts even if you learn only a few simple greetings. Perhaps you could take a formal course of instruction in one of the languages spoken by a significant number of students in your school building. Encourage students to learn some words and phrases in each other's languages.
- **Be flexible in your grouping arrangements.** Although you may often want students to work in mixed language groups in order to reflect the diversity of the classroom and to promote the use of English, you may occasionally want to provide opportunities for students to work with a partner or group of peers who speak the same language. If you do this, the students understand that you respect their languages and that when you place them in mixed language groups where

English is the only common language, you are not attempting to promote English at the expense of their languages.

- **Accept that you will not understand everything** that your students say or write. If students are in a situation where it makes sense for them to use their own language, they will naturally do so. You may feel that you will lose control over what is going on; but if the students are involved in a task that is interesting and cognitively challenging, and if you have clear expectations about the process and the product, the students are more likely than not to become engaged in the task. Instead of acting as 'language police' in the classroom, urging everyone to 'Speak English!' you can build in some expectations that require a shift to English once a task is completed or a concept is understood. For example, you can suggest that students discuss a mathematics problem with a partner in whatever language(s) they choose, but at the end of a specified period must be ready to verbalize their solution in English. When students are involved in group work, circulate from group to group and ask individual students to update you, in English, on their work so far.

  When it is important for everyone to be using English, explain why. Emphasize that the learning outcomes include proficiency in English as well as knowledge of content. Encourage discussion about how it feels to be shut out of a conversation, and establish some rules of etiquette. For example, if students need to use their first language occasionally to clarify ideas and information, they can excuse themselves briefly to confer with a language peer. Make sure that all students know what to say in English: for example, 'Do you mind if I check something with _____?'

  If you feel that a few students are unnecessarily using languages other than English, and alienating other students in the group, encourage the students to monitor their own language behaviour. At the beginning of the next group session, give one student in the group the task of monitoring the number of times that students use languages other than English. For example, the student could mark an 'x' on a tally sheet, or drop a plastic counter into a cup. At the end of the session, provide time for students to tally the total and to talk about when and why they resorted to other languages, whether it was essential, and how the other students felt about it. Set a goal for the next session: the group will reduce the use of languages other than English by a specified amount. You may have to do this several times, or do it again later in the year, until you feel that students are using other languages judiciously. Your goal is not to eliminate other languages entirely, but to make sure that students use them only when necessary and in ways that do not interfere with the group process.

- **Provide bilingual support** for newcomers with the assistance of classroom partners and cross-grade tutors. Help to train students for these roles by highlighting the key concepts that you want them to teach or translate, and by demonstrating some of the instructional strategies you would like the tutors to use. Acknowledge publicly the value of the bilingual skills of the students who are helping you.

- **Encourage beginners to write in their first languages.** For example, they could write their first journal responses in their own language, or they might insert words in their own language when they don't know the English word. If another students or a colleague can help with translation, you may be surprised by the quality of the students' writing in their own language, compared with what they are able to produce in English.
- **Communicate positive attitudes towards linguistic diversity.** For example, you can acknowledge that bilingualism is an asset to the individual and to the nation by displaying slogans in support of language learning.

> **'Monolingualism can be cured!'**
>
> **'Learn a language,
> touch the world!'**
>
> **'Many voices in one classroom
> Many voices in one world'**

- **Incorporate other languages into the classroom** and into the curriculum by creating multilingual displays and signs, by comparing how different languages do things, or to produce dual language versions of projects and assignments.

Encourage students to consult adult informants. This will help students to expand their knowledge of their first language, and provide parents with important opportunities for involvement in their children's education. Students whose first language is English can either be partnered with a bilingual student, or use a language they are learning at school. For some tasks, you will need to show students how to transliterate from languages that do not use the Roman alphabet. They will gain practice that will help to reinforce common spelling conventions in English.

You can design group activities that place a premium on languages other than English. For example, encourage students to produce dual-language versions of some of their written work. This allows students who are proficient in languages other than English to make important contributions. At the same time, it emphasizes that all languages are valid means of communication, and encourages students to maintain and continue to develop their first language skills. Provide opportunities for peer conferences in specific language groups so that students can receive feedback from their language peers. You can seek the help of parents and older students as well as colleagues in assessing the work.

History

- Why are English and French the official languages in Canada?
- Make a list of some Aboriginal place names and find out what they mean.
- Write about a country that has experienced conflict over language in the last 50 years.

Geography

- What is the Russian word for Moscow?
- How do Iranians pronounce Teheran?
- How do you say Canada in your language?
- How many people in the world speak your language? Where is your language spoken? What percentage of the students in this school/this class speak your language?

Language and literature

- How do stories begin and end in your language?
- What do animals say instead of 'Moo' or 'Miaow' in your language?
- Recite a poem in your language so that other students can listen for poetic features such as rhyme and rhythm. Be ready to explain in English what the poem is about.
- Translate English expressions such as 'in a pickle' into similar expressions in your language.
- Make a dual language collection of proverbs.

Science

- Make a dual language classification chart of the animal kingdom.
- Make a dual language picture book for children about the food chain.

Music

- Bring a recording of a song in your language, with a written translation.
- Make a dual language picture book or scrapbook about a musician who is important in your culture.

Mathematics

- Write a word problem in two languages.
- How do you count from 1 to 10 in Gujarati?
- How do you say '+' in Somali?
- What is the word for 'percentage' in Vietnamese?
- Make multilingual classroom signs for mathematical symbols and geometric shapes.
- Make a bar graph showing the top ten languages in this school.
- Write bilingual instructions for a number game that you know how to play.

Visual art

- Do all languages classify colours the same way?
- Label the colour wheel in different languages.
- Make multilingual labels for equipment in the art room.
- Make a dual language picture book or scrapbook about a musician who is important in your culture.
- Make a dual language picture book or scrapbook about an artist who is important in your culture.

- **Provide multilingual reading materials** in school and classroom libraries. Dual language materials are especially useful. Some popular children's books are available in several languages, and publishers will produce more if they feel there is an adequate market. Write to the publishers of some of the books you use, and let them know what languages you have in your classroom and how valuable it would be to have more material in those languages. The Multilingual Resources for Children Project (1995) provides a detailed discussion of the issues involved in developing multilingual classroom resources; this information would be very helpful to publishers.

  Monolingual books in other languages may be available in community bookstores in your area. Seek the help of parents and other community members in locating material from other countries. Some schools and school districts have recruited bilingual parents, teachers, and professional translators to provide translations that can be pasted above or below the English text in a children's picture book to create a dual language book. Before embarking on a project of this kind, consult the publisher about copyright requirements. Select your translators carefully. The best translators would be bilingual teachers who are familiar with the books and understand their pedagogical value. Discuss with the translators specific features of the text that you would like to retain in the translation, such as a repeated pattern or a rhyme. It is not always possible to retain these features, however, and it is important that the translation sound natural rather than stilted. Some books may lose so much in translation that it might be better to choose another title instead.

- **Respect language variety**. For example, Black English Vernacular in the United States (also known as African American Vernacular English and as 'Ebonics' in popular usage), and English-related creoles spoken by many students of Caribbean background are languages with their own systems of grammar; they are not deficient versions of English. Refer to these languages by name, such as Jamaican Creole. Encourage students who speak varieties of English other than standard English, and speakers of English-related creoles, to consider themselves bilingual (for a detailed discussion, see Coelho, 1991a).
- **Expose the learners to different varieties of English** and different accents. For example, if you make audiotapes of print materials, ask some of your colleagues to make some recordings. Seek out literature that represents varieties of English in print: for example, much of the literature from the English Caribbean features dialogue in Caribbean English Creole.

Classroom routines

All students are more comfortable in a classroom with predicable routines and expectations. This is especially important for students from other countries whose lives have been disrupted, and who may be unfamiliar with group work, learning centres, and student-centred learning. Set up routines that will ensure that you always know or can find out what each group is doing, and that you can quickly get the attention of the class as a whole in order to give additional instructions or information, get feedback, or check on progress. Have routines in place to take care of such matters as student attendance or absence, the distribution of resources, the collection of homework, and room set-up. Use co-operative learning groups to help you manage classroom routines. For example:

- **Assign tasks within each group.** Each day, or each week if groups will be working together for some time, have each group delegate a different member to fetch and distribute materials and equipment, collect and hand in homework, and so on. This person may be responsible for checking group attendance and reporting to you that everyone in the group has completed the homework, has brought the requisite materials, and is prepared for class.
- **Establish a classroom rota** allocating specific duties so that groups of students may take turns with general classroom responsibilities.
- **Give instructions once only,** and say, 'Now make sure everyone in your group knows what to do.' This may be done before or after the distribution of the material, and will result in a short, concentrated buzz of repetition and confirmation. If students use languages other than English to help each other, advise them to repeat the information in English in order to support second language learning. Use this technique at the end of class to review homework instructions as well.

- **Check homework daily.** Instead of collecting all the homework, visit groups of students to do random spot checks. Use a checklist system to keep track of homework on a group or individual basis.

   Homework check-up

   These instructions to students show how a teacher might use groups to check the previous day's mathematics homework. When students are reporting to the class, teammates can 'coach from the sidelines' if their representative gets flustered or confused. A second language learner with very limited English might write out the problem and solution on the board while another member of his/her group verbalizes each step.

   (1) At the beginning of each class, compare your answers with the rest of the group.
   (2) If you don't all agree on the solution to a problem, or if one of you had difficulty with it, try working it out aloud. You can use languages other than English to get an idea across, but then make sure everyone can explain the solution in English.
   (3) If you still have difficulty, get help from another group or from the teacher.
   (4) The teacher will choose a student from the group to demonstrate the group's solution to one of the problems.

- **Establish a signal** that lets the students know when to stop talking and look at you. This can be visual signal: for example, 'Stop talking when you see me raise my hand; raise your own hand as a signal to those around you who may not notice me.' Some teachers prefer a not-too-intrusive noise signal, such as a small bell, a rattle, or three hand claps.
- **Always have an extra chair** at every table. This is for you when you are visiting the group, or for students from other groups acting as consultants or interviewers. If you have visitors in your classroom, this chair is for them also. Encourage students to welcome people who join or visit the group by introducing themselves and describing what they are doing.
- **Make note of important announcements** and make sure that someone translates and explains them to newcomers and second language learners in the group. For instance, make sure that all students know when there is to be a public holiday or professional activity day.
- **Have students share telephone numbers** within the group. Advise students to call another group member if they are going to be absent from school that day. Group members take turns to call or visit and keep the absentee up to date on what's happening in class. When the absentee returns, the group is responsible for helping that student to catch up. Be sensitive to the needs of students of various cultural backgrounds: for example, some girls may be able to accept calls only from other girls.

- **Let the groups manage the problem of latecomers.** Suggest that those who come late need to apologize to their group as well as to you. They will have to rely on their group to fill them in on what they have missed. You may find that being accountable to their peers has a far stronger positive effect than anything you might do. Some teachers report that students in co-operative learning groups become more responsible because 'they have a sense of ownership for their work and get encouragement from peers. They come to class on time and they get to work more quickly. They are aware that they are responsible to themselves and their friends, not just to me' (Clarke *et al.*, 1990: 2).
- **Intervene** when a student is chronically absent or late, or does not behave co-operatively with group members. Investigate the reasons for the problem, and offer help in solving it. Sometimes this may mean working with the individual student, or contacting the parents, or it may be best to work with the group to resolve interpersonal conflict that may be going on among group members. You may decide to reassign groups before the next unit of work.

   Students who regularly disrupt the work of the group, or fail to meet their responsibilities, do not have the right to interfere with the work of others, and may lose the privilege of belonging to a group until their attendance and effort warrants it. Often, this will mean that they have more work and less fun than those who are working in groups, and will wish to be included next time.
- **Allow determined individualists the option of working alone;** if this is their preferred learning style, there is nothing to gain from an insistence on group work.

If your intended outcomes include social goals to be developed through the group process, your assessment and evaluation plan will include this component, so you will need to discuss with these students how they might practise and demonstrate social skills without being a permanent member of a group. For example, perhaps they might be willing to act as tutor to an individual student from time to time.

CONCLUSION

This chapter has suggested several ways of fostering an inclusive classroom community. The time teachers spend creating a social environment that is inclusive and supportive of all the learners is time well-spent, because a harmonious and orderly classroom promotes learning and cuts down the amount of time teachers might otherwise spend on classroom management and discipline. Most suggestions in this chapter require no additional resources and can be implemented immediately in every classroom in the school. The checklist below can be used to assess progress.

CHECKLIST: AN INCLUSIVE CLASSROOM COMMUNITY

This checklist is organized as a series of indicators under broad topic areas that correspond with the instructional strategies and approaches recommended in this chapter.

The checklist can be used by:

- Individual teachers: to assess their own classrooms as inclusive social and learning environments.
- School administrators, school department heads, and district curriculum advisers: to assess classrooms within their sphere of influence.
- Teacher educators: to guide and assess student teachers on practicum assignment.
- Students: to assess the classroom environment provided to them (perhaps using a simplified or translated form).

The rating system can be used and interpreted as follows:

yes = whenever appropriate
not yet = this is an area that the teacher might work on
n/a = not applicable, or not available at this time

yes not n/a
     yet

yes	not yet	n/a	
❏	❏	❏	Routines are in place for welcoming newcomers.
❏	❏	❏	Students and teacher can pronounce each others' names.
❏	❏	❏	Newcomers and beginning learners of English are seated beside peers who speak their first language for the first few weeks.
❏	❏	❏	The teacher makes personal contact with new students at least once during each lesson.
❏	❏	❏	The teacher uses interviews to help students to get to know each other.

yes not n/a
   yet

❏ ❏ ❏ The teacher uses class surveys to learn about the students' backgrounds, needs, and interests.

❏ ❏ ❏ Classroom displays are inclusive.

❏ ❏ ❏ Students are involved in creating classroom displays.

❏ ❏ ❏ Students often work with partners or in a peer tutoring relationship.

❏ ❏ ❏ Students often work in co-operative learning groups.

❏ ❏ ❏ The teacher creates a climate of support for language learning.

❏ ❏ ❏ The teacher knows some expressions in the students' languages.

❏ ❏ ❏ Classroom routines are predictable and explicit.

❏ ❏ ❏ There is a rota for classroom routines and responsibilities.

❏ ❏ ❏ Students take on some responsibility for monitoring and checking homework, making sure all group members understand a task, etc.

❏ ❏ ❏ The teacher monitors group relationships and helps students to manage group work and share responsibilities.

FURTHER READING AND RESOURCES FOR TEACHERS

Clarke, J., Wideman, R., and Eadie, S. (1990) *Together We Learn: Co-operative Small Group Learning*. Scarborough, Ontario: Prentice-Hall. Practical handbook, useful to teachers at all grade levels.

Coelho, E. (1991b) *Jigsaw*. Markham, Ontario: Pippin Publishing Limited. Content-based reading and discussion tasks and problem-solving activities for middle and secondary school students.

Coelho, E. (1994) *Learning Together in the Multicultural Classroom*. Markham, Ontario: Pippin Publishing Limited, 1994. The focus of this book is the implementation of co-operative learning in middle and secondary school classrooms where some or all of the learners are learning the language of instruction.

Coelho, E., and Winer, L. (1991) *Jigsaw Plus*. Markham, Ontario: Pippin Publishing Limited. Content-based reading and discussion tasks and problem-solving activities for secondary school students.

Coelho, E., Winer, L., and Winn-Bell Olsen, J. (1989) *All Sides of the Issue*. Hayward, CA: Alemany Press. US version of the *Jigsaw* materials.

Edwards, V. (1996) *The Other Languages: A Guide to Multilingual Classrooms*. Reading, UK: Reading and Language Information Centre, University of Reading. The language profiles in this booklet provide interesting and helpful information for teachers. The author also suggests ways of working with children to enhance the multilingual climate of the school, and provides models that teachers can use to conduct their own language surveys and develop new language profiles.

Kessler, C. (1992) (ed.) *Cooperative Language Learning*. Englewood Cliffs, NJ: Prentice-Hall. A collection of articles on how to organize group activities in classrooms that include second language learners.

CHAPTER 6

An Inclusive Approach to Instruction

INTRODUCTION

Teaching in multicultural classrooms demands a high level of expertise among teachers. Culturally diverse learners may have prior learning experiences that predispose them to learning in ways that may not be compatible with some methods of instruction in common use in many classrooms. Therefore, teachers need to adopt an inclusive and flexible approach to instruction, observing their student's responses and adjusting instruction to meet the needs of individuals and groups in the classroom.

This chapter begins with a discussion of instructional style, describes some effective instructional strategies, and suggests some ways of helping all students to expand their repertoire of learning strategies. The next section describes the effects of teacher expectations on student performance, and suggests some strategies for communicating high expectations to all students. The chapter concludes with a discussion of grouping practices, with special reference to the effects of 'ability grouping' on immigrant and minority students.

TEACHING AND LEARNING STYLES IN MULTICULTURAL CLASSROOMS

Many teachers in multicultural classrooms find that lessons that worked before, when classes were less heterogeneous, are no longer so successful. Most teachers work hard on lesson preparation, and it can be very frustrating to deliver a lesson that falls flat, or that does not seem to reach some of the students. One of the reasons that lessons may fail to engage some students is a mismatch between the teacher's instructional style and the students' learning styles.

Adopting a more inclusive approach to instruction may require teachers to re-think some of the assumptions they may make about teaching and learning. A teacher's instructional style is based partly on individual personality, and partly on the teacher's beliefs, explicit or otherwise, about the goals of education, how children learn, how teachers should organize learning experiences, and the role of the teacher. These beliefs are congruent with the teacher's own educational experiences and world view, but may not be congruent with the expectations or experiences of students and parents of other cultural and social class backgrounds.

When teachers and students do not share a common background, the potential exists for miscommunication or conflict. For example, a teacher may expect students to engage in behaviour that seeks to draw attention and praise to themselves, such as eagerly raising their hands to answer questions, or participating enthusiastically in competitive games. However, some students may avoid engaging in this behaviour, or participate without enthusiasm, and their aversion to it may be based on a set of cultural values about teaching and learning that do not match the teacher's assumptions about what is motivating or appealing to students.

When children do not respond to the learning situation in the ways that teachers expect, teachers sometimes assume that there is some deficit in the students. For example, if some students do not raise their hands to answer questions, the teacher may assume that these students do not understand or are not keeping up with the lesson, or they may become concerned about the students' 'passive' behaviour. If specific groups of students seem more reluctant than others to engage in the desired behaviour, teachers sometimes develop differential expectations for those groups. These expectations are often subconscious, but nevertheless are communicated to students in various subtle ways (see 'Communicating High Expectations' later in this chapter).

All children experience a great deal of informal learning before they arrive in school. Children's early experiences may predispose them towards certain ways of interacting with each other and with adults, and different ways of processing information; depending on the social and cultural environment in which the children are raised, these may not be the ways that the teacher expects. For example, in some families it is common for children to learn by following instructions; in others, learning by observing is more prevalent; and in others, children may be more likely to learn as 'apprentices' working side-by-side with an adult or a more competent sibling. In some families, children engage in physical activity, or use rhyme and rhythm as aids to learning; in others, children may be rewarded for sitting quietly and paying attention to an adult. In some families, children may be encouraged to label their world verbally; in others they demonstrate understanding of their world through non-verbal acts. In some families, children learn through experimentation; in others, they are expected to learn through the careful guidance of an expert adult.

Early experiences may predispose children to certain ways of approaching a learning task or processing information. Research on learning styles shows that learners have different strengths, strategies, or preferences for different kinds of cognitive activity, such as inductive or deductive reasoning; much of the research in this area emphasizes individual differences that transcend cultural and even family groupings (Dunn *et al.*, 1989). Learning style also includes perceptual preferences such as visual, auditory, or hands-on learning experiences. Other aspects of learning style include behavioural preferences such as different levels of physical mobility, or social preferences such as independence or interdependence.

'A sticky and tricky business'

Immigrant students are often uncomfortable in their new learning environment. Many newcomers have had formal learning experiences that are based on different concepts of teaching and learning, and they may be bewildered by their new classroom environment or intimidated by the learning tasks they are given. For example:

When I attended school, I experienced a new system of teaching and a different relationship between teachers and students. In Burma, when the teacher asks a question, a student must get up and fold hands before answering. Teachers give notes and the students must memorize the notes. Term marks are not counted; the final examination is everything. The exams are quite easy if one memorizes the notes. In Canada, however, the education is a 'sticky and tricky' business. I have many sleepless nights because of unfinished homework. I feel frustrated because of my poor, poor term marks. I'm in despair to do the play presentation in English since I loathe speaking in public. Now, I know life is a challenge. Jodie Chen (Porter, 1991: 20)

While there is no consensus on the relative importance of cultural background in the development of individual learning style, some researchers have observed the predominant learning styles of different social class and ethnocultural groups, and found that there is a mismatch between those learning styles and the instructional style of many teachers (Shade, 1982; Hale-Benson, 1986; Irvine, 1990; Guild, 1994).

An inclusive approach to instruction is responsive to the needs of all the students. In order to reach all the students, Banks recommends that teachers adopt an 'equity pedagogy' which consists of 'techniques and teaching methods that facilitate the academic achievement of students from diverse racial and ethnic groups and from all social classes' (Banks, 1993: 27). At the same time, according to Bowman, 'Children whose cultural styles are different from the mainstream may need help extending the range of their response patterns so that they can succeed in two worlds, not just their own' (Bowman, 1993: 131).

In the following pages, elements of teaching and learning style are identified, and suggestions are made on how teachers can diversify their instructional style and help students to diversify their approaches to learning. Although some of these ideas are the subject of continued research and controversy, they are offered here as possibilities to consider when teachers plan their lessons and select instructional techniques. The main topics of discussion are:

- Holistic and analytical approaches to learning
- Independence and interdependence
- Extrinsic and intrinsic motivation
- High and low levels of activity
- Teacher-centred and learner-centred instruction
- Implicit and explicit scripts

Each of these aspects of learning style is best viewed as a continuum rather than an either/or dichotomy. Flexible learners may adopt behaviour at either end of the continuum, or somewhere in between, when they are engaged in different tasks at different times. However, teachers often deliver lessons oriented more towards one end of the continuum, while some of the students may exhibit an overall preference that places them closer to the other.

The focus in the discussion that follows is on the possible link between culture and learning style. Where generalizations are made about minority students, or specific ethnocultural groups are mentioned as examples, it is important to remember that great differences exist among individuals within any group. Do not expect all minority students, or all members of a specific group, to behave in the same way. Also, although some behaviours and preferences appear to be more prevalent among minority students, they can also be found among students of the dominant cultural group.

Holistic and analytical approaches to learning

At one end of this continuum, a holistic approach to learning may lead students to view concepts or information holistically. The 'big picture' is more important than the details, at least initially. Some learning-style researchers use the terms 'field-dependent' and 'field-independent' to describe the extent to which the learner relates to the contextual 'field' in which an activity or concept is embedded. Field-dependent learners are believed to pay more attention to the overall field, or the whole context, than to the elements that make up the whole.

Holistic learners may prefer to reason inductively, by considering several examples from which a rule or pattern can be generated. Holistic learners tend to be intuitive rather than reflective in their approach to a problem or a task. The social environment of learning appears to be important for holistic learners, and they may function better in classrooms where peer-group relationships are used to support cognitive development — for example, through co-operative learning. Some writers believe that a holistic learning style is more prevalent among some cultural groups (see, for example, Gilbert and Gay, 1985).

At the other end of the continuum, analytical learners tend to approach problems reflectively and to think deductively: that is, they are able to learn an abstract rule or principle and then apply it to specific examples. These students tend to perceive and process information analytically: they can identify and categorize the parts or pieces of the information without being distracted by other elements in the learning context such as the whole picture, interesting tangents, or the physical and social environment.

The cognitive style that best matches the way learning is usually organized in schools is analytical. Curriculum is broken up into parts, labelled 'subjects', even in elementary school, and many concepts and skills are taught using a part-to-whole approach. For example, phonics instruction is sometimes used to introduce children to reading by teaching the sounds of letters and combinations of letters in isolation from meaningful text. Analytical learners are more likely to adapt successfully to the organizational structure of most middle and secondary schools, where separate subjects are often taught to different groups of learners in different classrooms by different teachers.

A successful learning style
According to Shade (1982: 232), students with the following characteristics are the most likely to succeed at school:

(1) An attention style that focuses on the task itself, rather than on the people in the situation.
(2) An abstraction ability that separates ideas and concepts into parts and reweaves them into a unified whole.
(3) A perceptual style that leads to the abstraction of both obvious and nonobvious attributes that seemingly link things, ideas, or principles.
(4) A perceptual style that facilitates the extraction of important information embedded in distracting influences.
(5) A long attention span with prolonged concentrating ability.
(6) An attending preference for verbal cues rather than nonverbal cues.
(7) A reflective rather than an impulsive style in problem solving.
(8) A highly differentiated or analytical thinking style that leads to abstract or logical reasoning.

Although analytical approaches are more highly valued in most classrooms, they are not superior to more holistic approaches. Both are useful for different kinds of tasks. For example, many of the most important scientific theories and discoveries were based initially on leaps of intuition, while reflection would be more appropriate in solving a problem such as weighing the advantages and disadvantage of a particular course of action. As Hilliard points out, 'Ideally, a student would be flexible enough to do either. Since schools traditionally give more weight to analytical approaches than to holistic approaches, however, the student who does not manifest analytical habits is at a decided disadvantage' (Hilliard, 1989: 23).

You can build on holistic approaches to knowledge by providing an integrated curriculum using cross-curricular themes. For example, a unit of study on 'English as a World Language' integrates language arts, history, and geography, as well as mathematics activities such as graphing or expressing ratio and percentage. You can also build on the holistic learner's affinity for interpersonal relationships as part of the learning process by providing co-operative group activities. At the same time, it is important to teach cognitive and metacognitive skills so that all students diversify their ways of perceiving and processing information, and know which kind of thinking to apply to specific kinds of learning tasks.

How to teach learning strategies:

- Allow some time for students to establish social relationships in the class, but set guidelines on how long students should spend on each phase of a task;
- Encourage students to reflect on the process of learning through the use of learning logs;
- Give explicit instructions about the approach the students should take: for example, advise students to rely on impulse and intuition in a group brainstorming session, but to survey and analyze all the information before making a judgment or attempting to solve a problem.
- Demonstrate how to distinguish generalizations from specific information or details and fact from opinion in text, visual information, or other media;
- Teach categorization and classification skills, using visual organizers such as charts, Venn diagrams and classification trees;
- Incorporate cognitive strategy instruction across the curriculum and across all grade levels: for example, by using graphic organizers to demonstrate logical relationships such as comparison and contrast or cause and effect in textbooks and lessons (see Clarke, 1990; Pressley et al., 1990; Hyerle, 1996);
- Teach students how to develop their own graphic organizers as reading and study guides;
- Teach students how to approach text of different types and for different purposes;
- Demonstrate how to use a problem-solving model;
- Highlight important transition words in a piece of text in order to teach students how to recognize and use language that indicates specific kinds of thinking such as generalization and example, cause and effect, sequence, etc.;
- Model reading and thinking skills by thinking aloud a specific approach or strategy. For example, to demonstrate the use of word analysis to figure at the meaning of words, you could read a short passage aloud and stop at a particular word and say, 'Here is a new word: *impure*. I recognize *pure* in this word, and *im* often means not, as in *impossible*, so I guess *impure* is the opposite of *pure*';
- Model the writing process by composing specific kinds of writing on the board or on chart paper, thinking aloud as you make word choices, add or delete words and phrases, check spelling, combine or extend sentences, etc.;

- Develop metacognitive awareness by labelling cognitive strategies as you model and teach them, and as the students use them: for example, 'Should we survey the text first or start reading in detail?'

Independence and interdependence

There are three basic methods of organizing classroom activities: competitive and individualized methods, both of which emphasize independence, and and co-operative methods, emphasizing interdependence among students (Johnson and Johnson, 1991). Independence and interdependence are both important ways of relating to the social environment.

Independence

In most classrooms, students spend most of their time working independently. When activities are organized competitively, students compete with each other for attention, praise, and high marks or grades, or higher quality work. Assessment of individual performance is usually norm-referenced: students are set the same goals and ranked on performance. In individualized activities, instead of working against each other, students work towards accomplishment of their individual goals. Assessment of performance is criterion-referenced, or students may be encouraged to compare their performance with their own previous performance.

The higher the grade level, the more independent work is assigned to students; by the end of elementary school, students spend most of their time sitting alone, working on individual tasks and assignments.

Interdependence

Students work in relationships of interdependence when they are involved in co-operative learning activities (sometimes called collaborative activities). In co-operative learning tasks, students work with a small group of peers towards a common goal, and assessment of group and individual performance is criterion-referenced. Peer assessment is also important in co-operative learning activities.

Activities that emphasize interdependence become less common as students advance through the grades, and in many secondary classrooms they are not used at all.

The case for increased interdependence

Students who are raised in cultural environments where independence and competition are highly valued, and where there is an emphasis on the needs, wishes, and successes of the individual, adapt well to competitive and individualized methods of organizing classroom instruction. However, some children are raised in a cultural environment that values collectivity and interdependence. These children may be culturally predisposed to co-operate rather than to compete, and therefore learn best in a classroom that supports and promotes their cultural values. Individual recognition may be less important than membership in a group, and peer approval is often more important than the approval of an authority figure such as the teacher. Contributing to the group enhances self-esteem, while the increased opportunities for oral interaction enhance language learning.

Co-operative learning has been shown to have important benefits for all students in terms of academic achievement and social development (Kagan, 1986; Slavin, 1990; Johnson and Johnson, 1991). Classroom activities that build on interdependence appear to be especially appropriate for some minority groups (Kagan, 1986; Slavin, 1983, 1990; Pine and Hilliard, 1990; McGee Banks, 1993; Banks, 1993, 1994). According to Kagan, 'The majority–minority school achievement gap may be attributed in part to the pervasive tendency of schools to rely almost exclusively on competitive classroom structures that provide more valued rewards for majority than minority students' (Kagan, 1986: 270).

Implementing co-operative learning is one of the most important changes that teachers can make in order to promote positive intergroup relations and academic success for all learners in culturally diverse classrooms. This does not mean that competitive and individualized activities are always inappropriate, or even that most classroom activities should be co-operative; but there should be a balance. According to Johnson and Johnson, 'Knowing how and when to structure students' learning

goals cooperatively, competitively, or individualistically is an essential instructional skill all teachers need' (Johnson and Johnson, 1991: 2). They point out that in most classrooms, co-operative learning is the least-used method for organizing instruction; they recommend that teachers use it more often, especially 'whenever teachers want students to learn more, like school better, like each other better, have higher self-esteem, and learn more effective social skills' (Johnson and Johnson, 1991: 14).

One reason that co-operative learning is under-utilized is that many teachers have received no specific training in this approach, and their own experience of schooling did not provide them with models. Many teachers have tried 'group work' with limited success, because some students do all the work and others don't seem to learn anything at all. Co-operative learning involves more than moving the desks together: the way that a learning activity or task is designed, and how the groups are structured and managed, will determine how effectively students will work together in small groups. For an overview of specific techniques, see 'Co-operative Learning Groups' in Chapter 5. For more detailed advice, see Clarke *et al.*, (1990) and Coelho (1994).

Extrinsic and intrinsic motivation and rewards

Motivation is a key component of learning. In the classroom, students may be motivated to complete a task by extrinsic rewards such as high marks or public attention and praise, or by intrinsic factors such as satisfaction from successful completion of a task, positive feelings about working collaboratively with peers, or enjoyment of the task itself.

In many classrooms, the focus is on extrinsic motivation. Marks or grades, praise, special privileges, stickers and other tokens are distributed by the teacher in recognition of individual effort and achievement. Students are expected to be motivated by disincentives as well: they are urged to stay on task, or to complete work that is boring or unpleasant, in order to avoid negative consequences such as poor marks, public criticism, or detentions. Sometimes the penalty for not completing a task is to be assigned more work of the same kind. This is paradoxical: how can students be motivated to do something that is so unpleasant that it can be effective as a punishment?

Extrinsic rewards may motivate some students, especially those from families or cultural backgrounds where there is an emphasis on the needs, wishes, and successes of the individual, where competition is valued, and where effort and achievement are related to incentives.

However, an extrinsic reward system may be unappealing to students from cultural and social class groups that have a collective rather than an individualistic orientation.

Some families and cultural groups value individual achievement when it brings benefit or credit to the group. For example, Mexican Americans are said to be motivated to do well if achievement is for the family, but motivation is lower if achievement is for themselves (Kagan, 1986). Among some groups, effort may be valued as much as actual achievement; in others, the focus is on the intrinsic value of a task — its importance, relevance or interest — and on achievement of the task itself, rather than the performer. In some African cultures, children learn important skills by observing and emulating successful performance; they receive corrective feedback if necessary, but praise is not offered to children who successfully complete the task (Kohn, 1993).

Children raised in families where rewards are not emphasized, or where praising an individual is not viewed as appropriate, may be uncomfortable in a classroom environment where individuals are singled out for praise or recognition. Some children are able to overcome this cultural mismatch without becoming involved in cultural conflict at home: for example, many Chinese immigrants have a pragmatic orientation that allows or encourages their children to behave in ways that promote academic success, even when these may be in conflict with traditional values (Ogbu and Matute-Bianchi, 1986). Some children strive to do well in order to satisfy family aspirations, or to contribute to the group they are associated with in the classroom. For example, African American children may 'tend to work together for the benefit of the group. The pace of the learning effort is set more by the momentum of the group than by some arbitrarily determined time allocated for the completion of an instructional task' (Gilbert and Gay, 1985: 134).

Most students of all cultural backgrounds will work hard if they find a specific task relevant and interesting. However, some children are so uncomfortable with public praise that they may actively avoid the teacher's attention, seldom volunteering answers or engaging in classroom discussion. Some students avoid teacher approval and high marks if these are viewed by their cultural peers as evidence of 'showing off', 'acting white', or 'sucking up'; for these students, being singled out for praise, being recognized as one of the 'top three spellers', or earning a gold star on a classroom behaviour chart may actually be a disincentive.

What about marks for effort?

In an attempt to 'motivate' students, teachers sometimes give marks for 'effort' on a task as well as, or instead of, marks for achievement. Many forms that are used for reporting to parents require teachers to give separate marks or grades for effort and achievement.

Gilbert and Gay argue that some students, especially African American children, 'place great value on efforts towards achievement: they will argue for recognition of their efforts to complete a task, even though they were unsuccessful' (Gilbert and Gay, 1985: 134). However, Kohn argues that rewards for effort represent 'an attempt to coerce children to try harder. The fatal paradox, however, is that while coercion can sometimes elicit resentful obedience, it can never create desire. A low grade for effort is more likely to be read as 'You're a failure even at trying.' On the other hand, a high grade for effort combined with a low grade for achievement says, 'You're just too dumb to succeed.' Most of all, rewarding or punishing the *child's* effort allows educators to ignore the possibility that the curriculum or learning environment may just have something to do with his or her lack of enthusiasm.' (Kohn, 1993: p. 209)

Non-specific marks for 'effort' may be inappropriate. However, teachers can use specific performance criteria to give students feedback on how they approach learning tasks — for example, seeking help from peers in group activities, consulting with the teacher, using a spell-check program to edit a final draft, using a problem-solving model, or demonstrating readiness to learn through specific kinds of behaviour.

Kohn argues against extrinsic motivation; from a survey of many studies, he concludes that extrinsic rewards do not promote lasting behavior change or improve performance; in fact, they often make things worse (Kohn, 1993). However, extrinsic motivation is so integral to the system that few students, teachers, or parents would be able to imagine school without marks, grades, and awards. Indeed, employers and post-secondary institutions often have no other way of sorting and selecting individuals for employment or college and university admission.

Grades and marks may be a fact of school life, at least for the foreseeable future, but individual teachers can make tasks more intrinsically important and appealing in their own classrooms. For example, you can:

- avoid trivial or material rewards such as stickers, stars, pencils, etc.;
- never use academic tasks as punishment;
- de-emphasize marks, grades, and ranking of student performance;
- offer constructive feedback on specific aspects of a task, rather than praising or criticizing the individual or offering non-specific assessment of the performance;
- offer feedback in quiet and unobtrusive ways;
- never offer public criticism;
- organize students to work in groups, and value the process and the product of group work;
- offer students some choice in the tasks they are assigned;
- ensure that assignments deal with significant content;
- value satisfactory completion of a task rather than the best performance in the class.

How to handle marks and grades

To minimize the importance of marks or grades, Kohn (1993) suggests that teachers

- limit the number of assignments that receive a number or letter grade;
- reduce the number of gradations by using ✓+, ✓, ✓–, or by using only 'A' and 'Incomplete' as grades;
- never mark or grade students while they are still learning;
- never give marks for effort;
- never grade on a curve;
- work with students to determine the criteria for assessment,
- involve students in peer and self assessment.

High and low levels of activity

Some students prefer a linear approach to classroom activities, attending to one task at a time. Such students may learn best in quiet, 'orderly' classrooms where children stay in one place, and give sustained attention to a task. In general, these are the students who are most successful in school. In contrast, some students prefer higher levels of physical activity and frequent changes of stimulus. They are comfortable in a busy environment where several things are happening at once. They may need to move around the classroom more often than others, and they may learn effectively if music and movement are associated with a task.

Neither of these preferences is 'better' than the other, but the classroom is generally more supportive of a sequential, relatively static style of learning. Students who need to move around the room from time to time, or accompany learning with physical activity such as tapping a pen against the desk, or like to sing or listen to personal stereos while they are working, tend to be regarded as disruptive or hyperactive.

Children who bring a high level of energy to the classroom or who like to attend to more than one task or stimulus at once may be just as 'ready to learn' as children who are more inclined to sit quietly and follow a specific linear sequence in their work. You can diversify your instructional style in order to appeal to learners of diverse cultural backgrounds, and to help all students learn to function in both high-activity and low-activity environments. For example, you can alternate tasks that require prolonged concentration with activities that involve frequent change of stimulus, physical movement, or high levels of interpersonal interaction. Lessons can include drama, music, dance and movement, learning centres, and small group discussion and problem-solving as well as teacher or media presentations, whole-class discussion, and independent seat work. Background music may help some of the students to focus on independent work. Explain to all students the importance of learning to function in many different environments — not only at school, but in many contexts outside the school as well — and establish some consensus about when movement, music, and talk are appropriate in the classroom, and when they are not.

Hyperactive children or boring classrooms?
Children's early socialization develops an affinity for certain levels of energy and physical activity. For example, many African American children are raised in homes where there is a high level of energy and activity; as a result, they develop an affinity for relatively high levels of stimulation (Boykin, 1978). Therefore classrooms that include high-activity, high-interaction learning experiences are more engaging and more relevant to the cultural learning style of many children of African ancestry. In contrast, middle-class white children raised in homes where activities are usually more linear or consecutive, and where the pace or intensity is more placid, seem to relate better to learning activities that are relatively slow in pace and linear in development. A study of middle-class white children's responses to television programs lends support to Boykin's argument: these children learned more effectively from 'Mr. Rogers', a slow-paced children's television program, than they did from 'Sesame Street', which is fast-paced and develops several concepts in a fast-switching format (Morgan, 1980).

Most classrooms are more like 'Mr. Rogers' than 'Sesame Street,' especially in the higher grades of elementary school and in secondary school. As students progress through the grades, they are expected to sit quietly and pay sustained attention for longer periods of time. By the time they reach secondary school, where each period of instruction may be more than an hour in duration, students are often expected to stay in their seats and concentrate one or two activities for the whole period. While this is undoubtedly boring for all students, those whose early childhood experiences have developed an affinity for this way of learning are better able to adapt to this kind of learning environment than children whose early socialization has fostered an affinity for a more frequent change of stimulus and a generally higher level of activity. Morgan describes a 'third grade syndrome' that afflicts many African American children: as classrooms become increasingly ill-attuned to their learning style, their performance declines in comparison with the performance of their white peers (Morgan, 1980). The disengagement of many African American children from the classroom program has often been regarded as a deficit, or labelled and even medicated as hyperactive behaviour; but according to Boykin, 'Black children are bored primarily because school is a relatively unstimulating, constraining, and monotonous place, and perhaps relatively more compatible with the more placid existence of suburbia' (Boykin, 1978: 347). In other words, the deficiency is in the classroom, not the children.

Teacher-centred and learner-centred instruction

Until recently, teacher-centred instruction was generally the norm. In most English-speaking and western European countries, recent developments in pedagogy emphasize the needs and interests of the learner, especially in the elementary grades. In most other countries, teacher-centred activities are still the norm.

Teacher-centred classrooms

In teacher-centred classrooms and activities there is an emphasis on the transmission of information from the teacher or some other authoritative source, such as a textbook, to the students. Students are not involved in choosing the information that is to be studied, and are not expected to challenge the validity or importance of the information they are given. Convergent rather than divergent or creative thinking is encouraged. Learners are expected to memorize large amounts of information, and teachers ask 'display questions' to which there is usually only one 'right' answer. Students seldom initiate questions except to seek clarification of the information. Learners are expected to learn in the ways that the teacher has demonstrated or prescribed: for example, students use the same approach for regrouping in mathematics, learn the same style of handwriting, or use the same format in writing a science report, down to the last detail. Errors are viewed as evidence of imperfect learning; students are given expert models to emulate, and practise a skill over and over until performance is judged perfect. Teacher-centred instruction is more prevalent in secondary schools than in elementary schools, and some subject areas tend to be more teacher-centred than others. For example, success in science requires the memorization of complex classification systems and a great deal of specialized vocabulary, while success in mathematics requires a knowledge of many number facts and formulae, as well as automaticity in many operations.

Teacher-centred approaches are congruent with the values of many traditional cultures. For example, most Chinese children are raised to respect elders and authority, to fulfil their roles as children and as students regardless of their personal preferences or goals, and to 'model themselves after authorities, to listen to authorities and watch what they do, and finally to practice again and again to achieve perfection' (Heath, 1986: 158). Many immigrant children are accustomed to an authoritarian, transmission-oriented learning environment, and often prefer teacher-centred classrooms. However, children from families or cultural backgrounds where non-conformity and divergent thinking are valued may have a great deal of difficulty in teacher-centred classrooms. Some children — especially the children of intellectuals and political activists — learn at an early age to distrust governments, military leaders, the media, and other institutions, including schools, that perpetuate a corrupt system or regime; these children may experience difficulty in authoritarian, teacher-centred classrooms. Students who are marginalized through poverty or discrimination may also be predisposed to distrust authority and may question the value of the knowledge that is being transmitted to them– especially if the curriculum they are offered is Eurocentric and contributes to their feelings of marginalization.

Learner-centred classrooms

Learner-centred classrooms are less authoritarian in style and less conformist in intent. The teacher supports learning rather than directing every phase of it. Students have opportunities to learn through experimentation and trial and error, and learning is viewed as developmental: children approximate adult or expert performance with increasing proficiency as they mature. Errors are viewed as part of the learning process, and students are given direct feedback on how to improve their performance. Learners are encouraged to think critically, to develop their own opinions, to

pursue their own interests, to engage in divergent thinking, and to demonstrate initiative. Students have opportunities to design and carry out their own research projects, making their own choices about topics and modes of presentation. Teachers welcome a certain amount of questioning and encourage risk-taking; indeed, this kind of behaviour is one of the attributes of 'giftedness' in school districts that provide differentiated programs for children identified as intellectually exceptional.

Not all learners are comfortable in a learner-centred classroom. Immigrant students, and students raised in families where conformity and respect for authority are emphasized, may have difficulty with activities that ask them to formulate an opinion, investigate a topic through independent research, or develop a hypothesis through experimentation and observation. For example, in most Chinese families, parents control the topic of conversation, decide how much the children will contribute to a conversation, and control the direction of the conversation (Heath, 1986). Some students are reluctant to engage in discussions that require them to suggest alternatives, make hypotheses, or question an authority such as the teacher or a textbook. Immigrant students, in particular, find it difficult to adjust to classrooms that expect them to take risks. For example, students from cultures where the preservation of 'face' is important may not challenge or criticise ideas, venture an opinion, or ask questions that may reveal a lack of understanding. Students whose cultural orientation emphasizes learning from and emulating 'the masters' and memorizing exemplary models may feel lost and uncomfortable without the structure to which they are accustomed, and may not benefit initially from student-centred activities.

Combining teacher-centred and learner-centred approaches

You can provide appropriate learning experiences for all the students by providing both teacher-centred and learner-centred instruction. It is appropriate to provide strong leadership and direct instruction when you are introducing knowledge or developing skills that all students need. For example:

- **Provide direct instruction** about specific features of standard English such as common spelling patterns, subject–verb agreement, or irregular past tense forms, so that all students have opportunities to become proficient users of standard English. Always embed this instruction in a meaningful context: for example, focus on passive verb structures when they arise in the context of science, and the use of past tense forms of the verb when they arise in the context of history.

  Cloze: a strategy for content-based language instruction

  Cloze activities based on the content of a lesson can be used to focus attention on specific language features:

To find the volume of a solid by using an overflow can and a graduated cylinder:

(1) The spout of the can _____ with a finger.
(2) The overflow can _____ above the level of the spout.
(3) The can _____ on a level surface and the water above the spout _____ out.
(4) The object _____ into the water, and the water that overflows _____ in the graduated cylinder.
(5) The volume of water in the cylinder _____ by reading the graduated cylinder.

The First People

The first people _____ in Africa more than three million years ago. Their brains _____ bigger than the brains of apes, and they _____ upright. They_____fruits, roots and berries for their food.

   During the next three million years, humans _____ to make tools and weapons. They _____ animals for their meat and their skins. They _____ to use fire.

   About 6,000 years ago, people _____ to live in settled communities. They _____ the land and _____ animals.

Many of the resources listed at the end of Chapter 3 provide detailed suggestions on how to integrate content and language instruction.

- **Use songs, chants, and oral recitation** to help student memorize important information such as the alphabet, multiplication tables and number facts, the parts of a cell, or the characteristics of living things. Songs and chants provide a change of pace and may be accompanied by physical movement as well.
- **Use mnemonic devices** to help students memorize a rule or a process such as 'BEDMAS' in algebra (Bracket Exponents: Divide, Multiply, Add, Subtract).
- **Provide some learning activities that promote convergent thinking** and help students to reach consensus or arrive a 'right answer' when there really is only one suitable approach or solution.
- **Provide some activities that encourage creativity and divergent thinking**. Some students may need guidance when they are working on tasks that build on the students' own interests, strengths, and curiosity, promote divergent thinking, and encourage initiative. For example, you can pave the way for new learning through prereading activities such as 'KWL' charts and brainstorming.

What we **Know**	What we **Want** to learn	What we **Learned**

• **Use visual organizers** to illustrate key ideas and the relationships among them in text, in lessons, and in units of work. In recent years, theorists and practitioners in cognitive strategy instruction have developed the use of graphic organizers as a way of representing specific thinking processes such as comparison and contrast, cause and effect, problem solving, or sequence (Clarke, 1990). Teachers often use 'generic' graphic organizers of specific types, such as Venn diagrams and flow charts, to show students how to think about a particular problem, or how to organize their work and ideas for a specific task.

Comparison and contrast

This example shows how the Venn diagram can be used to help students collect, compare and contrast information from different sources. The teacher may then teach the use of specific words such as 'neither . . . nor' and 'in contrast' to link ideas in writing.

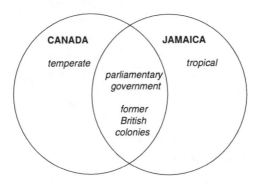

Teachers can also provide content-specific visual organizers show key ideas are related in a text, a lesson, or a unit of study. The organizer may be used before, during, or after a lesson. It may be provided to the students blank, partially completed, or completed. The teacher may complete the organizer with the class, or students can use it to guide their reading, to make notes from their reading, to guide their writing, or to plan their work on a group or individual project. A visual organizer is also useful in assessment, allowing second language learners to display their knowledge and understanding even though they may not yet know enough English to do so verbally. If students can complete an organizer with key words, perhaps selected from a list provided by the teacher, they have understood the key concepts and are able to provide examples.

Concept map

This organizer shows an overview of the concepts in a science lesson. The 'What's missing' box is for nuclear waste; this topic will be dealt with in another lesson, but the learners need to see how topics are related in the 'big picture'.

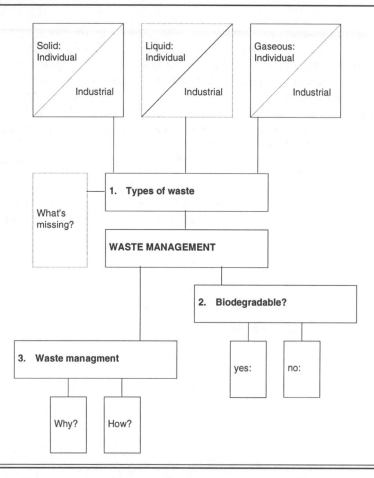

- **Provide strong support for students' writing** by providing writing scaffolds. Writing scaffolds are temporary frameworks that support the students and enable them to produce sentences and paragraphs of a quality that they are not yet able to produce unaided. As the learners become more proficient, they need less and less support.

Writing scaffolds
A writing scaffold may consist of a sentence completion activity based on the content of a lesson or text. This activity can be used to help learners recognize and use expressions that indicate a specific relationship of ideas, such as cause and effect.

The plant on the windowsill grew taller **because** . . .
The plant in the corner received less light. **As a result,** . . .
The plant in the closet received no light. **Therefore,** . . .
We conclude that . . . **in order** to grow.

This paragraph scaffold provides link words to help direct the students' thinking as they write.

Should we have a Christmas play this year?

In my opinion, we should/should not have a Christmas play this year, **because . . . Also, . . . In addition, . . . Therefore, . . .**

For ideas on how to support longer pieces of writing using 'writing frames' for specific genres of writing such as reports, explanations, and procedures, see Lewis and Wray (1995, 1996).

- **Promote exploratory learning** through co-operative learning tasks, and bring a unit of study to closure with an activity through which students can apply new learning, such as a group project.
- **Involve students** in planning and organizing special events such as field trips, and involved them in decisions about how the class should be run.
- **Invite students to give their personal responses** and reflect on their own learning in journal assignments and learning logs.
- **Encourage risk-taking**: explain that making errors is part of the learning process, and nobody in the class will 'lose face' for making mistakes. Talk about times when you have learned from your mistakes: for example, in your teaching methods.
- **Explain the instructional purpose** of all learning activities. Don't assume that all learners understand the purpose of learner-centred activities such as field trips or projects. Explain how the activity is linked to the curriculum; for example, if you are planning to involve the children in looking after a classroom pet, make sure they and their parents understand the pedagogical purpose, such as developing nurturing skills and responsibility, and providing background knowledge and experience for the science curriculum.
- **Provide strong guidance and support for new ways of learning,** such as research projects. Review the process each time you assign a project, and be ready to give direct individualized instruction to students who have less experience than others with project work. Make sure that the learning outcomes for these students are realistic. For example, if an important outcome is 'learn how to find information', then the volume of the information is not tremendously important. Beginners might start with finding and reporting five relevant facts to demonstrate mastery of this outcome at a level appropriate to their stage of proficiency in English, while other students might be writing a longer and more detailed report.

Guided projects

Follow this procedure to help your students with projects:

- Help students with choosing a topic. Strategies such as brainstorming will help students see how diverse the topic choices might be, and how they might relate to each other.

- **Encourage group projects**. This provides support for the second language learners and allows students to utilize each other's skills, talents, and interests. In addition, the process helps students to develop important social skills.
- **Provide a step-by-step checklist** of the various tasks involved, with time lines, and monitor completion of each step. This way you can give feedback at each step, redirect students who may be off track, offer extra help when needed, and help students to plan their work and organize their time. Provide constructive feedback on process as well as product, basing your assessment on observation, as well as students' notes, journals, or reading logs.
- **Show the learners a variety of models** of acceptable to outstanding performance. Show several different ways of presenting information, such as posters, videotapes, comic books, interviews and role plays, as well as traditional written reports. Discuss the criteria used in assessing the models. Students can discuss what makes the difference between satisfactory and excellent.
- **Help students to develop pre-writing charts or outlines** to organize existing knowledge and indicate where research is needed. A KWL chart can help students to get started. A concept map, flow chart, or other visual organizer can help them to categorize or sequence their ideas.
- **Introduce your students to the libraries** at the school and in the community. Ask the librarian to give your class an orientation to the facilities and services available to them there. Many students, especially those who do not have study space at home, may find the library an ideal place to do homework.
- **Teach students how to paraphrase**. Take a sentence or a short paragraph from a reference book, write it on the board, and show the students several ways of re-wording it. The provide several sentences for them to practise on. It is important not to penalize second language learners who paraphrase with spelling and grammar errors; if you do, they will revert to memorizing or copying from the text as a way of avoiding these errors.
- **Make sure that all students have access to the necessary resources**. Check that appropriate reference material is available in the library or in your classroom. Provide presentation folders, different kinds and sizes of paper, coloured markers and crayons, glue and scissors, concrete materials for models, magazine pictures, and other materials that some students may not have available to them at home. If you don't have computers in your classroom, arrange for your class to use the computer lab.

Project checklist

Use or adapt this form to help guide students and give feedback as they work on group projects or presentations. Change the wording for use with individual students.

Project Checklist

Use this checklist to help you plan and organize your group project. Check off each task as you go. Don't skip any steps.

Planning

- ❏ We have agreed on a topic.
- ❏ We have brainstormed some questions about the topic.
- ❏ We have predicted some possible answers to our questions.
- ❏ We have made a graphic organizer to organize topics and sub-topics.
- ❏ We have given ourselves sub-topics or tasks.
- ❏ We know what information we need.
- ❏ We have consulted the teacher about possible sources of information.
- ❏ Our teacher has seen and approved our work so far.
- ❏ We are ready to start our research.

Research

- ❏ We have planned research time in the school library, or for interviews.
- ❏ We have helped one another by sharing resources.
- ❏ We have made point form notes of the information we collected.
- ❏ We have discussed how our information answers our original questions.
- ❏ We have revised our graphic organizer and added notes under each sub-topic.
- ❏ We have asked the teacher for help when necessary.
- ❏ Our teacher has seen and approved our work so far.
- ❏ We are ready to start preparing our final product.

Report writing

- ❏ We have used the graphic organizer to plan an outline for our project.
- ❏ We have agreed on how we want to present our information.
- ❏ We have helped each other to revise our first draft.
- ❏ We have met ___ times to review progress and make sure we are all on track.
- ❏ We have asked the teacher for help when necessary.
- ❏ We have read through our report or rehearsed our presentation together.
- ❏ We are ready to share our finished product.

Implicit and explicit scripts

Teachers in multicultural classrooms, viewing children's behaviour and communication styles from their own cultural perspective, sometimes become frustrated with students who seem uncommunicative, passive, or timid — or, in contrast, loud, aggressive, or disobedient. Some of these difficulties may be attributed to cultural differences. The teacher and the students may have different 'scripts' or 'mutually understood ways of thinking and behaving'; when teachers and students come from different cultures, 'the meaning of their scripts may be mutually unintelligible . . . . they may be unaware of their different understanding because cultural knowledge is so tacit' (Bowman, 1993: 130). These differences can have significant effects on student–teacher interaction, as the following examples show.

Giving directions

There are important script differences in the ways adults direct the activities of children. Classrooms in most English-speaking countries have become far less formal and authoritarian than they were a few decades ago. They are much less 'strict' than the family environments of many children, and less authoritarian than classrooms in many other countries. Instead of asserting overt power and authority in their interaction with students, teachers often express directions and warnings as indirect requests or suggestions, as in 'It's time to put our paints away now,' 'Is this where the scissors belong?' or 'Someone else is talking now, we'll all have to wait' (Heath, 1983: 280). It is not uncommon, especially in elementary schools, for teachers to draw attention to appropriate behaviour instead of giving explicit orders to students who may be behaving inappropriately: 'I like the way this group is sitting so quietly and paying attention.' Rules are often implicit; even where there is a list of rules, they may be non-specific and couched impersonally rather than as direct orders, as in 'teachers and students will respect each other at all times.'

This kind of indirectness and vagueness may not be correctly interpreted by students from backgrounds where instructions, warnings, and rules are much more direct and explicit. For example, in many African American families, instructions to children are usually very direct and couched as imperatives. A child accustomed to this style of interaction may misinterpret or ignore a veiled command such as 'Where do the scissors belong?' and consequently be perceived as a 'behaviour problem'. The problem is not the child, but the teacher's indirectness; the child needs explicit directions in order to conform to the expectations of the teacher (Delpit, 1988). Students who are accustomed to a more direct, authoritarian style may be unable to discern the 'invisible discipline' that the teacher expects them to understand implicitly; they may conclude that there is no discipline or classroom structure at all. Some students withdraw from interaction in an unpredictable, incomprehensible environment. Others become boisterous and playful, testing the limits of this new cultural environment, sometimes with the result that they cross an invisible line and find themselves in serious trouble. Parents are sometimes critical of teachers whose way of relating to the learners does not conform with their expectations, believing that the teachers are not giving appropriate guidance and discipline to their children.

Exhibiting authority

Teachers and students from different cultural backgrounds may also have different scripts about how teachers and other authority figures behave towards subordinates.

Many teachers interact informally with their students and may treat them as equals. For example, teachers sit side-by-side with students to check on their work or offer help. They use colloquial language and exchange jokes with their students, and some teachers even trade mock insults with their students. They dress in casual clothes, tell students about their personal lives, play team sports against students, dress up in strange clothes for special events, and take part in skits at school concerts. In spite of this informality, there is an unwritten rule that a teacher is in charge, no matter how egalitarian things may appear on the surface.

This informality and egalitarianism is sometimes uncomfortable or incomprehensible to students from countries or cultural backgrounds where adults provide strong, authoritarian leadership to children and young people, and never treat them as equals. There is a distinct hierarchy among the generations in many traditional cultures; older siblings have authority over younger children and there may be ritualized forms of address that reflect a hierarchy of relationships. Many students and parents from other countries are accustomed to schools where teachers always behave as authority figures and children are expected to defer to teachers at all times. This relationship is manifested in many ways: for example, all the children wear uniforms and the teachers follow a dress code; the students stand when the teacher enters the classroom, and whenever they are called on to answer a question; teachers are addressed respectfully by name or title; students seldom ask questions or initiate discussion, but wait to be called on. These and other symbols of 'respect' are highly ritualized and visible; their loss can be deeply unsettling to newcomers.

As a result of these script differences, some minority children may behave towards their teachers in ways that seem timid or overly deferential; others may simply lose respect for the teacher who does not behave as a teacher should, according to the cultural norms of the students. For example, according to Delpit, African American children 'expect an authority figure to act with authority. When the teacher acts instead as a 'chum' the message is sent that this adult has no authority, and the children react accordingly' (Delpit, 1988: 289).

Non-verbal communication

Another area of difficulty in cross-cultural communication in the classroom is in non-verbal communication. Children of different cultural backgrounds learn different scripts for behaviour such as making eye contact: in some cultures, it is disrespectful to 'look someone in the eye', especially an elder or an authority figure. Children learn different cultural rules about personal space, such as how far apart people should stand or sit, about how loudly or quietly one should speak in specific situations, and about who may initiate a conversation between people of different status, such as teacher and student. Gestures may have completely different meanings: nodding the head means 'Yes' in some cultures and 'No' in others; similarly, shaking the head may mean 'Yes' or 'No' depending on cultural background. The gesture for 'Come here' in one culture may mean 'Go away' in another, and a gesture that may be insulting in one culture may be friendly or respectful in another. In some cultures it may be appropriate for a teacher to pat a child on the head or the shoulder, or put an arm around a child; in others this may be highly inappropriate, especially if the teacher and the child are of different genders.

These differences cause individuals of different cultural backgrounds to perceive each other inaccurately. In the classroom, teachers and students may misinterpret each other's non-verbal behaviour, with disastrous consequences. The child who does not make eye-contact with the teacher may be viewed as sullen or devious. The child who stands too closely may be viewed as pushy or invasive. The teacher may make a gesture signifying approval that has an insulting or obscene connotation in the culture of some of the students. Sometimes, students who are 'testing the system' and who know that the teacher does not understand some of their non-verbal signals may take advantage of the situation to communicate with each other in inappropriate ways, thus subtly undermining the authority of the teacher.

You can reduce the risk of cultural misinterpretation in your classroom by observing interaction patterns and analyzing your own behaviour and that of the students. Consult adults who can act as cultural informants. Find ways of observing students interacting with adults in their own cultural environment: for example, visit community centres, heritage language classes, and places of worship, and attend cultural events and celebrations. Include a home visit in the registration procedures for children entering school for the first time. In class, do not make assumptions when students do not behave as you expect; instead, ask non-judgmental questions such as 'What did you think I meant when I . . . ', 'I don't understand what just happened. Why did you . . . ?' Be explicit when you are giving directions to students. When you are establishing classroom rules or norms, give examples of specific behaviour: for example, 'respecting others' includes 'asking permission to use or borrow things' or 'taking turns in speaking'. Communicate warmth and enthusiasm but maintain your role as an authority figure, not as an equal. Learn to recognize behaviour that is inappropriate: for example, swearing in other languages, or making rude or suggestive noises, gestures, and comments. Include in the curriculum the topic of child–adult and student–teacher relationships and interaction patterns, so that cultural differences become 'visible'. Include non-verbal communication as a topic in the language arts or English program.

In addition to becoming skilled in using a wide variety of instructional strategies, and providing explicit instructions and explanations, teachers in multicultural classrooms need to behave in ways that communicate high expectations to all students, as discussed in the next section.

COMMUNICATING HIGH EXPECTATIONS

Expectations have long been believed to have a powerful effect on student performance (Rosenthal and Jacobson, 1968; Brophy and Good, 1974; Irvine, 1990; Ladson-Billings, 1994). Students who are consistently expected to do well often do, whereas students who consistently receive more negative messages often achieve much lower levels of performance. This is sometimes called the 'self-fulfilling prophecy' effect.

There is some evidence that some groups of minority students receive negative messages more consistently than others (Irvine, 1990; Ladson-Billings, 1994). Teachers convey subtle messages about their expectations of some groups or individuals through their behaviour towards them. Sometimes without even being aware of it themselves, teachers may hold differential expectations for different groups of students, and behave differently towards them. *The Swann Report* in Britain reported that 'boys and girls of different ethnic origins taught in the same multi-ethnic classroom by the same teacher are likely to receive widely different educational experiences' (Green, in the *Swann Report*: Department of Education and Science, 1985: 53). In North America, Asian students, especially those of Chinese background, are often viewed as a 'model minority' and their teachers view them as harder working and more academically able than their peers, especially in mathematics and science (Wong, 1980; MacLear, 1994). Black students, on the other hand, are more likely to be viewed negatively (Washington, 1980; Irvine, 1990). Some writers on antiracist education identify low teacher expectations as a major factor in the low levels of academic achievement among some groups of students (Irvine, 1990; Hilliard, 1994).

Teachers' expectations of their students are communicated in a variety of ways, often subconsciously. For example, a teacher's questioning techniques often reveal differential expectations. The teacher may address more questions to some students than to others. The teacher may give more 'wait time' for some students to answer questions; subconsciously the teacher expects these students to be able to answer, and so gives them enough time to formulate an answer. With other students, the teacher waits less time before giving the answer or moving on to another student. The teacher may coach some students to respond by repeating or rephrasing the question, or by providing key words or other clues; the teacher may offer less support for students on whom he or she subconsciously believes the effort would be wasted. Another way that teachers communicate their expectations is through the feedback they give to students. Some students receive feedback and are encouraged to re-do unsatisfactory work, while others receive less feedback, even if the work is not satisfactory, or have their work assessed by less demanding criteria. The teacher may seat the 'high-expectation' students at the front, so that they can receive the benefit of the teacher's attention, or at the back, because they don't need it. The teacher may engage in interaction with some students about the content of the lesson, inviting them to initiate ideas and introduce new new topics, while focussing on factual recall and behaviour control with others.

Teachers' expectations, it is believed, may be internalized by students as part of their self-concept, which in turn affects performance (Brophy and Good, 1974). Teachers are significant in the lives of their students, and from the time that they enter school many children spend more time with their teachers than they do with their parents. Teachers who are warm, kind, approachable, sensitive and enthusiastic communicate more positive expectations and have more positive effects on their students' attendance, conduct, self-concept and academic achievement than teachers who are more task-oriented. Negative expectations, on the other hand, are believed to act as a self-fulfilling prophecy which makes an originally false belief or expectation come true.

How to communicate high expectations

Observe your own teaching, or work with a colleague to observe each other, to make sure that you communicate positive expectations to all the students in the following ways:

- make questioning more effective by encouraging students to rehearse their responses orally, in small groups, and then selecting individuals to respond;
- give all students — especially those who need extra time to formulate answers in English — sufficient time to answer questions;
- if a student is stuck for an answer, try repeating or rephrasing the question, asking another student to help with translation, or providing clues;
- provide supportive feedback (never public criticism) to all students' responses by providing a model of more effective expression, or a more complete response;
- pay attention to all students and interact with them equally;
- call on all students equally often to respond to questions;
- call on all students to answer questions that demand higher-order thinking as well as factual recall;
- make sure that students change location when you choose groups so that everyone has a turn near the window, near to the teacher's desk, or other important locations;
- move your desk 'off to the side' and use this area for private conferences with individual students;
- move around the room, sharing your time more or less equally with all the groups and students in the room;
- use performance-based assessment: show students models of performance, including models of poor performance as well as satisfactory and excellent models, and invite them to figure out the criteria for assessment (see Chapter 9);
- if you have differential expectations for some students — for example, those who are learning the language of instruction, or newcomers who have missed some schooling — make sure that everyone understands that this is a temporary situation;
- when you have found the functional level of a student or a group of students, make sure that your expectations do not remain static; students should have to 'reach' a little more on each new assignment so that, over time, they close the gap between their performance and that of their peers. For example, if an

ESL learner can read material at a specific level in a series of graded readers, do not expect the student to read all the titles at that level, but to move on to the next level as soon as possible;

- recognize that performance may fall at first as a student adjusts to more challenging work — for example, when an ESL learner is first integrated into a mainstream subject classroom — and provide the support and encouragement the student needs to maintain the necessary self-esteem and effort.

Teachers convey subtle messages about their expectations for performance through their behaviour towards the students in their classrooms. Schools and school systems convey explicit messages about expectations when they divide students into different instructional groups on the basis of 'ability'. This issue is discussed in the next section.

GROUPING PRACTICES

Few practices communicate expectations more clearly than dividing students into 'ability groups' for different levels of instruction. This practice often occurs informally at the classroom level from the very earliest years of schooling — for example, when students are grouped within the class for reading instruction. Systematic ability grouping usually begins formally at secondary level. Students may be directed to different kinds of secondary schools, such as academic, technical and vocational schools. In some school districts, students go to the same school but are placed in different 'tracks', 'streams', or 'levels' where they receive different kinds of instruction.

It is difficult to conceive of an 'inclusive learning environment' in classrooms that have been systematically designed to include some groups of learners and exclude others. Supporters of ability grouping often argue that students with different levels of ability learn best in very different kinds of instructional program: higher achievers learn best in challenging programs alongside other high achievers, while lower achievers learn better and maintain their self-esteem in classrooms where they do not have to compete with higher achievers. Opponents of ability grouping argue that the practice perpetuates social inequality by providing an inferior education to children of immigrant, minority, and low socioeconomic background, who are often over-represented in lower level programs.

An inferior education

In theory, students are placed in lower levels so that they may receive an instructional program of equal quality to that offered to their high-achieving peers, but more appropriate to their needs. The reality is somewhat different: students placed in lower levels are offered a curriculum that is less stimulating and more restricted to lower-level modes of thinking than that offered to the higher-functioning groups (Goodlad, 1984; Oakes, 1985, 1995; Wheelock, 1994). One reason for this may be the lower expectations that teachers have for these students. Another may be that the least effective teachers are often assigned to teach in lower level programs where, even if they perform incompetently, there is less likelihood of a negative response from politically active parents (George, 1988).

In theory, lower-achieving students can maintain higher self-esteem if they are not competing with high achievers. However, research has shown, and most teachers would probably agree, that students placed in lower levels have lower self-esteem, lower aspirations, and more negative attitudes towards school (Oakes, 1986; George, 1988). Even when teachers approach their lower-level classes with commitment, skill, and enthusiasm, it is often difficult to establish an effective learning environment because students consigned to these classes 'resent their status, respond defensively, and refuse to engage in the very academic efforts which might bring them more success' (George, 1988: 23). Students placed in lower levels are more likely to drop out of secondary school (Radwanski, 1987), and immigrant students are especially at risk (Watt and Roessingh, 1994).

The quality of instruction

Goodlad's famous study of schools in the United States included a look at the quality of instruction in three different tracks or streams, and concluded that students in lower-level programs — students whose greater needs demand the most skilful instruction — actually received instruction that was inferior to that offered to their higher-achieving peers (Goodlad, 1984). For example:

- Students in the academic stream spent more class time on instruction, and were expected to do more homework and independent study, than their peers in the lower level classes.
- Students in the academic stream spent more time on higher level cognitive processes such as making inferences, synthesizing information, making judgments, or using symbolism, while students in the lower level or vocational streams spent more time on rote learning and the application of knowledge and skills.
- Teachers in the academic stream valued and promoted more independence, creativity, critical thinking, and active learning, while teachers in the lower streams valued more conforming types of classroom behaviour.
- Effective instructional practices were more prevalent in the higher stream, while students in the lower streams were less likely to experience the types of instruction that promotes achievement.
- Teachers in the academic classes communicated their expectations more clearly, and their students perceived them to be more enthusiastic in their teaching.

As Oakes observes, 'Tracking propels children through the system at different speeds — even though the goal for the slower-paced groups is to have them 'catch up' ' (Oakes, 1995: 61). It seems that those who need the most receive the least; the high achievers receive the best quality instruction, and, year by year and grade by grade, the gap between high and low achievers grows larger.

Over-representation

Many academic researchers and government studies have recognized the over-representation of some groups of students — especially immigrant and minority students — at lower levels of instruction (for example: Department of Education and Science, 1985; Oakes, 1985, 1986, 1995; Radwanski, 1987; George, 1988; Black, 1992; Curtis *et al.*, 1992; Troyna and Siraj-Blatchford, 1993; Watt and Roessingh, 1994; Braddock and Slavin, 1995; Page and Page, 1995). In 1986, Oakes' studies of tracking in American schools showed that 'Poor and minority youngsters (principally black and Hispanic) are disproportionately placed in tracks for low-ability or non-college-bound students. By the same token, minority students are consistently underrepresented in programs for the gifted and talented' (Oakes, 1986: p. 14). Almost a decade later, Braddock and Slavin (1995: 9) report that 'One of the most consistent impacts of ability groupings is to create classes that have disproportionate numbers of students from certain races or social classes'.

Students are directed to or selected for differential educational treatment on the basis of their levels of achievement, as assessed by their teachers and, sometimes, by standardized tests. Achievement is often believed to indicate a student's 'ability' or 'potential'. Immigrant and minority children may have lower levels of achievement, and therefore be judged to have lower levels of ability, because:

- the teaching methods may have been unsuited to their needs, as suggested earlier in this chapter;
- negative expectations on the part of teachers may lead to lower performance on the part of students, as discussed in earlier in this chapter;
- the curriculum provided to them has not been inclusive of their needs or perspectives (see Chapter 8);
- not all students have had opportunity to learn the knowledge or skills being assessed (see Chapter 9);
- not all students have had the opportunity to become proficient in the language in which the assessment is conducted (see Chapter 9).

Instead of seeking to attribute achievement differences to differences in the students, it may be more appropriate to adjust the curriculum, especially in multicultural teaching and learning environments. According to Pine and Hilliard (1990: 598), 'traditional pedagogical approaches and educational delivery systems that have been used to deal with at-risk minority students have often proved to be dysfunctional and anachronistic'. (See 'Assessment Reform in Multicultural Schools' in Chapter 9 for a discussion of 'opportunity to learn'.)

Alternatives

According to prominent writers on antiracist education, the elimination of ability grouping may be one of the most important ways of improving educational opportunity for minority students (Pine and Hilliard, 1990; Banks, 1993, 1994). This can be done — at least through the middle and early secondary grades, before curriculum specialization — with positive effects, including higher academic achievement for all students, positive social interaction among different groups of students, and higher levels of motivation and self-esteem (George, 1988). However, the elimination of ability grouping is a long-term proposition that may require political action beyond the school level. In the meantime, what are schools and teachers to do?

At the school level, it would be appropriate to to examine aspects of curriculum content and delivery that may contribute to lower levels of achievement among some groups; to delay tracking or streaming until as late as possible in the students' schooling; to examine and adjust the assessment procedures which determine the students' placement levels; to provide the academic and linguistic support that immigrant students and second language learners may need in order to perform adequately at higher levels; and to ensure that students at all levels receive instruction from committed and competent teachers.

At the classroom level, individual teachers can group students heterogeneously for most activities. Many writers advocate the skilful use of co-operative learning as an important strategy for heterogeneous classrooms (Kagan, 1986; Slavin, 1983, 1990; Pine and Hilliard, 1990; Banks, 1993, 1994). The Jigsaw strategy (described earlier in this chapter) is especially useful because students may work in homogeneous 'expert' groups to work on tasks and use resource material suited to their current level of development, and then contribute the results of their work to the work of their heterogeneous home groups.

Teachers can also provide learning experiences that appeal to a variety of learning styles, are intrinsically motivating, are culturally relevant, and offer students some choices, as has already been suggested earlier in this chapter. Another important approach is curriculum integration, involving cross-curricular thematic units of study. Working within a common conceptual framework, students may be engaged in some common tasks and some that are designed to give more time for some students to master concepts, or to provide opportunity for enrichment for others. Cohen's Program for Complex Instruction uses a variety of grouping patterns, materials, and academic tasks to provide all children in culturally and linguistically diverse classrooms with access to advanced instruction that involves higher order thinking skills (Cohen, 1990). In some schools, teacher collaboration and team teaching assignments help teachers to build on each other's strengths and broaden the scope of activities in the classroom. Finally, it is important to use a variety of assessment procedures and criteria (see Chapter 9).

CONCLUSION

This chapter has suggested several ways to transform the process of instruction in order to meet the needs and build on the strengths of students of all backgrounds. Most of these changes can be implemented by individual teachers in their own classrooms. It may be better to focus on one aspect of the classroom program at a time, rather than attempting to implement everything at once. For example, a teacher might decide to start by using some of the co-operative learning strategies suggested in this chapter (see also 'Co-operative Learning Groups' in Chapter 5).

The following checklist can be use to assess progress in developing an inclusive instructional style and promoting high levels of performance among all students. It may be helpful to work with a partner or a small group of teachers in the same school; collegial support and peer coaching can provide valuable support to teachers who are analyzing their own practice and transforming the way they work in the classroom.

Some changes, such as the elimination of ability grouping, or a change in the way students are assigned marks and grades, would take years of advocacy and concerted action to achieve. In the meantime, teachers can connect with colleagues and parents to discuss these and other issues raised in this chapter.

CHECKLIST: AN INCLUSIVE APPROACH TO INSTRUCTION

This checklist is organized as a series of indicators under broad topic areas that correspond with the instructional strategies and approaches recommended in this chapter. The checklist can be used by:

- individual teachers: to assess their own classrooms as inclusive social and learning environments;
- school administrators, school department heads, and district curriculum advisers: to assess classrooms within their sphere of influence;
- teacher educators: to guide and assess student teachers on practicum assignment;
- students: to assess the classroom environment provided to them (perhaps using a simplified or translated form).

The rating system can be used and interpreted as follows:

yes = whenever appropriate
not yet = this is an area that the teacher might work on
n/a = not applicable, or not available at this time

Teaching and learning styles

yes not n/a
    yet

❑ ❑ ❑   There is an emphasis on cognitive and metacognitive skills so that all students diversify their ways of perceiving and processing information.

❑ ❑ ❑   The teacher models effective learning and problem-solving techniques.

❑ ❑ ❑   Students are involved in learning tasks that promote interdependence as well as activities that develop independence.

❑ ❑ ❑   Most learning activities are intrinsically important or appealing.

❏ ❏ ❏   There is usually a choice of assignments.

❏ ❏ ❏   Lessons include some activities that require sustained concentration and others that involve high levels of activity or movement.

❏ ❏ ❏   The teacher provides direct instruction when introducing new knowledge or skills.

❏ ❏ ❏   Important knowledge is reinforced through chants, mnemonics, and fast-paced drill activities.

❏ ❏ ❏   Teacher-directed activities are balanced with student-centred activities and projects.

❏ ❏ ❏   The teacher's 'script' is explicit, and examples of miscommunication are explored with the students in order to make implicit norms and expectations more 'visible'.

Communicating high expectations

yes not n/a
    yet

❏ ❏ ❏   The teacher encourages group rehearsal before selecting individuals to respond to questions.

❏ ❏ ❏   The teacher provides sufficient 'wait time' for students to answer questions, and coaches students by repeating or rephrasing the question, asking another student to help with translation, or providing clues.

❏ ❏ ❏   The teacher provides supportive feedback to all students' responses.

❏ ❏ ❏   The teacher pays attention to all students and interacts with them equally.

❏ ❏ ❏   The teacher calls on all students equally often to respond to questions.

❏ ❏ ❏   The teacher calls on all students to answer questions that demand higher-order thinking as well as factual recall.

❏ ❏ ❏   The teacher groups students heterogeneously for most activities.

❏ ❏ ❏   The teacher makes sure that students change location when they change groups.

❏ ❏ ❏   The teacher's desk is at the side or in a corner, and is used for private conferences with individual students.

❏ ❏ ❏   The teacher moves around the room, sharing time more or less equally with all the groups and students in the room.

❏ ❏ ❏   The teacher uses performance-based assessment, showing students models various levels of performance, inviting them to figure out the criteria for assessment.

❏ ❏ ❏   If there are differential expectations for some students — for example, those who are learning the language of instruction, or newcomers who have missed some schooling — it is understood that this is a temporary situation.

❏   ❏   ❏   Expectations do not remain static, and students have to 'reach' a little more on each new assignment.

❏   ❏   ❏   If performance falls as a student adjusts to more challenging work, the teacher provides the support and encouragement the student needs to maintain the necessary self-esteem and effort.

Grouping practices

yes not n/a
     yet

❏   ❏   ❏   Students are grouped heterogeneously for most activities.

❏   ❏   ❏   When students are grouped in homogeneous groups, this is a temporary arrangement: e.g., Jigsaw 'expert groups'.

❏   ❏   ❏   When students are grouped in homogeneous groups, this is for a specific instructional purpose: e.g., to use alternative materials, to receive additional assistance from peer tutors or the teacher, etc.

❏   ❏   ❏   Working within a common conceptual framework, students may be engaged in some common tasks and some that are designed to give more time for some students to master concepts, or to provide opportunity for enrichment for others.

❏   ❏   ❏   Teachers collaborate and work as teams in order to build on each others' strengths and broaden the scope of activities in the classroom.

❏   ❏   ❏   Teachers use a variety of assessment procedures and criteria (see Chapter 9).

FURTHER READING AND RESOURCES FOR TEACHERS

Clarke, J.H. (1990) *Patterns of Thinking: Integrating Learning Skills in Content Teaching*. Needham Heights, MA: Allyn and Bacon. This book links cognitive strategy instruction with graphic organizers that help to teach students how to use certain kinds of thinking for specific learning tasks.

Clarke, J., Wideman, R., and Eadie, S. (1990) *Together We Learn: Co-operative Small Group Learning*. Scarborough, Ontario: Prentice-Hall. Practical handbook, useful to teachers at all grade levels.

Coelho, E. (1991) *Jigsaw*. Markham, Ontario: Pippin Publishing Limited. Content-based reading and discussion tasks and group problem-solving activities for middle and secondary school students.

Coelho, E. (1994) *Learning Together in the Multicultural Classroom*. Markham, Ontario: Pippin Publishing Limited, 1994. The focus of this book is the implementation of co-operative learning in middle and secondary school classrooms where some or all of the learners are learning the language of instruction.

Coelho, E., and Winer, L. (1991) *Jigsaw Plus*. Markham, Ontario: Pippin Publishing Limited. Content-based reading and discussion tasks and group problem-solving activities for secondary school students.

Coelho, E., Winer, L., and Winn-Bell Olsen, J. (1989) *All Sides of the Issue*. Hayward, CA: Alemany Press. US version of the *Jigsaw* materials.

Cohen, E. (1986) *Designing Groupwork: Strategies for the Heterogeneous Classroom*. New York, NY: Teachers College Press. This book deals with 'status problems' in classrooms where students of many different backgrounds, including recent immigrants, are learning together, and provides guidance on the development of activities that build students' individual strengths in order to promote effective group work.

Delpit, L. (1995) *Other People's Children: Cultural Conflict in the Classroom*. New York, NY: New Press. The author describes some of the cultural miscommunication that can take place in classrooms where teacher and students do not share a common culture, and suggests how teachers can adapt their instructional approach in order to assist students to acquire the language and academic skills they need for success in school.

Erickson, T. (1989) *Get It Together: Math Problems for Groups*. Berkeley, CA: Regents of the University of California. Materials for cooperative group learning in math, grades 4–12. There is a good introduction for the teacher, and the materials consist of reproducible clue cards for distribution to students. This book is one of several curriculum resource books from the 'Equals' program at the Lawrence Hall of Science, Berkeley. 'Equals' is a program of staff and curriculum development designed to promote the equitable participation of minorities and females in mathematics and science. For more information, contact: EQUALS, Lawrence Hall of Science, University of California, Berkeley, CA 9720.

Genesee, F. (ed.) (1994) *Educating Second Language Children: The Whole Child, the Whole Curriculum, the Whole Community*. Cambridge: Cambridge University Press. This collection of articles includes several related to effective instruction in multicultural and multilingual classrooms.

Helmer, S. and Eddy, C. (1996) *Look at Me When I Talk to You*. Toronto: Pippin Publishing. An introduction to cross-cultural communication in the classroom, with practical suggestions for teachers.

Hyerle, D. (1996) *Visual Tools for Constructing Knowledge*. Alexandria, VA: Association for Supervision and Curriculum Development. This helpful book shows how to use brainstorming webs, task-specific organizers, and thinking-process maps to demonstrate and help students to use specific kinds of thinking.

Kessler, C. (1992) (ed.) *Cooperative Language Learning*. Englewood Cliffs, NJ: Prentice-Hall. A collection of articles on how to organize group activities in classrooms that include second language learners.

Ladson-Billings, G. (1994) *The Dreamkeepers: Successful Teachers of African American Children*. San Francisco, CA: Jossey Bass. An inspirational book that uses portraits of exemplary teachers to document a variety of approaches and methods that provide academically challenging and culturally relevant educational experiences to children of diverse cultural backgrounds.

Lewis, M. and Wray, D. (1996) *Writing Frames: Scaffolding Children's Non-fiction Writing in a Range of Genres*. Reading, UK: Reading and Language Information Centre, University of Reading. Provides a variety of templates or writing frames to support student's writing in a variety of genres.

O'Malley, J.M., and Chamot, U.A. (1994) *The CALLA Handbook: Implementing the Cognitive Academic Language Learning Approach*. Reading, MA: Addison-Wesley. An instructional model for classrooms where students are learning the language of instruction. The model incorporates cognitive strategy instruction and provides model units for several subject areas.

Nehaul, K. (1996) *The Schooling of Children of Caribbean Heritage*. Stoke-on-Trent: Trentham Books. This book describes classroom-based research in schools where teachers were committed to meeting the educational needs of their students of diverse cultural backgrounds. The book identifies elements of the classroom experience and factors in the school that contribute to achievement.

Pool, H. and Page, J.A. (eds) (1995) *Beyond Tracking: Finding Success in Inclusive Schools*. Bloomington, IN: Phi Delta Kappan Educational Foundation. This collection of articles includes several on practical alternatives to 'tracking' or 'streaming'.

Pressley, M., and Associates (1990) *Cognitive Strategy Instruction that Really Improves Children's Academic Performance*. Cambridge, MA: Brookline Books. Presents procedures for teaching cognitive strategies that can be incorporated across the curriculum.

Scarcella, R. (1990) *Teaching Language Minority Students in the Multicultural Classroom*. Englewood Cliffs, NJ: Prentice Hall. This book suggests some principles for the provision of culturally responsive education in multicultural schools.

Wheelock, A. (1994) *Alternatives to Tracking and Ability Grouping*. Arlington, VA: American Association of School Administrators. This booklet deals with practical approaches to 'untracking'.

Wisconsin Department of Public Instruction (1991) *Strategic Learning in the Content Areas.* Madison, WI: Wisconsin Department of Public Instruction. Analyzes the linguistic and conceptual demands of several subject areas, and provides examples of graphic organizers and other learner strategies that can be developed through model activities and applied to academic tasks.

CHAPTER 7

An Antiracist Approach to Education

INTRODUCTION

This chapter explains why antiracist education is important for all students, and describes the benefits for students of a school-wide program of antiracist education. The rest of the chapter consists of an overview of several approaches to antiracist education, with an emphasis on the curriculum. The chapter serves as background information for the more detailed suggestions on curriculum development in Chapter 8. The discussion draws extensively on the principles and practices of antiracist education, focussing mainly on developments in Canada and the United States, although the discussion is relevant to many educational settings.

A note on terminology

In this chapter, and elsewhere in this book, the term 'antiracist education' refers to a broad set of institutional practices intended to reduce prejudice and discrimination, promote academic equity, and develop in all students the skills for social action and interaction in a racially and culturally diverse society.

In the United States, the term 'multicultural education' is more commonly used (for example, see Banks, 1988a, 1993). However, in Canada, a distinction is often drawn between 'multicultural education' and 'antiracist education'. 'Multicultural education' refers to educational practices that recognize the experiences and contributions of diverse cultural groups (Ministry of Education and Training, 1993), and is often regarded as a developmental stage on a continuum toward antiracist education, which 'provides teachers and students with the knowledge and skills to examine racism critically in order to understand how it originates and to identify and challenge it' (Ministry of Education and Training, 1993: 42). In Britain, the term 'antiracist multicultural education' is sometimes used to imply implementation beyond the superficial level that

195

'multicultural education' may imply (for example, see Massey, 1991). I have avoided using the phrase 'multicultural education' because these differences are problematic, although I have retained it in all quotations from other sources.

An inclusive curriculum, as described in this chapter and in Chapter 8, is one component of antiracist education. Other components are discussed in other chapters of this book.

WHO NEEDS ANTIRACIST EDUCATION?

Antiracist education is for all students, whether they belong to the cultural majority or a minority group, and whether they go a culturally diverse school or a school populated mainly or entirely by white English-speaking students. All students need an education that will help them reach their academic potential, learn the skills for living in a multicultural society, and develop the global awareness that is essential for future citizens of the world.

Antiracist education for the silent majority

A. Alan Borovoy, General Counsel for the Canadian Civil Liberties Association, identifies the well-meaning 'silent majority' as the real barrier to equity in society, and suggests that the antiracist curriculum should be directed towards them:

It is very important to see as the primary enemies of human rights and racial equality, not the ill-intentioned wrong-doers, but the well-intentioned non-doers. It is critically important to note that whatever educational programs we have on the issues of racism, they should focus on the large numbers of nice people who are against racism but who will not take a stand if it means compromising their comforts. ... Our educational efforts should be primarily directed to these people: not the fanatics, but the moderates; not the bigots, but the decent who won't take a stand. (Borovoy, 1989)

The limitations of a Eurocentric curriculum

The traditional curriculum in most English-speaking countries is Eurocentric: it is mainly concerned with the perspectives, experiences, achievements, contributions, inventions, discoveries, creations, beliefs, and daily life activities of people of European ancestry, and may distort or omit those of other groups (Pine and Hilliard, 1990; Ministry of Education and Training, 1993). Such a curriculum is limited in its selection of knowledge that students should learn, and provides students with a limited or biased view of the world. For example:

- Most North American students study literature by Europeans, or by North American authors of European ancestry, but read little or no literature from other cultures.
- Students' experiences with the arts are limited by an unquestioned assumption that to be 'cultured' one needs to know a lot about the arts of Europe, but may

remain ignorant of the artistic forms and creations of the rest of the world. For example, students study the paintings and sculptures of European artists in the visual arts program, while the music program exposes them to European classical music and to mainstream North American popular music. The contribution of other cultures to Western art, music, and drama is acknowledged cursorily, if at all.

- In social studies, students learn that the family usually consists of two parents and two children, and that people in the 'Third World' are poor because they have too many children. In the history class, students learn about the arrival of the European explorers and colonists from the European perspective.
- In mathematics, science, and technology, students learn little of the involvement of other cultures in those fields.
- Most English-speaking students graduate with limited proficiency in any other language.

The achievements and perspectives of Europeans and people of mainstream North Americans are worthy of study — but so are many others. A curriculum that includes only the knowledge, experiences, and achievements of people of European ancestry, to the exclusion of all others, is a biased curriculum.

Curriculum bias is seldom intentional; it is usually the result of a particular world view among those who develop it. Most educators, especially those in policy development and curriculum leadership, have traditionally been members of the dominant culture. They may not have the knowledge and experience that would enable them to include other perspectives — but most would undoubtedly agree that students of all racial and ethnocultural heritages need to learn to get along with each other and have equal opportunity to develop their individual potential.

The effects of a Eurocentric curriculum

Curriculum bias may be unintentional, but it is unjust. Curriculum bias is an institutional problem that can have negative effects on students. These include the perpetuation of cultural stereotypes, and low academic achievement among some groups of minority students.

Cultural stereotypes

Many students of all backgrounds bring stereotypical attitudes to the school, and these attitudes are formed by forces outside the school, such as the family, the media, and patterns of interaction in the community. The school may unintentionally reinforce these attitudes through the curriculum it offers to students. For example, if the only languages that students can formally study at school are European, there is an implicit message about the value of other languages. If the literature that students read at school presents them with a world view that is predominantly that of one cultural and socioeconomic group, the exclusion of other perspectives and experiences carries a subtle message about their importance. Such messages are harmful to all students, including those of the dominant cultural group.

Students of the dominant culture are harmed by a curriculum that represents, affirms, and celebrates only their own cultural background and experience. They are likely to develop an exaggerated sense of the importance of their own group, and are not helped to an understanding of the experiences of their classmates. They may develop a distorted world view, and thus are victims of racism. This is a process that begins when children are very young; Derman-Sparks gives several examples of three-, four-, and five-year-olds with strongly stereotypical views of themselves and others (Derman-Sparks, 1989).

Racism: a distortion of reality
Racism harms those who hold racist views as well as the victims of racism. Pine and Hilliard describe racism as:
[A] mental illness characterized by perceptual distortion, a denial of reality, delusions of grandeur (belief in white supremacy), the projection of blame (on the victim), and phobic reactions to differences. (Pine and Hilliard, 1990: 595)

Meanwhile, students whose cultural backgrounds are not validated by the curriculum receive the implicit message that their cultures are not worthy of study, and that people of these cultures have achieved little and contributed nothing to the human story. The effects of this kind of message are profoundly damaging; some students learn not to value themselves or their communities, and develop poor self-esteem, or become so alienated that they become disengaged from the educational process. As one student comments, 'When I was going to school the teachers focussed on European history, European this... when you sit in a classroom full of twelve white people and all you hear is white this white that you think so what am I here for... and they don't tell you about great African stuff or... Indian or East Indian... there's nothing like that, so a lot of the students that are minorities don't feel interested or are left out' (reported in Dei, 1996: 55).

All students need opportunities to develop balanced and non-stereotypical attitudes towards their own racial and cultural group and towards people of other cultural and racial backgrounds — whether the school serves a diverse population or is attended mainly by children of the white mainstream community (Massey, 1991; Banks, 1993). They also need to develop the skills to interact effectively in intercultural settings, to think critically about the society they live in, and to become involved in social action to challenge and change inequity of all kinds. Globally as well as nationally, intercultural understanding and co-operation will be essential to the solution of many of the problems that face future generations. On an individual level, antiracist education is important for mental health and cultural enrichment. It is dysfunctional to react to racial and cultural diversity in the school, the community, or the workplace in an emotional and illogical way — for example, with fear, suspicion, contempt, or aggression. Moreover, a monocultural perspective on life is culturally impoverished.

Antiracist educators advocate the inclusion of various cultural perspectives and experiences in the curriculum, so that all students feel validated by what they learn at school, and learn to value cultural diversity while recognizing fundamental similarities among all human beings. The curriculum can play an important role in counteracting the negative messages that children may receive elsewhere, and in promoting positive messages about cultural diversity. In this way, the school becomes more than a reflection of the community; it acts as an agent of social change, in the interests of social harmony and justice.

Low academic achievement

An issue of urgency in schools and school districts that serve culturally diverse communities is the differential academic achievement of students of different social class and ethnocultural groups. At present, the school system in most English-speaking countries is generally effective, in terms of academic outcomes, for students of the dominant social and cultural group in the society — that is, middle-class, white, English-speaking students. However, there is great concern about lower levels of academic achievement and eventual life prospects of some groups of minority students, and students of lower socioeconomic status of all cultural backgrounds (Department of Education and Science, 1985; Sue and Padilla, 1986; McGee Banks, 1993; Lewis, 1992; Ministry of Education and Training, 1993). This is not to say that all immigrant or minority students are doing badly. Some groups and individuals are doing very well, and there are greater achievement differences within all ethnocultural groups than between them (Department of Education and Science, 1985). Nevertheless, there is disproportionate failure among some immigrant and minority groups.

Academic failure among some groups of students may be attributed to several factors, including poverty (Hess, 1989; Lincoln and Higgins, 1991; Carey, 1997; Philp, 1997), unequal distribution of educational resources (Kozol, 1991), and lack of proficiency in, or lack of opportunity to learn, the language of instruction (Cummins, 1984, 1996; Watt and Roessingh, 1994). Low teacher expectations and a mismatch between teaching and learning styles may also contribute to lower academic achievement, as discussed in Chapter 6. Another important factor may be a loss of identity and self-esteem among students who do not see themselves positively and equitably reflected in the curriculum. Pine and Hilliard explain (1990: 596):

> They experience conceptual separations from their roots; they are compelled to examine their own experiences through the assumptions, paradigms, constructs, and language of other people; they lose their cultural identity; and they find it difficult to develop a sense of affiliation and connection to a school. They become 'universal strangers' — disaffected and alienated — and all too many eventually drop out of school.

Many writers on antiracist education recommend transformation of the traditional Eurocentric curriculum into one that is more inclusive of the experiences and perspectives of diverse cultural groups in order to improve the academic performance of minority students (Banks, 1993; Hodson, 1993; Pine and Hilliard, 1990).

STUDENT OUTCOMES OF ANTIRACIST EDUCATION

Antiracist education is a philosophy based on concepts of social justice and equity, and promotes these outcomes for students:

- positive and non-stereotypical attitudes towards cultural diversity, and a balanced view of the relative importance of different cultural and racial groups, including their own, among all students: indigenous minorities, established residents, and recent arrivals, and students of all racial, cultural, and linguistic and cultural backgrounds, including the English-speaking mainstream;
- ability to interact effectively in mixed cultural settings at school, in the community, and in the workplace;
- critical thinking skills required for recognizing bias and inequity;
- problem-solving strategies for counteracting prejudice and discrimination in many contexts, including the school;
- cultural enrichment through the arts, literature, and other cultural forms of expression;
- equitable levels of academic achievement among students of all ethnocultural backgrounds.

Achievement of these outcomes involves almost every aspect of the school program. Important components of a school-wide approach to antiracist education include culturally and linguistically sensitive procedures for reception, assessment, and placement (see Chapter 3), an inclusive school environment (see Chapter 4), classrooms that foster a sense of community (see Chapter 5), teachers who use a variety of instructional strategies to meet the learning needs of all their students (see Chapter 6), a curriculum that includes diverse cultural perspectives (see Chapter 8), and equitable assessment policies and practices (see Chapter 9). In all of these aspects of the school program, antiracist education may begin with small changes to traditional practice, and gradually move along a continuum towards transformation, as described in the next section.

APPROACHES TO ANTIRACIST EDUCATION

There are several approaches to antiracist education. Massey describes six stages, from 'Laissez-faire' to 'Anti-Racist Multiculturalism' (Massey, 1991) while Banks identifies four levels of implementation, from the 'Contributions Approach' to the 'Decision-Making and Social Action Approach' (Banks, 1988b).

The four approaches described here are based on Banks' model. These approaches may evolve as a series of developmental stages. However, schools and individual teachers may have different starting points, and a school or a teacher may use several aspects of different approaches simultaneously.

'Food, festivals and famous men'

Educators in North America often use this term, or 'the 3 Fs of multiculturalism' to characterize an approach that focusses on superficial aspects of culture and is often sexist. In Britain, this approach is often called the 3Ss version of multiculturalism: 'Saris, samosas, and steel bands'. Common features of this approach include the staging of school concerts featuring the music, dance, and traditional clothing of various cultures, and the invitation to parents to contribute 'ethnic foods' for these special events. These events can be a lot of fun but are not usually regarded as essential to the serious business of education, and have little impact on the curriculum. Also, the approach is based on a limited definition of 'culture', and can trivialize the concept through an emphasis on the exotic and the different. A major problem is that 'Multicultural Night' usually highlights only the cultures that are seen as 'different'; the mainstream culture is not considered as one of the diverse cultures in the school, because it is seen as 'normal'.

Another feature of this approach is the observation of special days such as Martin Luther King Day, or the celebration of festivals such as Chinese New Year. This is a positive development, of value to all the students in the school. However, unless these events are given similar prominence to 'mainstream' festivals such as Halloween or Christmas, which are sometimes the focus of several weeks of classroom work in elementary schools, these special days are merely 'tokens' of diversity and can serve to underline the fact that some cultures and heroes are peripheral to the mainstream activity of the school.

Avoid some of the pitfalls...

To make these special events more meaningful, teachers can:

- Make sure that examples of traditional dance, music, food and clothing from the mainstream culture are included in multicultural celebrations and events.
- Recognize the difference between special events and daily life. For example, women and girls who wear saris for special occasions probably wear suits to the office, and jeans or a uniform to school.
- Include some classroom activities to explore the significance of special days or festivals. For example, develop parallel themes such as 'Spring Festivals' or 'Days of Reflection and Atonement'.
- Include women among the heroes.
- Include heroes associated with resistance as well as those who represent success in mainstream terms.

The 'add-on' approach

This approach is a response to the under-representation of some cultural and racial groups in the curriculum. In response, special stand-alone units are added to the curriculum. Some of these new units are devoted to a specific culture or geographic region, and are especially common in social studies. Examples are units on 'Native People of Canada', 'African American Inventors and Scientists', 'Heroes of Latin America', or 'Black History Month'. Other units are devoted to a theme that examines a concept in several cultures or geographic locations. For example, the cooking class might include a unit on 'Foods of the World', while the sewing class might study 'Clothing Around the World'. Meanwhile, in the Social Studies class, children study examples of 'Housing Around the World' or 'Heroes from Many Cultures', and music teachers add 'Songs from Many Cultures'. In literature, students read 'Folk Tales and Legends from Around the World'; at the secondary level they might read stories and poems reflecting 'Our Multicultural Heritage', or study a novel or play related to 'The Black Experience'.

While this approach is a major advance on the unexamined, assimilationist, 'colour-blind' approach of earlier decades, it has serious limitations. For example, students do not learn to view diversity as part of a multicultural mainstream; rather, they learn to view the presence and experiences of cultures other than the dominant culture as an appendage to the core curriculum (Banks, 1988a). Cultures other than the dominant culture are often viewed from a mainstream perspective; for example, the arrival of European colonizers and settlers in other parts of the world is often viewed from the point of view of the heroic explorers and brave settlers, rather than from the point of view of the people who were already there. Their heroic acts of resistance, and the impact of the European conquest on their cultures and systems of government, may receive little or no acknowledgement. In spite of good intentions, the add-on approach may actually promote stereotypical views of specific cultures and, far from making students of minority racial and cultural groups feel more accepted, this approach often makes them feel more singled out. Also, the approach does not address important issues such as racism and inequality, and does not encourage students to question existing stereotypes and power relationships.

Avoid some of the pitfalls...

Careful planning and selection of content and resources may help to minimize problems and keep the process of curriculum development moving forward. For example:

- Check the perspectives and images presented in curriculum guidelines and learning materials. The students themselves, as well as their parents and other community members, may be able to help with this.
- Make sure that multicultural themes such as 'Housing Around the World' include parallel examples from different countries, such as urban and rural housing from equivalent social strata. If students look at a picture of a shanty

town in an African country, make sure that they also see a picture of a run-down slum or tumbledown rural cottage or shack in Canada, the United States, or Britain. If the students see examples of high-rise apartments or affluent suburbs in developed countries, show them similar examples from cities and suburbs in countries such as Nigeria, India, China, and Colombia as well.

In spite of its limitations, this approach represents progress. Banks comments, 'I think it's OK to start with Black History Month, as long as you don't stop there. And I think it's fine to start by adding good books to the existing curriculum… You can't transform the curriculum overnight. It took 300 years to get the current curriculum structure — the Renaissance, the Middle Ages — and it's going to take a long time to transform the curriculum into new patterns' (Banks, interviewed by Brandt, 1994: 28).

Transformation

In this approach, the curriculum is transformed through the integration of multicultural content across the curriculum, and through the inclusion of multiple perspectives on specific topics, events, or problems.

Instead of adding 'stand-alone' units to the curriculum, teachers integrate multicultural content into every unit of work. Examples from a variety of cultures are used in a matter-of-fact way to illustrate concepts in different subject areas, without drawing self-conscious attention to them as examples of 'multiculturalism'. Content integration helps students to see cultural diversity as 'normal', and to recognize fundamental commonalities among cultures, as well as interesting differences. Students are presented with models of competence and excellence from many cultural and racial backgrounds. Teachers also draw on the cultural experience and knowledge of the students as a resource.

Multicultural content across the curriculum

Multicultural content can be integrated into many areas of the curriculum. For example:

- Children in kindergarten and the primary grades play with dolls, toys and games that reflect a variety of cultural and racial backgrounds. Their parents help the teacher to find and select appropriate resources.
- Students in a music class listen to lullabies from several cultural backgrounds, and talk about the common elements and purpose as well as the different tone systems, instruments, and musical conventions.
- Students in a cooking class learn about the need for protein in the diet and learn about the many different ways that various cultures supply protein in their food. They also learn about some of the environmental, religious and cultural factors that underlie the dietary practices of different groups. Stu-

dents create a display of 'protein foods' using advertisements and labels from a variety of sources and in different languages.

- Students in a mathematics class examine geometric and number concepts in textile patterns and architectural designs from many places and cultures. Students bring in examples, photographs, books, and magazines to illustrate the themes.
- Textbooks include examples and illustrations of people of diverse backgrounds in a variety of roles, presenting students with models of competence from a variety of backgrounds and both genders in a routine and matter-of-fact way.

Scientists and scientific achievements

Gather some biographical information on noted scientists from a variety of cultural backgrounds. Provide the following scenario and instructions, using the Jigsaw technique for organizing group work (see 'Co-operative Learning' in Chapter 5):

A new stamp

The Post Office plans to design a new series of stamps to celebrate the achievements of scientists. The Post Office has asked the public to recommend the names of people from various cultural backgrounds who have made a contribution to science. Whose name would you recommend?

(1) In your group, each of you will choose a different scientist and read some information about his or her life and achievements.
(2) Share your information with your group.
(3) Which of these scientists do you think the Post Office should honour with a new stamp? Why?
(4) Choose your personal favourite from the list of names.
(5) Write a letter to the Post Office or to the editor of the local newspaper, recommending that this scientist be honoured with a special stamp, and explaining why.

Note: The activity can be adapted to different curriculum areas by focussing on writers, musicians, athletes, political leaders, human rights activists, or artists.

The curriculum is further transformed by the inclusion of several perspectives. For example, a traditional unit titled 'The Discovery of the Americas', focussing mainly on the exploits of Europeans and viewing events from their perspective, might alter its perspective and begin from the point of view of the indigenous peoples who were already there, having 'discovered' the Americas many thousands of years before. Students learn that the arrival of the Europeans in the Americas can be viewed from the perspective of the Europeans, who gained new lands, wealth, adventure, and fame, and from the point of view of the indigenous peoples, who lost land, language and culture, their independence, and even their lives. *Rethinking Columbus*, a special issue of *Rethinking Schools*, is a helpful resource for this curriculum unit (Bigelow et al., 1991). Additional examples of themes and activities involving multiple perspectives are provided in Chapter 8.

In some subject areas such as social studies and language arts, the amount of new material is significant, and teachers have to 'move [the] European perspective over to the side to make room for other cultural perspectives that must be included' (Lee, interviewed by Miner, 1994: 19). However, 'moving to the side' does not mean 'setting aside' or 'eliminating'; the European cultural heritage and European perspectives will still be clearly present, sharing the stage in a balanced way with many others.

Social action

In this approach, the focus of antiracist education is on teaching students how to effect social change inside and outside the school. The curriculum deals directly with issues of bias, prejudice, and discrimination, and students learn how to think critically about 'taken for granted' institutions, practices, and beliefs. Students also learn how to take action related to problems such as biased texts and other resources, or other inequities in the school and local community.

The Christmas concert

Many schools have a December concert where students sing Christmas carols and songs, perform plays and skits related to the Christmas theme, and sometimes present a Nativity play. A teacher could organize some group discussion about whether this event is inclusive of all the cultures and religious groups represented in the school. The students then gather information by surveying a representative sample of students, staff, and community members about their opinions on the purpose and content of an end-of-year concert. The students synthesize, record, analyze, and evaluate the information they gather, and then take action by writing a report and recommendations, and presenting these to the different classes in the school, the school principal, the student council, and the Parent–Teacher Association. In addition to developing the students' skills for full participation in a democratic society, this activity incorporates a variety of cross-curricular skills.

Students as concerned citizens

[At] the social change stage, . . . the curriculum helps lead to changes outside of the school. We actually go out and change the nature of the community we live in. For example, kids might become involved in how the media portray people, and start a letter-writing campaign about news that is negatively biased. Kids begin to see this as a responsibility that they have to change the world.

I think about a group of elementary school kids who wrote to the manager of the store about the kinds of games and dolls they had. That's a long way from having some dinner and dances that represent an 'exotic' form of life.

In essence, in anti-racist education we use knowledge to empower people and to change their lives. (Lee, interviewed by Miner, 1994: 20).

Images on television

Help older students to recognize and challenge subtle forms of bias and stereotyping by giving them a focussed viewing assignment:

- Organize students in groups, and make each group responsible for a different television channel.
- Give each group member a specific viewing assignment: for example, one student watches a news program, another watches an evening drama show, another watches two half-hour situation comedies, and another watches 20 different commercials.
- Give students a chart to complete by adding a check mark (Ú) in the appropriate box as they watch their assigned programs.
- Next day, students meet in their groups to share their information and compile it into one chart. Each group reports the finding to the whole class
- Each group writes a letter and a report with specific recommendations to the appropriate television channel or to the entertainment editor of the local newspaper. Send a covering letter of your own, explaining the purpose of the project.

	Main roles: news anchor, hero/heroine, most important or powerful figure in a commercial	Minor roles: news and weather reporters, minor characters and 'sidekicks', victims, minor characters in a commercial	Bad Guys: criminals and wrongdoers, villains and fools, negative characters in a commercial
African			
East Asian			
South Asian			
Latin American			
Middle Eastern or Arab			
White or European			
Male			
Female			

Antiracism work is often challenging and sometimes discouraging, so it is important to promote enthusiasm, optimism, and fellowship. One way to do this is to designate and celebrate 'antiracism week'. This works best if every class does some work on antiracism, using a cross-curricular, integrative approach. For example, students could make posters in the art class, create plays in the drama class, collect and present surveys and statistical data in the mathematics class, write essays, poems, and stories in the English class, and study the work of human rights activists from around the world in the social studies program. The school's antiracism leadership group or club could organize special assemblies and displays, and honour the antiracist work of individual students and teachers. It would be a good idea to invite parents and community members to participate.

CONCLUSION

Antiracist education important for all schools and for all students. All schools need to help all students to reach their academic potential, to learn how to live, study, work, and participate as citizens alongside people whose cultural and linguistic backgrounds may differ from their own, and to develop the global awareness that is essential for future citizens of the world. An important component of antiracist education is an inclusive curriculum, as described in the next chapter.

FURTHER READING AND RESOURCES FOR TEACHERS

Banks, J. A. (1988a [1981]) *Multiethnic Education, Theory and Practice*. Second edition. Newton, MA: Allyn and Bacon. Provides a philosophical orientation towards multicultural education, and makes suggestions for implementation in schools and classrooms.

Derman-Sparks, L. and the A.B.C. Task Force. (1989) *Anti-Bias Curriculum: Tools for Empowering Young Children*. Washington, DC: National Association for the Education of Young Children. A helpful book for teachers of pre-school and early elementary classes. Includes a useful list of resources.

Massey, I. (1991) *More Than Skin Deep: Developing Anti-Racist Multicultural Education in Schools*. London: Hodder and Stoughton. This book emphasizes the importance of antiracist education for all students, and provides a case study of implementation in an 'all-white' school.

CHAPTER 8

An Inclusive Curriculum

This chapter is about transforming the curriculum so that it becomes more inclusive in orientation and more equitable in effect. In the context of this chapter, 'curriculum' consists of the knowledge that students are expected to learn or to bring to the learning process. In an inclusive curriculum, the approach to knowledge is transformed so that students are exposed to multiple perspectives and experiences. An inclusive curriculum also helps students develop the skills for social criticism and action. Such a curriculum comes about not through minor adjustment, but major redesign.

The design process requires teachers to rethink accepted practice in terms of the content that students are required to learn, the cultural values that are promoted through the curriculum, the knowledge and experiences that students are expected to bring to school, and the selection of learning resources. The process is more rewarding if teachers work collaboratively with each other, with their students, and with parents and other community members to identify and solve problems.

This chapter begins by proposing some changes in curriculum content, and provides specific examples in various subject areas. Next there is a discussion of the way 'mainstream' cultural values may be transmitted through the traditional curriculum, and recommends that teachers adopt a more inclusive orientation towards the variety of beliefs that their students may hold or be familiar with. This is followed by some examples of the assumptions that the traditional curriculum may make about the knowledge and experiences of the students, as well as some suggestions on how to link new learning to students' prior knowledge and how to provide the necessary background knowledge. Next there are some suggestions on choosing resources for an inclusive curriculum. At the end of the chapter there is a checklist that students can use to assess the school as an inclusive multicultural environment.

CURRICULUM CONTENT

An inclusive curriculum does not eliminate traditional or European content, but places it alongside content and perspectives from other cultural backgrounds. Therefore, some traditional content will be dropped or reduced in order to make way for new material; essential content will be retained in order to develop central concepts and allow students to move ahead in the subject. New content will be selected that will capitalize on students' previous knowledge and experience and develop a more inclusive perspective; this may require teachers to become learners in order to gain the necessary knowledge.

Some teachers and parents may be concerned that an antiracist curriculum is socially divisive and potentially dangerous. They may fear that re-examining previous beliefs and practices may stir up anger among some groups, and threaten the identity and security of others. It is important, therefore, to maintain a balance among viewpoints, rather than to substitute one for another, and to avoid 'blaming' the descendants of previous generations for past injustice. In discussions with parents, students, and colleagues, point out that *not* addressing these issues in a constructive way, and failing to ensure a just society for all, is far more dangerous to everyone. Focus on the benefits to *all* groups of a just and harmonious society.

In the following pages, aspects of the traditional curriculum are contrasted with some approaches and activities that reflect a more inclusive orientation to knowledge. The examples are drawn from the following subject areas:

- arts education;
- language studies;
- literature;
- mathematics;
- science and technology;
- social studies.

TRANSFORMING THE CURRICULUM: ARTS EDUCATION

The Traditional Arts Curriculum   An Inclusive Curriculum

Most students have some experience with the arts, and barriers of language that may limit students' performance in other areas of the curriculum are less significant in the arts. However, opportunities for cultural enrichment are not always recognized, and some aspects of the program may conflict with students' cultural values. The following examples are drawn from physical and health education, visual arts, music and drama.

In an inclusive arts program, students learn to appreciate the artistic styles and traditions of many cultures, as well as their own. In addition, the program offers choices to students whose cultural values may be in conflict with some aspects of the program. For example:

Physical and health education provides excellent opportunities for social integration and language development. However, the program is not always sensitive to the needs and values of all students. For example, some recently arrived students may be unfamiliar with some of the games and sports that are played, and contact sports may not appeal to all students. Some students may be intimidated by the competitive atmosphere that exists in many physical education programs.

In an inclusive physical education program, there is a wide variety of sports, games, and physical activities available to students, and student have choices about the activities they will be involved in. Teachers welcome the introduction of sports, games, and dance that students from other countries may be able to demonstrate or teach to their peers. There is a balance of competitive and co-operative activities, and an emphasis on individual fitness and health as well as team sports.

TRANSFORMING THE CURRICULUM: ARTS EDUCATION

The Traditional Arts Curriculum	An Inclusive Curriculum
Some students may be reluctant to participate in the program if it is in conflict with their religious beliefs and cultural norms. For example, some students are not allowed to participate in co-educational sports or dance activities, and may have restrictions about the kind of clothing they may wear. The health education or sex education components of the program may cause extreme embarrassment and discomfort to some students, especially if it is taught in a co-educational setting, or if 'mainstream' values about dating and sex are presented as the norm.	In order to encourage participation by all cultural groups, parents are consulted about their expectations for their children. For example, teachers and parents might agree that female students may wear loose-fitting clothing rather than shorts or bathing suits. Schools that offer a co-educational program may decide to offer some or all of the program to single-sex classes.

The health education program includes diverse cultural perspectives and experiences: for example, the sex education component may be taught in single-sex classes, and dating is presented as only one way to find a life partner. In health and nutrition, eating meat is presented as one of the ways of including protein in the diet, and various cultural practices, rules, and taboos about food are explored for their sanitary and social significance. |
| In visual arts, students usually learn about technique by studying European art forms, and about art history by studying the work of European artists. Students recognize the names and some of the works of artists such as Michelangelo and Reubens, but learn little about art and artists from other cultural traditions. | In an inclusive visual arts program, students learn about art and artists from many cultures, including western art and European artists; they also learn how one cultural tradition borrows from another. Students are encouraged to work in the traditions of their own cultures as well as experiment with new forms of expression. They see, and are encouraged to produce, work that reflects cultural and racial diversity. |

TRANSFORMING THE CURRICULUM: ARTS EDUCATION

The Traditional Arts Curriculum

The work of female artists all over the world — especially work derived from the domestic sphere, such as textiles — is not accorded the same status as 'art' to which the artist (usually a male) has devoted a lifetime.

Students from some religious backgrounds may have little or no experience with representational art, or may be prohibited from depicting the human figure or animals.

An Inclusive Curriculum

Activities for an inclusive visual arts program

- Provide crayons and paints in a variety of true skin colours so that students can produce realistic representations of themselves, their families, and their communities.

- In Art History courses and projects, include a variety of cultures and a variety of forms such as architecture, clothing, and the decoration of the home and the person, as well as painting and sculpture.

- Give students opportunities to use or explore art forms from their own or other cultures: for example, Islamic design, Rangoli patterns, Chinese brush painting and calligraphy, Aboriginal styles of painting and carving, African styles of sculpture, masks, dolls, puppets, textile designs, jewellery and ceramics of many different styles and cultural origins. Encourage students to develop their own styles using a combination of traditional motifs and individual expression.

- In 'Artist in the Schools' projects, include artists of many different cultural backgrounds.

- Display a wide variety of students' art and illustrations and examples of art from around the world around the school.

- Encourage students to design notices and posters for cultural events or to promote an antiracism message throughout the school, using a variety of languages and artistic styles.

- Provide appropriate choices for students who may be uncomfortable with or prohibited from participating in some activities: for example, assignments in calligraphy, line pattern, texture, and colour may be offered instead of life drawing, and students can apply these skills in ceramics, textile and architectural design, page borders, title pages, posters, book marks and book covers, and other activities that do not require the depiction of humans or animals.

TRANSFORMING THE CURRICULUM: ARTS EDUCATION

The Traditional Arts Curriculum

Music education is often limited in scope, and most children have been exposed to only a narrow sample of the world's music. In daily life they are surrounded by popular contemporary music, commercial jingles, and theme music from television and movies, all within a Western tradition. Their musical education at school focusses mainly on Western classical and traditional music, and students learn to play instruments associated with this music. Many of the folk songs that students learn are from Britain, or reflect the experiences of British settlers in other parts of the world. Students' ears are trained to appreciate western forms in music, and other kinds of music, if included at all, are exotic or weird, and not to be considered on a par with Bach or Beethoven.

An Inclusive Curriculum

In an inclusive music program, students are exposed to many kinds of music in addition to western music, both classical or traditional and modern. Musical conventions and traditions vary enormously from one culture to another and they provide a rich source of material illustrating cultural diversity. By including some examples of music from different cultural traditions in the program, music education can help students to recognize that, while music is universal, its forms are not. For example, the human voice is a musical instrument all over the world, but singers of western opera, Chinese opera, classical *ghazals* and *ragas* from South Asia, the Islamic call to prayer, western rock music, Indian movie music, or Inuit throat music all use very different techniques. Also, the western concept of musical scales is not universal; other cultures have devised different scales and some use no scales at all, while some music, such as traditional African music, emphasizes rhythm more than melody (Walker, 1990). A study of different kinds of instruments would help students to see that although they vary, there are fundamental similarities in the technology (for instance, there are wind instruments, string instruments, and percussion instruments). For example:

TRANSFORMING THE CURRICULUM: ARTS EDUCATION

The Traditional Arts Curriculum

The prevalence of western music, both classical or traditional and modern, around the globe is testimony to its importance as a commercial commodity rather than its inherent superiority as music. Music education that restricts itself to only this musical tradition limits the opportunities that students might have for cultural enrichment, and may promote Eurocentric attitudes towards the music of other cultures.

Note: Some groups have beliefs that prohibit all or some forms of music. For example, some Muslim children may be allowed to sing but not to learn how to play an instrument.

An Inclusive Curriculum

Activities for an inclusive music program

- Explore the music of other cultures. Include the study of different tone systems, instruments, and the role of music in various cultures.
- Include vocal music, so that students can be involved in music without having to buy expensive instruments, and develop a lifelong joy of singing.
- Expand the student's horizons by including songs from a variety of cultural traditions. Students could also sing or listen to songs that promote social justice, some of which deal with issues related to race and culture (see Peterson, 1994).
- Help students to form groups interested in playing, singing, or listening to specific types of music.
- Play different kinds of music in the morning before school, and during other non-instructional time, over the public address system; students can play the role of DJ by providing a brief introduction to the music.
- With school music or choir groups, rehearse and record the national anthem in different cultural styles. Whenever the anthem is used in the school, different renditions could be featured, either live or on tape.
- Offer choices to students whose cultural values may be in conflict with some aspects of the program.

TRANSFORMING THE CURRICULUM: ARTS EDUCATION

The Traditional Arts Curriculum

Drama education tends to focus on the work of Western European and North American writers and performers. Shakespeare was a great playwright, and it is important for students in English-speaking countries to study and perform the works of Shakespeare and others writing in English, but there are other writers and other dramatic forms that students could explore as well.

Dramatic productions provide an important and enjoyable way for schools to show off the talents of teachers and students. However, the plays chosen for school performances are usually from the European or North American repertoire. In elementary schools, stories such as Snow White or Cinderella are often chosen for the class play. It is rare for a school to put on a play that has important roles for students of colour, who often have to play minor characters in stereotypical roles: for example, the character of Titubah in *The Crucible*.

An Inclusive Curriculum

An inclusive drama program provides opportunities for students to explore classical and modern dramatic forms from a variety of cultures, in addition to the works of Euripides, Shakespeare, Molière, and other European playwrights. For example, students could learn about Japanese *Noh* and *Kabuki* drama, classical Chinese opera, and the role of the *griot* as the keeper of oral history in many West African cultures.

Student activities such as improvisation, roleplays, student-scripted drama, and storytelling provide opportunities for students to explore issues relevant to their own lives, or to themes in specific subjects such as social studies. These activities could involve themes of social justice and equity. For example, students can prepare drama or storytelling activities for younger children, dealing with topics related to cultural diversity and equity in a way that is appropriate to the audience.

Activities for an inclusive drama program

- Experiment with non-traditional casting in school plays and other dramatic performances.
- Rather than producing one full-length play, select several shorter pieces from different cultural backgrounds. An additional benefit of this approach is that there are more roles, so that more students have a chance to be involved; moreover, each short play or excerpt could be produced by a different staff member and stage crew.
- Include the study of dramatic works and performers of diverse cultural backgrounds.

TRANSFORMING THE CURRICULUM: ARTS EDUCATION

The Traditional Arts Curriculum An Inclusive Curriculum

- Provide opportunities for students to improvise and write their own plays exploring different cultural experiences and dealing with themes in cultural diversity and equity.

- Give students the opportunity to experience, through role play and improvised drama, the experiences of different cultural groups. For example, students could roleplay the arrival of Columbus in the Americas, portraying the experiences, feelings, and responses of the Arawak population as well as the Europeans.

- Include many opportunities for different kinds of oral performance: oratory, storytelling, choral recitation, call-and-response styles of presentation, and poetry reading.

- Use multicultural literature as a source for drama activities. Older students may present performances to younger children in the local elementary school.

TRANSFORMING THE CURRICULUM: LANGUAGE STUDIES

The Traditional Curriculum	An Inclusive Curriculum
Schools need to consider what is meant by terms such as 'language', 'literacy', or 'standard English', which are often narrowly defined in the school curriculum. For example:	**In an inclusive, multilingual school,** all languages are seen as equally valid, and students' languages have a high profile in the school. For example:

The Traditional Curriculum text continues:

'Language' is often used as if it were synonymous with 'English', as in 'language development', 'language arts', or 'language skills'. The underlying assumption is that only English counts as 'language'. Similarly, 'literacy' usually means literacy in English, and 'reading and writing' refers to reading and writing in English — as if the reading and writing that the student may do in other languages were of no value (de la luz Reyes, 1992). When English is viewed as the only acceptable language for use in school, speakers of other languages are devalued, while monolingual English speakers are viewed as 'normal'.

Second and third language programs may be narrowly defined. When students learn a language other than English in the school, it is usually a European language such as French or German. Where students do have an opportunity to learn their heritage or ancestral languages, it is often after school or on weekends; these programs, good as they often are, do not have the same status as language programs that are included as part of the mainstream curriculum of the school.

An Inclusive Curriculum text continues:

- There is a multilingual orientation to language. For example, 'Language development' means development in the students' first languages. 'Second language development' or 'English language development' means development English. 'Literacy development' means literacy development in all languages, unless 'literacy skills in English' is specified.
- Students have opportunities to develop their first language at school, and all students have opportunities to learn community languages such as Punjab, Twi or Cantonese as well as European languages. Students read in their first language as well as in English, and bilingual projects and assignments are encouraged.

TRANSFORMING THE CURRICULUM: LANGUAGE STUDIES

The Traditional Curriculum	An Inclusive Curriculum
'Standard English' is often used as if it meant 'correct' or 'good' English. Students who speak other varieties of English often receive the message that their own language is substandard in some way, and may be regarded not as learners of standard English, but as English speakers who are careless or lazy. These students need teachers who value language variety while providing focussed instruction on the forms of standard English.	• Language variety is respected. Varieties of English and English-related creole languages have a place in the language and literature of the classroom. At the same time, students receive focussed instruction on the forms of standard English that are required for success at school.
The language program includes little instruction *about* language. Teachers and students in all classrooms talk about language — which usually means 'English' — in terms of organization, spelling, grammar, punctuation, and other conventions of writing . These are valid components of the language program, but the language program could also include Language Awareness activities designed to help students to develop a broader view of language, to become better language learners, and become more conscious of the many ways they use language, in the school and beyond (Hawkins, 1987).	• 'Standard' varieties of European languages such as Spanish or French are taught in a manner that does not devalue other varieties such as Latin American varieties of Spanish, or Caribbean, Canadian and African varieties of French.
	• Language Awareness activities are incorporated across the curriculum to help all students learn about language in general, about English in particular, and about each other's languages. For example, students might learn about the writing systems of different languages — and in so doing develop a better understanding of both the regularities and irregularities of English spelling.
	Teachers can refer to their students as expert informants on various aspects of language awareness. Acknowledging the students' expertise in this way effectively changes the 'balance of power' in the language classroom: the teacher no longer has all of the knowledge, and English-speaking students are not always advantaged.

TRANSFORMING THE CURRICULUM: LANGUAGE STUDIES

The Traditional Curriculum

Awareness of language is especially important in multilingual schools because it helps students to value their own and each other's languages, and challenges linguistic prejudice and parochialism.

An Inclusive Curriculum

Many language topics and activities are interdisciplinary in nature and can be used to support curriculum integration. For example:

Mathematics and social studies: graphs and charts about language distribution, or percentage and ratio problems related to literacy statistics;

Social studies: the movements of peoples that contributed to English and the evolution of varieties of English; English around the world; how children learn language; how to raise bilingual children; language rights and language conflict, locally and around the world;

Computer studies: various uses of technology for communication;

Drama: oral performance and storytelling in English and other languages;

Visual arts: calligraphy, printing, and graphic arts;

Science: Latin and Greek nomenclature; symbols, acronyms, and abbreviations.

TRANSFORMING THE CURRICULUM: LITERATURE

The Traditional Curriculum	An Inclusive Curriculum
The literature program is one of the most powerful in shaping students' attitudes and informing them, through vicarious experience, about the world they live in. The traditional program has some limitations when viewed from an antiracist perspective. For example:	**To provide multiple perspectives**, and help students develop a more balanced view of the world, keep some of the classics and old favourites, add literature from diverse cultures dealing with similar themes, and teach students how to read literature or view media critically. For example:
The literature program is often narrowly conceptualized, especially in secondary schools. 'Literature' usually means 'literature in English,' mostly by British and American men, about the experiences of white English-speaking people.' In secondary schools, the 'literary canon' celebrated in English programs consists mainly of Greek and Roman mythology and classic British and North American works reflecting the experiences and values of people of the dominant culture. This Eurocentric approach to literature provides students with a limited perspective on literature and the world.	• Diversify the literary canon. There is no shortage of good literature by writers from diverse cultural backgrounds. Kezwer's detailed bibliography (1995) provides information on multicultural books for children. Jobe (1993) focusses on books for children aged 9 to 12. For teachers of older students, Oliver (1994) provides a list of titles from a variety of cultures, as well as suggestions on how to teach literature from a multicultural perspective.

TRANSFORMING THE CURRICULUM: LITERATURE

The Traditional Curriculum

The books that students read at school may reinforce cultural stereotypes. From a very early age, children are exposed to stereotypical material in children's literature, as well as in other media such as children's cartoons on television, or computer games. From this material they learn about male and female roles; they also learn that beauty, goodness, and heroism are associated with youth and with the physical attributes of white people.

Students may also learn that people of colour are rarely important enough to be in a story, and if they are, they play villains or peripheral roles such as servants. Poor people are often present but not in central roles unless they escape poverty through luck or magic or their own individual efforts (not by collective action). Although these biases are seldom intentional, they can have a lasting impact on the students' self-esteem and world view.

An Inclusive Curriculum

- Develop multicultural themes through literature. Choose novels, stories and poems that provide a multicultural perspective on universal human values and practices. For example, Ngugi's *Weep Not, Child* explores some of the same themes as *A Tale of Two Cities* (Ngugi, 1985 [1964]). You can also create new theme units: topics such as 'Birthdays', 'Families', 'Coming of Age', 'Heroes and Role Models', 'Getting Married' and so on provide opportunities for students to share and understand cultural diversity in a way that emphasizes the underlying commonality of human experience. Jobe (1993) and Kezwer (1995) provide guidance on multicultural themes that can be explored through children's books.

- Introduce diverse perspectives through children's literature. When you introduce children to traditional stories such as Red Riding Hood and Cinderella, use children's literature that deals with the same situation in another cultural context or from a different perspective. Alternative perspectives help children to explore the social messages that traditional stories convey about, for example, the roles of men and women, the lives of the poor, and so on. For instance, *Flossie and the Fox* (McKissack, 1986) is an African American version of Red Riding Hood, with a twist: this little girl needs no woodcutter to rescue her; instead, she outfoxes the fox with her own wit and courage. Students could be invited to write or tell their own alternative versions of stories; this activity is appropriate for older students as well as young children.

TRANSFORMING THE CURRICULUM: LITERATURE

The Traditional Curriculum

Some works studied in secondary school English classes portray individuals of some cultures, religions, social classes, or racial backgrounds in limited or stereotypical ways that are reflective of the time in which they were written: for example, the portrayal of Shylock in *The Merchant of Venice* or the portrayal of Jim in *Huckleberry Finn*. Even in books that attempt to deal with issues of racism, cultures other than the dominant culture are often viewed from a mainstream perspective. For example, *To Kill a Mockingbird* is studied in many high school English classes. This book, although intended to raise awareness of the unequal treatment of black people in the Southern United States, has some limitations: it was written by white writer and has a white hero, and the black man he defends is helpless, passive, and much less well developed as a character.

An Inclusive Curriculum

- Use literature study circles. Instead of having everyone read the same book at the same pace, provide four to six copies each of several different books. These may be thematically related. Include some books that the second language learners in the class will be able to read. Samway and Whang (1996) suggest presenting a book-talk, after which the students choose the book they will read. Meet periodically with each book group, helping the students to set targets for reading a certain number of pages per day, organizing group discussions, and giving directions for a written responses, encouraging children to relate events in the story to their own experience and to view them from other perspectives.

TRANSFORMING THE CURRICULUM: LITERATURE

The Traditional Curriculum

An Inclusive Curriculum

- Help students to become critical readers. It is not necessary to exclude all literature that may have negative or stereotypical portrayals of different cultural groups. You can use some of this literature, in spite of its limitations, in order to confront issues of racism and sexism, and help students recognize and challenge stereotypes in literature. For example, students might discuss how *To Kill a Mockingbird* or *Huckleberry Finn* might be different if written from the black character's perspective, or how *The Merchant of Venice* might be different if it had been written by a Jew. Never ignore the issues: students draw their own conclusions when teachers do not face up to problems of bias or examples of racism.

  Even young children can learn to be critical readers. Campbell (1983) suggests helping children to write book reviews that are published in the classroom and shared with others in the school. Use concrete examples to get children thinking and talking about what is 'fair' or 'not fair': for instance, ask questions such as, *What would you do if your teacher decided that children with brown hair couldn't go on a trip? Would that be fair?* Schniedewind and Davidson (1998) provide many activities designed to promote this kind of discussion.

  Help students develop some simple guidelines for choosing books, and publish their reviews. The teacher or an older student can write the review for younger children; read it to them and invite their reactions before sharing it with others.

TRANSFORMING THE CURRICULUM: MATHEMATICS

The Traditional Curriculum

Curriculum bias may not seem relevant to mathematics teachers, who often feel that their subject is neutral. However, rethinking the mathematics curriculum from an antiracist perspective leads to the conclusion that there are many neglected opportunities to address issues related to cultural diversity, and many omissions that are not neutral in effect. For example:

The tasks and problems that students deal with in the mathematics curriculum are often not reflective of cultural diversity. The items being counted, manipulated, measured, or calculated, and the names of people and places used in the problems usually relate to the cultural experiences of the mainstream.

There are few images of people of diverse ethnocultural backgrounds and both genders as problem-solvers and models of competence in mathematics.

An Inclusive Curriculum

There are opportunities in mathematics to help students develop see cultural diversity in a positive and a matter-of-fact way, and to learn some important cultural content along with the mathematical skills. You can incorporate multicultural content and raise students' awareness of equity issues by including some of these activities:

- Include problems with multicultural content. Rewrite some of the problems using a variety of cultural contexts, conveying that the same mathematical operations can be used to solve problems in many cultural settings, and making students other than those of the dominant culture 'experts' as well. For example, some of the problems can be couched in terms of the amount of rice required to feed the guests at a wedding, or the cost of a pound of mangoes. The names of people and places can reflect a multicultural community and a diverse world, and the examples and illustrations can depict problem solvers of all backgrounds and both genders. Some questions could be written by groups of students, featuring sports or other contexts familiar to different cultural groups; representatives of those groups teach the rules of the game or other cultural information required so that others can deal with the mathematical problem.

TRANSFORMING THE CURRICULUM: MATHEMATICS

The Traditional Curriculum	An Inclusive Curriculum
Problems seldom relate to equity issues. Mathematics can be an important tool in antiracist education because equity is a mathematical concept, as well as a moral one. In most mathematics programs, however, students spend a lot of time making calculations such as the ratio of red apples to green ones, or the percentage of students who scored above the average. How much more would they learn about the world around them if they were sometimes engaged in solving mathematical problems that involve equity issues such as the representation of different groups in various aspects of the school program, or the per capita consumption of certain resources in different regions of the world?	• Teach about mathematical principles and application in many contexts. Examine geometric and number concepts in textile patterns and architectural designs from around the world. Integrate mathematics, geography, and fine arts through the analysis of symmetry in folk art such as quilts and rugs. Compare calendars, number systems, and recording devices from several ancient and modern civilizations. Students could learn about games from different cultures that use numbers and a variety of counting or scoring devices, and look at some common concepts. (For more ideas, see Zaslavsky, 1994, 1996; Burnett and Irons, 1993; Krause, 1986.) • Involve students in demographic surveys. Teach students how to create surveys to find out the countries of origin or languages represented in the class, and record the information in a number of ways: as a graph, as an expression of ratio, as a percentage, as a fraction, and so on. Students can also use census and immigration data in the same way that social scientists use them: to make projections or predict trends, or to identify disparities and needs, such as the need to balance an aging population through immigration. Involve students in research projects on Arab, South Asian, and South and Central American mathematicians and mathematical innovations. For example, the concept of zero is believed to have come to Greece from India via contact with the Arab world. Ancient cultures in South America also used this concept. Also, the vocabulary of mathematics indicates the origins of many concepts in the Arab and Muslim world: *algebra, algorithm*, etc. Useful sources for this kind of activity include CD-ROM encyclopedias.

TRANSFORMING THE CURRICULUM: MATHEMATICS

The Traditional Curriculum	An Inclusive Curriculum
	• Teach students how to apply mathematics to equity issues. Assign groups of students to develop, conduct, and record and analyze the results of surveys that reveal information on equity issues, and how to present the data convincingly to others. Suitable topics for investigation include the ethnocultural composition of the student population and the school staff; the representation of languages in the student population and in various aspects of the school program; the representation of males and females or specific ethnocultural groups in the student population and in in specific aspects of the school program. Students could also use the techniques of data collection and analysis to examine the representation of different ethnocultural groups in the media.
	• Include problems with global content. Help students to develop a global perspective by using relevant content in some of the problems that students have to solve. For example, students could work with international data from United Nations agencies or OECD in some of the problems involving percentage, ratio, and graphs. Suitable topics include educational spending or the provision of public health care. Students could analyze how the results differ if expenditures are reported in a variety of ways: e.g., as total expenditure, as per capita spending, as per capita spending as a % of the gross national product, or as % of GNP compared with another national expenditures such as defence. Other topics of global significance include the distribution of the world's population, resources, and consumption; the loss of the world's forests or growth of the deserts over a period of time and projected into the future, expressed as percentage of global land area or in any other way that students find meaningful; global population statistics analyzed in terms of distribution by region or continent, age group, levels of education, gender, race, language group, etc.

TRANSFORMING THE CURRICULUM: SCIENCE AND TECHNOLOGY

The Traditional Curriculum

Science and technology are often considered to be factual, objective, and empirical in nature, and therefore neutral and 'culture-free'. But no area of human activity is separate from its social context. For example:

Science is involved in racism. Far from being uninvolved in issues of race and culture, science has been used to justify racist beliefs (Gould, 1981; Young, 1987). Science and technology were used in Nazi Germany, where the scientific method was meticulously used to find and document an effective technology for genocide. Science and technology are not neutral, and a science curriculum that deals only with natural laws and phenomena avoids dealing with important moral issues such as how science is used in society.

Science and technology are narrowly defined. For example, the inventions of women receive little recognition. Textile technology, agriculture, food processing, the design and manufacture of food vessels and other domestic utensils, and the development of a pharmacopoeia and the healing arts can probably be attributed to women in non-technological societies all over the world. These inventions have affected the lives of every person on earth, and now form the basis of major industries and fields of study.

An Inclusive Curriculum

You can offer your students a more inclusive curriculum by broadening the traditional concepts of science and technology and viewing these fields of human development from a variety of perspectives. For example:

- Diversify the image of the scientist.
  The science curriculum may be more more attractive to minority to students, and culturally enriching for everyone, if it includes the achievements of scientists and mathematicians, ancient and modern, in many parts of the world. Much of modern Western science and technology depends on discoveries and inventions made in Chinese, Arab, Indian, and African cultures. Important contributions to science include the Chinese inventions of paper and printing, explosives, and the navigational compass; theories of Islamic scientists about the circulation of blood and the movements of the solar system that predate Harvey, Copernicus, and Galileo; the use of a steel-making technology in East Africa 1500–2000 years ago, and many other African achievements in science and technology (Hodson, 1993; Van Sertima, 1983).

  Choose or create texts and other resources that counteract the image of the scientist as a white male by providing examples of female scientists and scientists of colour. Include scientists whose work contributed to major innovations or discoveries that are usually credited to one person.

TRANSFORMING THE CURRICULUM: SCIENCE AND TECHNOLOGY

The Traditional Curriculum

Minority groups are under-represented in science and technology. One reason may be that science is taught in ways that makes the discipline unattractive or inaccessible to many minority students. According to Hodson (1993: 687):

It seems that the science curriculum does little to raise the self-esteem of children from some ethnic minority groups and is seen by many as irrelevant to their experiences, needs, interests, and aspirations. Among the several causal factors are the following:

- *Science curriculum content is often exclusively western in orientation.*

- *Many curriculum materials are covertly racist, just as many are still covertly sexist.*

- *Teaching and learning methods are sometimes inappropriate to the cultural traditions of minorities.*

- *The image of the scientist as the controller, manipulator, and exploiter of the environment is in conflict with the cultural values of some children.*

An Inclusive Curriculum

- Provide role models.
  Invite people of many different cultural backgrounds who work in a scientific or technological field to come and talk to students about the work they do, how and why they became scientists, and the ethics of science and technology.

- Emphasize interdependence in science.
  Explain that many of the greatest discoveries did not come about as the result of one scientist's independent work, and that discoveries credited to Newton, Galileo, and other great scientists often built on the work of others, not always European, who advanced knowledge to a point at which the 'great discovery' could be made.

- Value intuition and imagination.
  Do not over-emphasize 'the scientific method' as the only way that scientists think and work; include some discussion of the importance of intuition and great leaps of imagination in some of the great scientific discoveries.

TRANSFORMING THE CURRICULUM: SCIENCE AND TECHNOLOGY

The Traditional Curriculum

An Inclusive Curriculum

- Include 'ordinary science'.
  Expand the concept of science and technology to include important but undocumented innovations related to the domestic and agricultural needs of ordinary people. Encourage students to view modern technological developments such as electricity, the computer, the pharmaceutical industry, or genetic engineering, as the most recent steps in a continuum that began with ancient knowledge and skills such as the use of fire, the healing properties of plants, the manufacture of textiles, the observation of the planets and the seasons and the development of a calendar, and other achievements of unknown inventors and technologists all over the world.

- Develop social awareness.
  Discuss important social issues related to science. For example include some discussion of how the problem-solving approach to science, without an awareness of the societal impact of new inventions and processes, can lead to long-term problems and disasters. Use examples such as Chernobyl and Bhopal, the effects of oil spills in the Arctic, or the disappearance of flora and fauna in many parts of the world.

TRANSFORMING THE CURRICULUM: SCIENCE AND TECHNOLOGY

The Traditional Curriculum

An Inclusive Curriculum

- Develop a critical awareness of 'scientific racism'. Help students to become critically aware of how science has contributed to racism, through the invention of the concept of race as a biological classification system, and racist theories about intelligence and aptitudes. Discuss the concept of race as an artificial, pseudo-scientific classification of humans that emphasizes superficial differences resulting from adaptation to specific environments, rather than the fundamental similarities among human beings that are so much greater than these differences. It is important for students to lean that there are greater differences within a group than among the different racial groups, and many biologists no longer use race as a classification system (Hodson, 1993).

TRANSFORMING THE CURRICULUM: SOCIAL STUDIES

The Traditional Curriculum

A Eurocentric curriculum views the world from a European perspective. For example, the concept of 'civilization' is usually associated with Europe, and the study of ancient history traditionally focusses on Greece and Rome. When Egypt is studied, it is seldom related to the African continent.

The history of continents other than Europe is often presented as if it began when Europeans arrived. For example, the study of African history often starts with colonization and the slave trade. This is a distortion of the total African experience, which includes epic sagas, inventions, and monuments that parallel those of Greece and Rome. Indeed, Africa is thought to be the birthplace of humankind, and therefore of all civilizations. Oppression and degradation are important parts of a people's story, and we can all learn from these experiences, but they are not the whole story.

An Inclusive Curriculum

To help students to view the world from a variety of cultural perspectives, and to challenge social inequities, incorporate some of these topics, themes, and activities into the social studies program:

- Teach about ancient civilizations. To promote positive images of cultures whose history has traditionally been omitted or distorted, delete some of the European content, and substitute units on the ancient civilizations of other peoples and continents. Use parallel themes to develop continuity of concept and language.

- Teach cross-cultural themes. You can help students to see that human beings around the world have the same needs and basic values by teaching cross-cultural themes. Depending on the age of the learners, some of these topics might be appropriate: the lives of children; games, sports, and other leisure activities; myths, legends, and folk tales related to particular themes; school; families; work; agriculture, trade, and the rise of cities; housing, clothing, and other material aspects of culture as responses to the environment; social class, caste, and slavery; the role of women; cultural practices associated with childbirth, the naming of children, marriage, death, and other important life events; religious beliefs and practices.

TRANSFORMING THE CURRICULUM: SOCIAL STUDIES

The Traditional Curriculum

Modern 'third world' countries are sometimes presented in distorted ways. For example, most students are aware of population problems and widespread poverty in South Asia, but they may not be aware that South Asia has an ancient history, an awe-inspiring tradition in architecture, and a rich heritage of classical, religious, and contemporary music and literature, or that many of the industrialized world's engineers, lawyers and doctors are from South Asia.

The history of indigenous peoples is often viewed from a European perspective. For example, in Canada, there is often a "museum" approach that is mainly concerned with traditional legends and traditional ways of life. Students learn much less about the systematic destruction of those traditional ways of life as a consequence of the European invasion.

An Inclusive Curriculum

• Teach about global interdependence. Make explicit the interdependence of human historical and economic development. Provide opportunities for students to learn that the 'development' of the west and the 'underdevelopment' of the 'Third World' are strongly interrelated. For example, a discussion of the industrial revolution, commonly presented as a story of the ingenuity of a group of white male scientists and inventors, could include information about how colonization and the slave trade financed it, how the displacement and exploitation of a new class of urban labourers fuelled it, and how the largely unrecognized domestic work of unenfranchized women supported it.

  In a discussion of natural resources and other environmental issues, provide a balanced global view. For instance, deforestation is a shared responsibility, and hunger in some countries is directly related to over-consumption in others.

• Teach about cultural conflict. Explore different cultural values involved in conflicts, local and global, historical and contemporary. For example, students growing up in North America need an understanding of the perspectives of First Nations cultures, how these perspectives were and are in conflict with the values of other cultures in North America, and how the values of the dominant culture became entrenched in the law. Encourage students to discuss alternative solutions to these conflicts.

TRANSFORMING THE CURRICULUM: SOCIAL STUDIES

The Traditional Curriculum

History often consists of the exploits of monarchs, religious and political leaders, entrepreneurs, and explorers — almost all men, almost all from the highest socioeconomic levels of their societies, and almost all white. This serves to discount the lives of most people, especially women, the poor, and cultural minorities.

An Inclusive Curriculum

• Teach about the lives of ordinary people. Help students to view society and history from many perspectives, not only from the point of view of the rulers and leaders whose words and deeds are recorded. History includes those whose contributions to and participation in historical events have been largely unchronicled: for example, the role of women as producers of most of the world's food, or the role that North America's First Peoples played in assisting the first Europeans to survive and learn how to live on the land.

• Teach about democracy and human rights. Discuss with all students, whenever the opportunity arises, the value of democracy. Make sure that students understand the relationship between democracy and the law: for example, the equality of men and women, the rights of children, and basic human rights are explicit in the law — even though all citizens may not agree with these concepts. Explain that cultural practices that detract from the rights of others are not morally or legally acceptable. At least once each school year, hold a special assembly or devote a designated school period to 'Rights and Responsibilities'.

  Celebrate the lives of human rights activists around the world. Study local human rights issues as well; make sure that all students are familiar with the human rights legislation or code that is in force in your jurisdiction and that they understand the relationship between this legislation, your school district's policy on ethnocultural equity, and the school rules or code of behaviour. Make sure that all students know how to use the process for initiating a complaint about racial or sexual harassment, within and outside the school.

CULTURAL VALUES

A Eurocentric curriculum is assimilationist in effect, if not always in intent. Values of the dominant culture are assumed to be universal, or are promoted on the assumption that they should be. As a result, students of other backgrounds may find it difficult to relate to a curriculum that seems to contradict or threaten the value system that they have grown up with. For example, themes in language arts, family studies and personal life management, physical and health education, social studies, and other subjects at both elementary and secondary level often involve discussion of issues such as gender roles, family roles and relationships, the rights of children, courtship and marriage, sexuality and birth control, and personal life goals. In these discussions, some students may not share the attitudes and experiences that may be assumed or promoted in classroom discussions. For instance, a discussion of 'dating' may be conducted as if this were the only way that males and females could interact and find mates. This kind of one-dimensional discussion validates the cultural values and practices of the mainstream while, by omission or by inference, bringing into question the values and practices of families whose teenage children interact with the opposite sex only in very closely supervised situations, or of parents who plan to arrange their children's marriages.

Some students, anxious to 'fit in' at school, or attracted by the version of the 'mainstream' lifestyle they see on television, are very troubled by the conflict between mainstream values and the traditional values of their homes and communities. Immigrant parents, in particular, are often anxious to preserve aspects of their former lives in the way they raise their children. Concerned that they will lose their children to the new culture, they may restrict their activities more than they would even in the homeland, where their values are generally upheld in the wider community.

It is important that the school does not contribute to these conflicts by presenting one view of how life should be lived. Instead, the school can help students to see that there are choices, and that each comes with benefits and costs. For example, students whose parents give them a great deal of independence may also expect their children to take on responsibilities in the home, or to take paid work outside the home, and to solve most of their own problems. Children in more protective homes may have less personal freedom but can count on a great deal of family support. Even if they are in conflict with their own parents, there is often an uncle, and aunt, a cousin, or someone else in the extended family to offer support and advice.

In an inclusive curriculum, teachers help students to explore many perspectives on issues, themes, and concepts, and encourage their students to articulate the beliefs and values that are part of their family and cultural background. All students and teachers need opportunities to learn about other points of view. Sometimes we only know what our own values are when we articulate them and compare them with others. This helps us to evaluate our own beliefs; sometimes we confirm them, and sometimes we shift our value system in response to new information and other points of view.

Antiracist educators respect the cultural values of their students — up to a point. Banks makes this plain: 'Our critics misinterpret multiculturalism by claiming we are cultural relativists. Nowhere in my writing, or in the writing of other multicultural educators, do we advocate cultural relativism. Rather, we make a strong, unequivocal commitment to democracy, to basic American values of justice and equality. And that means values that contradict justice and equality are not acceptable' (Banks, interviewed by Brandt, 1994: 31).

Antiracism is about social justice and equality. Some cultural values or practices that are prevalent among some cultural groups contradict these principles. For example:

- Members of some cultural groups espouse the subservience of women, and antiracist educators do not condone this or any other injustice in any culture. Rather, they communicate to their students and to the parents of their students that individuals in a culturally diverse society have the right to espouse a set of values and cultural practices that affirm their freedom and identity, as long as those values and behaviours do not damage the freedom or identity of anyone else– including members of their own families, such as their children.
- In most English-speaking countries the law requires teachers to report suspected child abuse, even though what constitutes 'child abuse' in mainstream culture may sometimes be considered responsible parenting in other cultures. This is often a source of conflict between some communities and the school. It is extremely important to establish open communication with parents in order to explore the issue and help parents to develop alternative ways of disciplining their children that enable them to maintain their authority in the home without coming into conflict with mainstream institutions or the law.
- As Hodson observes, 'Sex education highlights another major problem for multicultural education: the apparent incompatibility of contemporary feminist perspectives with the traditional views of certain ethnic and cultural groups. Even to debate the position of women may be a contravention of strict Islamic principles . . . there is a potential conflict between regard for diversity and the need to forge a socially cohesive set of educational goals (Hodson, 1993: 694).

Schools can play an extremely important role in explaining mainstream culture and helping parents and community groups to make some accommodations that reduce the potential for conflict between themselves and institutions such as the school, as well as between their children and themselves. At the same time, the school must be willing to make some accommodations that recognize the concerns of parents. There is, for example, no reason why sex education *must* be provided to co-educational groups of students. Nor is there any reason why the school cannot provide space and designated times for prayers for Muslim students, or organize chaperoned social events for females only. Many schools have overcome the reluctance of some students to participate in physical education and sports by offering classes for girls only, and allowing them to wear full clothing instead of shorts in the gym, or even in the swimming pool. If the school has a uniform or dress code, it can include culturally appropriate clothes and head covering; parents can be invited to advise on what is appropriate.

BACKGROUND KNOWLEDGE AND EXPERIENCE

Effective teaching involves activating the conceptual frameworks that children already have, and building on them to expand the children's knowledge and introduce new concepts. But teachers' assumptions about the knowledge and experiences that all students can be expected to have, are often culturally-based, and all students do not share the experiences and background knowledge that teachers, lessons, and textbooks may assume. This is not to say that they are *lacking* in knowledge or experiences; they have knowledge and experiences that are *different*.

Cultural capital
Bourdieu uses the phrase 'cultural capital' to describe those culturally esteemed advantages that people acquire as part of their life experiences, their peer group contacts and their family backgrounds . . . He argues that the cultural capital that is valued in schools is not equally available to children from different backgrounds, yet schools operate as if all children had equal access to it. By basing their assessments of school success and failure and their award of certificates and qualifications on children's possession of this high status cultural capital, which is unequally available, schools act in such a way as to reproduce the social arrangements that are favourable to some but which disadvantage other social groups. (Corson, 1990: 222)

When lessons or textbooks are based on a conceptual framework that is not shared by everyone, some students — those who possess the necessary 'cultural capital' — are more likely to make the expected connections and integrate the new learning. Students who do not have this knowledge are sometimes deemed to be 'deprived' at home and therefore 'disadvantaged' at school. Another way of looking at this is to consider how the curriculum may be limited in perspective. If a given lesson connects to the knowledge and experiences of only some of the students in the class, this is a deficiency in the lesson, not the students.

Cultural capital in the inner city
Bowman (1993) points out that teachers need to link new learning to children's prior knowledge and experience in order to make it meaningful. Teachers who do not know about the backgrounds and experiences of their students find it difficult to make those connections. For example, in the inner city:

Many teachers . . . find that they know so little about how children live their daily lives that they have little to draw upon . . . . Children from inner-city communities, for example, often do not come to schools or centers having had the experiential background that ties easily to the reading materials considered

> *most appropriate for young children. Books focus on baby animals, zoo animals, pets, milkmen, kind policemen, grass, and flowers — ideas and concepts not frequently encountered in children's daily lives. When children do not have the relevant background, they do not learn 'naturally' in the seamless and organic way that teachers have been led to expect.* (Bowman, 1993: 133)

Young children come to school with a store of knowledge and experience that is related to specific contexts. Bowman (1993) gives the example of 'setting a table' as a context that teachers sometimes use to develop the concept of one-to-one distribution. This is effective if all the children have had experience with the activity 'setting a table'; but there is no reason to assume this, or to assume that children who have not are therefore 'deprived'. There are other ways that families make sure each family member gets what he or she needs.

Setting tables
Many children's home experience, ... does not include such distributive activities. In their homes, people do not regularly mete out goods and services all at once; instead, each person draws on the common supply as needed. For them, the context (setting tables) that is meant to elicit knowledge of one-to-one relationships does not evoke what the teacher expects. This does not mean that the children have no informal knowledge to draw on; it does mean that the activities traditionally used may not be the best point of reference. The same children who have never set a table may have sophisticated knowledge of one-to-one relationships in jumping rope to rhymes and in basketball scoring. (Bowman, 1993: 131)

'Traditional' stories, bible stories, and classical mythology are often used as important reference points in teaching. Young children are expected to be familiar with nursery rhymes and stories such as 'Red Riding Hood' or 'The Three Little Pigs'. In fact, these stories cannot be assumed to be part of the early literacy experiences of all children, or to be equally engaging for all children. Some of the stories may be inconsistent with the values that some children have grown up with: for example, anthropomorphic representation of animals may not be common in all cultures, and for some children, stories about pigs may be deeply offensive.

It is important to remember that students from cultures other than the mainstream are not deprived of cultural knowledge; on the contrary, they bring a rich background of cultural knowledge and experiences to school with them. This knowledge is as valid as 'mainstream knowledge.' Children from all cultural backgrounds are raised on stories, rhymes, songs and chants that retell important events in history, celebrate heroic deeds, illustrate cultural values, and teach moral precepts. Most children have some exposure to religion and many are well-versed in stories and scriptures from a particular religion. Muslim children have detailed knowledge of the Qur'an, while Sikh and Hindu children have knowledge of complex stories and scriptures from those religious traditions. But this rich store of knowledge is seldom validated in the traditional curriculum.

Knowledge of 'traditional' stories is so deeply embedded in mainstream culture that they are used as cultural reference points throughout the curriculum. For example, there are some books for older children that parody traditional stories such as 'The Three Little Pigs' or 'Red Riding Hood', or present them from a new perspective. These books can be used to introduce the concepts of parody and point of view, and provide excellent models for students to develop their own humorous or alternative re-tellings of traditional stories. However, these stories are not 'traditional' for everyone, and only the children who recognize the source stories as 'classics' can recognize the humour or the switch in perspective, and participate effectively in related activities.

At secondary level, students are expected to recognize common themes from traditional stories, Greek and Roman mythology, and the Old and New Testaments of the Christian Bible in the adult literature they read and the media they study in their English courses. Teachers and textbooks in all subjects areas sometimes explain or exemplify concepts by referring to concepts and themes in Western history, European mythology, the Judaeo-Christian tradition, and local events and personalities. Some of these references are so much a part of mainstream culture that students encounter them in every aspect of school life. Texts and lessons that make use of these references as examples or analogies to introduce or illustrate a concept are helpful only to the learners who understand the references. For those who do not, these references constitute a barrier to their learning. This is not an argument for 'purging' the curriculum of all traditional or classical references or all European content. But it is important to explain cultural references that are not clear to everyone, and to make links to the knowledge that students do have.

Students who come from other countries are especially likely to have 'gaps' in their knowledge, when judged from a 'mainstream' point of view. They may have less experience than their peers with computers, environmental science, life skills, or physical and health education, but they have experienced a curriculum centred on their own cultural background, and focussing on subjects considered important in that cultural environment. For example, schools in some countries provide formal instruction in subjects such as philosophy, religion, and citizenship, and immigrant students have usually learned a great deal about the literature and history of their own country. Many recently-arrived students have a sophisticated awareness of contemporary issues and events, especially those involved in the family's decision to emigrate.

The curriculum in many countries is sequenced differently, so that newcomers might not yet have learned some skills that their native-born or mainstream peers learned in previous grades — or they may be ahead in some areas. For example, algebra is introduced earlier in some countries. Students may have learned different skills, too: for example, there are several different ways of approaching mathematical operations such as long division or regrouping.

Same skill, different drill
Students may learn different formats for **division.**

For example: $41 \underline{\lfloor 9 \rfloor} = 9 \overline{\lfloor 41 \rfloor} = 41 \div 9$

Regrouping (borrowing, paying back, and carrying) may be conceptualized differently. For example, in **subtraction:**

$$\begin{array}{ccc} {}^{4}\cancel{5}\ {}^{13}\cancel{4}\ {}^{1}2 \\ -\quad 8\quad 3 \\ \hline 4\quad 5\quad 9 \end{array}$$

Ones: Can't subtract 3 from 2. Take 1 ten from the 4, to leave 3, and put with the 2 to get 12. 3 from 12 is 9.

Tens: Can't subtract 8 from 3. Take 1 hundred from the 5, to leave 4, and put with the 3 to get 13. 8 from 13 is 5.

Hundreds: 0 from 4 is 4.

Another method of regrouping:

$$\begin{array}{ccc} 5\quad {}^{1}4\ {}^{1}2 \\ -_{1}\ 8_{9}\ 3 \\ \hline 4\quad 5\quad 9 \end{array}$$

Ones: Can't subtract 3 from 2. Borrow a ten from the tens column, and put with the 1 to get 12. Pay back one ten at the bottom to make 9. 3 from 12 is 9.

Tens: Can't subtract 9 from 4. Take 1 hundred from the hundreds column, and put with the 4 to get 14. Pay back 1 hundred at the bottom. 9 from 14 is 5.

Hundreds: 1 from 5 is 4.

Teachers who do not investigate students' educational background may regard some students as lacking knowledge or skills, or having knowledge and skills that are wrong. Thus it is not uncommon for students who have learned different ways of setting out a mathematical calculation, or who have been taught to do many steps in their heads without writing out each calculation, to be required to learn 'the proper way'. Sometimes students from other countries are actually penalized for using a method that the teacher has not taught. Not only is this unfair to those students; other students are deprived of opportunities to learn alternative ways of approaching tasks — ways that might be more appealing to their way of thinking than the one way that the teacher has taught.

In many curriculum areas, the selection of topics for study sometimes assumes knowledge or values that all the students may not have. For example, in many elementary schools, the school year and the instructional program revolve around themes such as Thanksgiving, Halloween, Christmas and New Year, Valentine's Day, Winter Sports, and Easter. These themes may not be meaningful to all children. Another common classroom theme is 'Pets'; but not all cultures value animals as pets, and some animals are considered unclean in some cultures. Therefore some children may not relate to sentimental depictions of animals in some children's books, and may not understand why keeping a classroom pet is an important classroom activity.

Cultural and linguistic barriers in mathematics

Word problems in mathematics are often difficult for newcomers, because they have to 'decode' unfamiliar content and terminology before they can begin to apply mathematical skills to the problem. For example:

Wendy is flying from Toronto to Seattle, WA, to visit her aunt and uncle during the summer holidays. Her plane leaves Toronto at 1400 EDT, and takes about an hour. She has a 75 min layover in Chicago. The flight from Chicago to Seattle is approximately 3.5 h. At what time can she ask her relatives to meet her at the airport?

Required knowledge: 24-hour clock; locations of Seattle and Chicago relative to Toronto; time zones; the meaning of 'layover'; abbreviations 'WA', 'EDT', 'min' and 'h'.

The Tigers lose 3 m on first down, gain 12 m on second down and 3 m on third down. What is their final position relative to their original position?

Required knowledge: American football; 'Tigers' as a team name; 'down' as a noun; the mathematical use of 'relative'; abbreviation 'm'.

Lee's batting average after 13 games was 0.395. Five games later it had dropped to 0.348. If Jackson was at bat 23 times during the 5 games, how many hits did he get during those 5 games?

Required knowledge: baseball; the concept of 'batting average'; the term 'at bat', 'hit' as a noun.

A baseball manager insists on having his pitcher bat third and his best hitter bat last. How many batting orders are possible?

Required knowledge: baseball; the number of players in a team; the concept of 'batting order'; the meaning of 'have someone do something'; the baseball terms 'hitter' and 'pitcher'.

Teachers who are aware of the knowledge and experience that students bring with them are better able to design effective lessons that build on that knowledge and, at the same time, to teach the background knowledge and give all students the experience that they need for success. How can teachers do this?

- **Find out** what knowledge and experience the learners have, and validate their world view. Pre-reading strategies such as brainstorming and KWL charts ('Know,' 'Want to know', and 'Learned') are very helpful (see Chapter 6).

    You may need to adjust the focus of a specific topic or unit to incorporate the students' own experiences and perspectives. For example, if your curriculum includes a unit on pets, start by talking about all the possible functions animals have in relation to humans: in many cultures animals are more important as food than they are as companions — and what is food in one culture may be unclean in another. Animals are also valued for the work they do, and different animals do different work in different parts of the world. In some cultures, animals have a particular religious or symbolic significance, or there may be taboos associated with certain animals. When you are dealing with animals as pets, include all levels of experience within the 'range of normal': although many people have or would like to have pets, it's also normal not to have a pet, not to want a pet, or to dislike certain animals. Offer children a choice: some students may prefer to explore the concept of animals as symbols, as work animals, or as food, rather than animals as pets.

- **Link new learning** to the students' own conceptual frameworks. Instead of starting with a culturally-based example or analogy, start with the fundamental concept, and encourage learners to discuss their experience or knowledge of that concept. For example, if you are starting a unit on 'The Quest' in literature, explain the concept of 'a quest', invite students to think of stories that deal with this theme, and share these stories with the class. Some students — those with more experience with mainstream culture — may know the story of Odysseus/Ulysses, or you may tell the story to the class. The story of Moses and the Israelites seeking the Promised Land is also a quest. Some students may know the story of Rama's quest in the *Ramayana*. Others may know the story of Prince Gautama's physical and spiritual quest for enlightenment through an ethical life; this story is the basis of Buddhist philosophy. You can also make links to more recent events and issues: the histories of Gandhi, Kenyatta, Martin Luther King, or Nelson Mandela can be viewed as contemporary quests that are becoming or likely to become immortalized. Students may also be interested in discussing the question of why women have not traditionally been celebrated in quest mythology.

- **Share the knowledge:** tell the stories and 'unpack' cultural references so that everyone has the 'cultural capital' they need. As part of your introduction to a new topic you can tell or read a specific story or piece of information to the class, or invite a student from the class to do so. Most students enjoy having stories read or told to them, even when they know the stories already. You can also provide additional resource material so that students can explore the story or the background information in more depth on their own. Children's books and simplified classics can be especially helpful to students who are learning English as a second language, and need to 'catch up' on traditional stories and classics from the mainstream culture — as long as it is made clear why they are reading children's books: not because they are not cognitively developed, but as a way of expanding their knowledge of the new culture.

- **Group students** so that each group includes at least one mainstream 'cultural informant' as well as students who can act as informants on other cultures. For example, when they are reading word problems in mathematics, students could brainstorm: *What knowledge do we need in order to understand this problem?* If some of the problems involve mainstream cultural knowledge, while others involve knowledge that relates to other cultures, everybody has an opportunity to act as cultural informant, and everyone learns a little more about the world.

Pay special attention to background knowledge on topics that students from other countries may not have been exposed to. Activate prior knowledge by drawing parallel references to events and issues in other parts of the world in order to clarify concepts.

Activating prior knowledge

In the Canadian social studies program, to prepare for a unit on contemporary French–English relations, students could discuss questions designed to help them to share background knowledge and draw parallel references:

What do we mean by 'French–English relations' in Canada?
Do you know of other countries where there are tensions between different linguistic and cultural groups?
Have you ever had the experience of living in a country where your linguistic or cultural group is a minority?

LEARNING RESOURCES

The learning resources include the textbooks and other print material that students read, or that teachers read to students; audiovisual resources such as classroom posters, videos and audiotapes; electronic resources such as computer games, CD-ROMs and simulations; the field trips and other out-of-class experiences that enrich the program; and guests invited into the classroom.

The resource material to which students are exposed has important effects on their attitudes towards themselves and towards members of other groups. According to Banks, 'social scientists have learned a great deal about how racial attitudes in children develop and about ways in which educators can design interventions to help children acquire more positive feelings toward other racial groups ... This research tells us that by age 4 African American, white, and Mexican American children are aware of racial differences and show racial preferences favouring whites. Students can be helped to develop more positive racial attitudes if realistic images of ethnic and racial groups are included in teaching materials in a consistent, natural, and integrated fashion' (Banks, 1993: 27).

In recognition of the role that curriculum resources play in the development of students' self-concept and their view of others, many educational jurisdictions publish guidelines on the selection of resource material. Teachers are advised to avoid resource material that presents biased or stereotypical images of specific groups such as women, the disabled, the old, or ethnocultural groups. Publishers are advised to make their material more inclusive and, at the same time, to ensure that it does not promote stereotypes (Ministry of Education, 1980; North York Board of Education, 1989). Recent publications do include more images of people of colour and other minority groups; however, simply counting the number of times various groups are represented is not an adequate guide to the content. Some texts that include images of diversity may provide information that is superficial or inaccurate (Swartz, 1992).

The issue of inclusion and representation in textbooks and other learning resources has been discussed for many years. According to Garcia (1993), progress has been made over the last 40 years, to the extent that 'multicultural content has increased in the prose, the illustrations, and the highlighted material' in elementary and secondary school textbooks (p. 29). A comparison of textbooks in subjects such as science and mathematics shows greater representation of females and persons of colour as models of competence. However, in many instances, the insertion of multicultural content is superficial. For example, in American history textbooks, the amount of material on African Americans has increased, but often remains focussed on specific topics such as slavery and the civil rights movement, rather than permeating every topic (Garcia, 1993). Therefore, it is still important to evaluate learning resources carefully, to supplement them with additional material, and to help students to recognize bias in the material they read.

- Choose classroom and library material that provides realistic and positive images of different cultural and racial groups, that reflects many types of family structure, different socioeconomic status, and different cultural values, but also communicates the fundamental similarities among cultures and peoples.
- Include a variety of material in the languages of the school in school and classroom libraries. It is important to help students to maintain their first languages because 'books in other languages offer cognitive benefits and raise the status of bilingual pupils, at the same time as broadening the horizons of monolingual peers' (Multilingual Resources for Children Project, 1995: 18). Students and their parents can help you to find, evaluate, and create first language and bilingual material for use in the school. The Multilingual Resources for Children Project suggests many ways of incorporating multilingual texts and other resources — including human resources such as bilingual storytellers, parents, and the students themselves — into the school program (Multilingual Resources for Children Project, 1995).

- Establish a process for evaluating textbooks and other resource material. To ensure that many perspectives are involved in evaluating texts and other resources, students and parents can be involved as reviewers. If there is an active antiracism group in the school, its members could assist in the process. It may be necessary to gather several books and media resources together in order to provide a variety of perspectives on a theme or topic. Several bibliographies of multicultural literature and other resources are available: see 'Further Reading and Resources for Teachers' at the end of this chapter.

How to choose resources for the multicultural school

These questions will help in balancing the selection of resources for libraries and classrooms:

- **Background knowledge:** Does the text make realistic assumptions about the background knowledge of the learners? The amount of previous knowledge the reader brings to the task will significantly influence comprehension. If the text assumes knowledge and experiences not shared by all readers, the teacher can intervene between students and text and provide the background knowledge and experiences to bridge the gap between the student's starting point and that of the text.
- **Perspective:** Does the text present a global view of the subject, and show participation in this field of men and women of a variety of racial and cultural backgrounds? For example, does a text on Ancient History give equal treatment, in terms of importance, depth of treatment, and respect, to the civilizations of the Americas, Asia, Africa and Europe? Does the text refer to and depict experts in the field, such as archeologist and linguists, representing different racial and cultural groups and different countries of origin? If the content is limited in perspective, but the text otherwise has some merit such as a clear organization of topics or useful visuals, you can supplement it with additional resources that provide other points of view or include other cultural experiences.
- **Values:** Is there anything in this material that may conflict with the values and belief systems of some of the students? Ask parents and other community members to help to assess texts and to suggest alternative resources that may present different points of view.
- **Sources:** Who was involved in writing this text? If diverse cultures are presented in the material, what perspective do the authors and illustrators bring to those cultures?
- **Parallel themes:** In a book with multicultural content, are themes given parallel treatment? For example, in a book dealing with homes around the world, a rural hut in Africa is not an appropriate parallel to a suburban house or city apartment in a European or North American city — but a suburban house or city apartment in Accra or Nairobi might be.

- **Illustrations:** Do the illustrations include people of diverse racial and cultural backgrounds in a variety of roles? Are males and females of a variety of backgrounds shown in strong or central roles in more or less equal proportions? Are the illustrations realistic? Be especially careful with cartoon illustrations: since cartoons often depend on caricature and stereotype, these could be offensive.
- **Vocabulary:** Some choice of vocabulary may reveal the writer's perspective. From a Eurocentric or western perspective, the clothing of some cultures may be described as 'costumes', and places that are home to millions of the earth's people may be described as 'exotic' or 'mysterious', etc. Terms such as 'rabble', 'mob', and 'horde' communicate quite different messages from terms such as 'protesters', 'demonstrators', or an 'army'. 'Fearless explorers' in one account might be 'ruthless invaders' in another. The use of terms such as 'freedom fighters', 'patriots', 'rebels', 'terrorists', 'fanatics', and so on also depend on the author's point of view.
- **Examples of bias:** Does the material provide clear examples of bias? It may be appropriate to retain some of the biased material in order to teach students how recognize bias and to become critical readers and media consumers.
- **Quality of writing:** a book that includes multicultural material but is otherwise boring or poorly written is not a good choice. There has been so much new multicultural material published in the last few years that it should not be necessary to choose poor quality material.

CONCLUSION

Multicultural schools and classrooms educate students of diverse cultural backgrounds, including some who have arrived from other countries and are learning the language of instruction. In these schools it is essential to examine and adjust the curriculum so that everyone in the school feels equally valued and included. In all schools, all students need to learn how to live and work in a multicultural society and a culturally diverse world.

There is no area of the curriculum or the school system as a whole that can remain unexamined or unchanged in pursuit of the goals of antiracist education. Indeed, the scope of antiracist education is so huge as to appear overwhelming, or at least the work of a lifetime. However, there are some changes that teachers can make immediately in their own classrooms. All teachers can begin to redesign their own curriculum, independently or with a group of colleagues, one unit at a time, to include diverse cultural perspectives and help students to develop their skills of critical thinking and social action, as suggested in this chapter. All teachers can initiate or become involved in one of the activities suggested in Chapter 4. All teachers can create a sense of community in their classrooms, as suggested in Chapter 5. All teachers can begin to transform their instructional style, focussing one one aspect of lesson design and classroom interaction at a time, as suggested in

Chapter 6. And all teachers can begin to use alternative methods of assessment, as suggested in the next chapter.

The following checklist is intended for students to use in assessing the school as an inclusive multicultural environment.

CHECKLIST: AN INCLUSIVE MULTICULTURAL ENVIRONMENT

This checklist is designed for students to use in assessing the education they receive. The items on the checklist relate to topics discussed in this chapter and in other chapters in the book. Some students may need to use a translated version of the checklist.

Students respond 'yes' or 'no' to each statement. Teachers could encourage group discussion of each item on the checklist before asking students to complete it individually. A pattern of 'no' responses indicates an area that needs attention.

Multicultural Education at _____ School

Multicultural education is important in this school. All students need to feel proud of their own backgrounds. All students need to learn about other cultures, and learn to get along with people of other cultural backgrounds. All students need to learn how to work together to stop racism and discrimination at school and in the community.

How are we doing? Circle 'yes' or 'no' to help improve multicultural education in our school.

yes   no   I learn about other cultures at school.
yes   no   I learn about my own culture at school.
yes   no   I feel comfortable talking about my own culture at school.
yes   no   Teachers and other students respect my language and culture.
yes   no   We have teachers from many different cultural backgrounds.
yes   no   Teachers help me to see different points of view.
yes   no   There are teachers in the school who speak my language.
yes   no   There are signs and notices in my language around the school.
yes   no   There are books in my language in the school library.
yes   no   We use books, videos, and other materials that show people of different backgrounds doing many different things.
yes   no   When we learn something new, the teachers begin with something we already know.
yes   no   At this school we learn about how to fight against racism and discrimination.
yes   no   If I have a problem with racism or discrimination, I know where to go for help.

yes   no   The displays in the classrooms and the hallways show people of many different cultural backgrounds.

yes   no   Our school concerts and other special events include all the cultures in the school.

yes   no   My parents feel comfortable coming to the school and talking to the teachers.

My comments and suggestions:

_____
_____
_____
_____
_____
_____

My first language is _____
My cultural background is _____

FURTHER READING AND RESOURCES FOR TEACHERS

Alladina, S. (1995) *Being Bilingual: A Guide for Parents, Teachers and Young People on Mother Tongue, Heritage Language and Bilingual Education.* Stoke-on-Trent, England: Trentham Books. This illustrated book could be used with older students in English classes to stimulate discussion on multilingualism and bilingualism.

Bigelow, B., Miner, B. and Peterson, B. (1991) *Rethinking Columbus.* Milwaukee, WI: Rethinking Schools. 96-page special issue of *Rethinking Schools* on teaching about Europeans in the Americas from several perspectives. Includes lesson plans and an annotated bibliography.

Bigelow, B., Christensen, C., Karp, S., Miner, B. and Peterson, B. (1994) *Rethinking Our Classrooms: Teaching for Equity and Justice.* 208-page special issue of *Rethinking Schools.* Filled with short articles written by practising teachers, outlining the changes they have made in their classrooms to support an antiracist, social justice curriculum. Highly recommended. Order from Rethinking Schools, 1001 E. Keefe Ave, Milwaukee, WI 53212.

Blakey, L., Hattiangadi, M., and Stanton, S. (1995) *Our Wonderful World.* Toronto: Ginn. These materials introduce concepts and language patterns through multicultural content and the arts. There are big books for shared reading and small books for individual children or partners, as well as audio cassettes and teacher resource books. The reading level is suitable for the early grades, but the material could be used with older learners at the beginning stages of second language acquisition.

Borovilos, J. (1990). *Breaking Through: A Canadian Literary Mosaic.* Scarborough, Ontario: Prentice-Hall Canada. Anthology of multicultural literature in a variety of genres for middle and secondary school students.

Borovilos, J. (1995). *Breaking Free: A Cross-Cultural Anthology.* Scarborough, Ontario: Prentice-Hall Canada.Anthology of multicultural literature for middle and secondary school students.

Burnett, J. and Irons, C. (1993) *Mathematics in Many Cultures.* San Francisco: Mimosa Publications. A series of kits showing a wide variety of mathematics applications around the world. Each kit include a big book, 7 full-colour posters, and a teacher's guide with suggestions for classroom activities. The posters in each kit provide excellent display material for school libraries, hallways, and classrooms.

Cummins, J. and Sayers, D. (1995) *Brave New Schools: Challenging Cultural Illiteracy.* Toronto: OISE Press. Fascinating book about using new technology to help students become critical thinkers, engaged in cross-cultural dialogue and problem-solving through electronic communications networks.

Day, F.A. (1994) *Multicultural Voices in Contemporary Literature: a Resource for Teachers.* Portsmouth, NH: Heinemann. This book celebrates the lives and work of authors and illustrators from many different cultural backgrounds, and suggests ways of using multicultural literature in the classroom and around the school.

Derman-Sparks, L. and the A.B.C. Task Force. (1989) *Anti-Bias Curriculum: Tools for Empowering Young Children.* Washington, DC: National Association for the Education of Young Children. Handbook for developing an anti-bias curriculum for young children. Each chapter focuses on a specific aspect of bias, discusses some basic principles, and provides practical classroom activities.

Gill, D. and Levidow, L. (eds) (1987) *Anti-Racist Science Teaching.* London: Free Association Books. Collection of articles by scientists and science teachers on the politics of science and the development of an antiracist science curriculum.

Golden, R. (1992) *Dangerous Memories: Invasion and Resistance Since 1492.* Chicago: Chicago Religious Task Force on Central America. This book provides alternative perspectives on the history of the Americas.

Harris, V. J. (ed.) (1993) *Teaching Multicultural Children's Literature in Grades K–8.* Norwood, MA: Christopher-Gordon Publishers. The articles in this book provide advice on how to select and use multicultural children's literature. Includes helpful reviews of many children's books from a variety of cultures.

Hawkins, E. (1987[1984]) *Awareness of Language: An Introduction.* Revised Edition. Cambridge: Cambridge University Press. A helpful and interesting introduction for teachers, curriculum planners, and teacher educators.

Hawkins, E. (ed.) (1984, 1985) *Awareness of Language Series.* Cambridge: Cambridge University Press. This is a series of short topic booklets, each on a different aspect of language, for students in the upper elementary grades and up. Many of the activities draw attention to interesting similarities and differences among languages, and introduce concepts such as register and language variety. Teachers could adapt many of the activities to the linguistic context of their own classrooms.

Jobe, R. (1993) *Cultural Connections.* Markham, Ontario: Pembroke. Helpful suggestions on using literature to enhance children's multicultural awareness. A central chapter focusses on four major themes: cultural encounters, cross-cultural experiences, cultural conflict, and reawakenings. Includes suggestions on how to use the books in the classroom with young adolescents, as well as bibliographies of thematically linked children's literature from a variety of cultures.

Kezwer, P. (1995) *Worlds of Wonder: Resources for Multicultural Children's Literature.* Toronto: Pippin Publishing. Annotated bibliography of multicultural material. Includes a thematic index that helps teachers to include several cultural perspectives in themes such as 'Friendship' or 'The Environment'.

Krater, J., Zeni, J., and Cason, N.D. (1994) *Mirror Images: Teaching Writing in Black and White.* Portsmouth, NH: Heinemann. The story of how a group of teachers changed their teaching methods, the classroom climate, and their own cultural awareness in order to increase the participation and success of African American students in high school English classes.

Krause, M.C. (1986) *Multicultural Mathematics Materials.* Reston, VA: National Council of Teachers of Mathematics. A collection of activities from different cultures, grouped as African (e.g., Egyptian Numeration System), Asian (e.g., Tangrams and Magic Squares), Middle Eastern (e.g., Tessellations), and North American (e.g., Navajo and Hopi designs).

McCloskey, M.L. and Stack, L. (1992, 1993, 1996) *Voices in Literature.* Boston: Heinle and Heinle. Series of three books for language development through experiences with multicultural literature in a broad range of genres; organized thematically. Includes pre-reading and follow-up activities. Teacher's manual also available. Suitable for upper elementary to secondary level.

Multilingual Resources for Children Project. (1995) *Building Bridges: Multilingual Resources for Children.* Clevedon, England: Multilingual Matters. This book is filled with interesting ideas for bringing community languages into the school, and for finding and creating multilingual resources.

Oliver, E.I. (1994) *Crossing the Mainstream: Multicultural Perspectives in Teaching Literature.* Urbana, IL: National Council of Teachers of English. Provides a rationale and suggests appropriate resources for a multicultural approach to the study of literature.

Rethinking Schools. This quarterly journal for teachers provides practical advice on how to teach for educational equity and social justice. Order from Rethinking schools, 1001 E. Keefe Ave, Milwaukee, WI 53212. Special issues also available, consisting of several articles that focus in detail on specific topics (see Bigelow *et al.*, 1991, 1994).

Samway, K.D. and Whang, G. (1996) *Literature Study Circles in a Multicultural Classroom.* York, Maine: Stenhouse Publishers. Provides detailed practical advice on using literature study circles with children. Includes bibliographies of children's literature and lists of authors from various cultural backgrounds.

Schniedewind, N. and Davidson, E. (1998) *Open Minds to Equality: A Sourcebook of Learning Activities to Promote Race, Sex, Class and Age Equity* (2nd edn). Englewood Cliffs, NJ: Prentice-Hall. A book of co-operative learning activities to help students recognize and change inequities based on gender, race, class, and age. Some activities need adaptation for secondary students.

Shan, S., and Bailey, P. (1991) *Multiple Factors: Classroom Mathematics for Equity and Justice.* Stoke-on-Trent, UK: Trentham Books. A guide to multicultural and antiracist mathematics; discusses the mathematical contributions and achievements of many cultures, and the use of mathematics to investigate equity issues. Includes many examples for classroom application.

Yolen, J. (1992) *Encounter.* New York, NY: Harcourt Brace Jovanovich. For students aged 10–14, this illustrated book views the arrival of the Europeans in the Americas from the point of view of an Aboriginal child.

Zaslavsky, C. (1996)*The Multicultural Math Classroom: Bringing in the World.* Portsmouth, NH: Heinemann. A rich source of ideas for teachers, with practical suggestions for topics and activities to help all students learn about mathematical applications and inventions from many cultures: number systems, measuring systems, calendars, architecture, art, and games.

CHAPTER 9

Assessment in Multicultural Schools

INTRODUCTION

Schools in multicultural communities often receive students who have recently arrived from other countries, or who first start learning English when they begin school. Before placing newcomers in classroom programs, it is important to use linguistically and culturally appropriate ways of assessing their linguistic and educational background, as suggested in Chapter 3. In addition, teachers need to find appropriate appropriate and equitable ways of assessing students' linguistic and cognitive development as they progress through the school.

This chapter begins by providing background information on some of the assessment reforms that many school districts are implementing, and how these initiatives may affect linguistically and culturally diverse students. This section includes a discussion of 'opportunity to learn', and suggests that this should be a fundamental principle in designing assessment tasks and standards for linguistically and culturally diverse students. The next section provides advice on how to assess students' progress in acquiring academic skills and content, and suggests the use of alternative assessment methods and the provision of additional support for students who are learning the language of instruction. In the third section, teachers will find suggestions on how to assess language and literacy development in the first language as well as in English. The chapter concludes with a brief consideration of the question: when should students who are learning the language of instruction be included in large scale assessments such as district-wide testing in literacy and mathematics? Following the chapter is a checklist to help teachers and school administrators plan and review the assessment procedures that are in use in the school.

ASSESSMENT REFORM IN MULTICULTURAL SCHOOLS

Students are involved in many forms of assessment in the classroom and at the school district or national level. In recent years, the assessment reform movement has had a considerable impact on the kinds of assessments that are used and how the results are reported.

While many of the changes in assessment practices are intended to inform and improve instructional practice, which is a very positive outcome, many of these changes do not take into account the cultural and educational experiences of some groups of students — especially those who are learning the language of instruction. In order to consider the implications of assessment reform for teachers and students in linguistically and culturally diverse schools, it is helpful to compare the traditional 'measurement and ranking' model of assessment with the 'standards' model that many school districts are implementing. It is also important to plan assessment and instruction in accordance with the 'opportunity to learn' principle.

The measurement and ranking model

Until recently, the predominant model of assessment in many schools and school districts has been the measurement and ranking model. This model relies mainly on 'summative' assessment (also called 'evaluation'), which gives students marks or grades based on how much they have learned by the end of a term or school year, or the knowledge and skills they can demonstrate on an examination at specific points during their schooling. At the school and classroom level, teachers usually design their own tests and other curriculum-related tasks, such as question-and-answer worksheets, research projects, reports, and essays, almost all of which are heavily dependent on reading and writing skills in the language of instruction. Often, the first and frequently the only time students perform a specific kind of task is also the time when their performance is evaluated. In this model of assessment, students may be graded 'on a curve', often without regard to absolute standards of perform-ance, so that the percentage of students gaining high marks, average marks, and low marks remains more or less constant from class to class within a school, and from year to year. In some countries and school districts, students also take public examinations or standardized tests at the end of elementary or secondary schooling. In addition, many colleges and universities require specific levels of performance on tests such as the Scholastic Aptitude Test or the Test of English as a Foreign Language for admission to post secondary education.

The measurement and ranking model is based on an implicit belief that not all students have 'what it takes' to be successful, and the job of schools is to find those who do, and to nurture them. Closer examination often shows that 'what it takes' consists of proficiency in the language of instruction, congruence between the cultural values and experiences of the home and those promoted in the school, educated parents, and higher socioeconomic status. Measurement and ranking helps to sort or select students for different kinds of educational treatment and, ultimately, different life paths. According to the Ford Foundation, the American testing system acts as a 'hostile gatekeeper' that has set up barriers for many, especially women and cultural minorities (Freeman and Freeman, 1991).

The standards model

Today, schools are expected to help *all* students to reach high standards of academic achievement. In the standards model of assessment, common standards of performance are clearly articulated and each aspect of performance is assessed according to a common set of standards and criteria. Many assessment tasks now involve a broad range of skills and talents, provide helpful feedback to the learners on how well they perform, and inform the learner of what they need to do in order to improve. These tests are more authentic than most tests and examinations.

These changes represent a major shift of philosophy about children's capacity to learn. School success is increasingly believed to be related to the kinds of educational experiences that students receive rather than to innate psychological differences (Farr and Trumbull, 1966). Therefore, the purpose of assessment is to assess instruction as much as it is to assess students. Many recent reforms in assessment are intended to help teachers understand how students learn, and to make informed decisions about the kind of instruction that students need in order to help them move towards the expected outcomes or standards.

Although summative assessment or evaluation are still used in most school districts — for example, in reporting to parents at the end of the school year, or determining a student's placement in the coming school year — there is also a strong emphasis on 'formative' assessment. Formative assessment takes place continuously, in many ways, and is intended to help form or shape the curriculum, and to give helpful feedback to students so that they can improve their performance. Assessment may take place even before instruction begins: for example, to find out what the learners know or can do before the teacher introduces a new skill or topic. The kinds of assessment tasks have changed too: instead of tests that measure a narrow range of performance, students are involved in performance-based assessment tasks that assess a wider range of skills and knowledge.

Many aspects of assessment reform are very positive, and offer the prospect of better instruction for all students. However, many of the reform initiatives have not taken into account the needs of some groups of students, including those who are learning the language of instruction, recently-arrived immigrant students, and students from cultural groups other than the mainstream. As a result, in many schools and school districts all students are expected to reach certain standards of performance — standards that were not designed with their needs and life experiences in mind. Farr and Trumbull argue that current reforms 'risk serious failure if they cannot truly address the needs of all students' and that 'a priority of all reforms should be the needs of underserved students before those of any others, because without such concerted attention, their needs are likely to go unmet again. Existing inequities will be perpetuated if not multiplied' (Farr and Trumbull, 1996: 2).

Opportunity to learn

A fundamental principle in equitable assessment is 'opportunity to learn'. It is not fair to assess students on knowledge and skills they could not possibly be expected to have gained, given their educational background and life experience. Many immigrant and minority students have not had the opportunity to learn the knowledge and skills that they are required to demonstrate through various kinds of assessment tasks. For example:

- Students may be required to express knowledge or demonstrate skills in a language that they are still learning. Whether traditional 'measurement' tasks or performance-based assessment tasks are used, proficiency in the language of instruction is still a critical factor in success.
- Immigrant students may be expected to meet outcomes or standards that are not appropriate in terms of their educational experience. For example, subjects such as social studies assume prior knowledge about their new country that recent arrivals have not had an opportunity to learn. The same problem exists with regard to academic skills. In an education system that aims to develops skills in self-directed learning, independent research, and projects, there is often an assumption that the learners have had opportunities throughout the elementary grades to develop the required sub-skills such as finding, selecting and collating information without copying verbatim. Many recent arrivals have not had experience with this kind of learning. (See Chapter 6 for advice on how to provide guidance and support for project work.)
- All students, including many native-born students, do not have equal access to high-quality instruction (Kozol, 1991; Farr and Trumbull, 1996). For example, almost 25% of the students who are learning the language of instruction in US schools do not receive specialized ESL or bilingual instruction (McKeon, 1994). Even when students do receive specialized instruction, this may be for only a small portion of each day; the rest of the time, when students are integrated into mainstream classrooms, their teachers may not have the requisite training or experience — or even the interest — that would enable them to provide second language learners with appropriate instruction and support. Farr and Trumbull remind educators who are developing standards as a way of improving schools to 'maintain a parallel focus on standards that ensure access to learning' because otherwise it would be unfair 'to impose standards on students who do not have access to the teaching and resources necessary to ensure the highest level of learning' (Farr and Trumbull, 1996: 60).

It is important, then, to take into account opportunity to learn in determining outcomes and setting standards, and in designing the assessment tasks through which students are required to demonstrate progress towards those outcomes and achievement of those standards. For example, many students — especially those who are still learning English — cannot immediately be assessed according to standards devised for native speakers of the language. While teachers may hold the same long-term goals for all students, and expect all students eventually to achieve common outcomes and high standards of performance, all students will not take the same route towards those outcomes, and will not reach them at the same time. For example, most students who arrive from other countries during their high school years as beginning learners of English *are still in the process of second language acquisition when they graduate* and when they enter the workforce or post secondary education; therefore those institutions, too, share the responsibility for assisting them to reach the highest possible levels of proficiency in English.

Setting appropriate standards, designing alternative assessment tasks, and using equitable criteria for the assessment of student performance are only part of what must happen to raise levels of performance among minority students and second language learners. The other part is the provision of an appropriate instructional program that conforms with 'opportunity to learn' standards. As Farr and Trumbull point out, 'those who are developing standards [for student performance] . . . must maintain a parallel focus on standards that ensure access to learning' (Farr and Trumbull, 1996: 60).

Setting the standards for opportunity to learn

In the context of multilingual and multicultural schooling, opportunity to learn standards include:

- teachers who understand cultural diversity and are knowledgeable about the life experiences of their students (see Chapters 1 and 2);
- a welcoming and inclusive school environment that helps all students to feel valued, and helps parents to become involved in their children's education (see Chapters 3 and 4);
- classroom experiences that help every student to feel valued as a member of the classroom community (see Chapter 5);
- an inclusive learning environment where teachers use a variety of instructional strategies in order to meet the learning needs of all students (see Chapter 6);
- teachers who support the goals of multicultural and antiracist education (see Chapter 7);
- an inclusive curriculum that provides multiple perspectives on the world and validates the cultural backgrounds of all students (see Chapter 8);
- teachers who take into account opportunity to learn in developing learning outcomes and standards, and who use alternative assessment strategies and criteria for students who are learning the language of instruction (see the suggestions on curriculum-related assessment later in this chapter);

- long-term support for second language acquisition through skilled instruction in specific features of English, delivered through the content of a meaningful and relevant academic program (see, for example, Rigg and Allen, 1989; Gibbons, 1991; Spangenberg-Urbschat and Pritchard, 1994; Chamot and O'Malley, 1994; Genesee, 1994).

CURRICULUM-RELATED ASSESSMENT: ACADEMIC KNOWLEDGE AND SKILLS

Language is a critical factor in the assessment of student learning. This creates special problems for teachers in classrooms where some or all of the students are learning the language of instruction. For example, most classroom-based assessment tasks — traditional tasks such as writing answers to test questions and performance-based assessment tasks such as writing explanations for mathematical solutions — measure reading and writing skills in English as much as, or even more than, academic knowledge and skills (Genesee and Hamayan, 1994; Farr and Trumbull, 1996).

Meeting the standards

McKeon (1994) points out that meeting standards for performance in subjects such as mathematics or social studies will be disproportionately difficult for students who are learning the language of instruction. They will have to perform at much higher cognitive and linguistic levels than their English-speaking peers. In designing new assessment policies and procedures, therefore, it is important to acknowledge that:

- meeting content standards is a more complex and cognitively demanding task for second language learners than it is for students who are proficient in English.
- second language learners may know as much as their English-speaking peers, but they may have knowledge and skills that are different; as McKeon (1994: 46) points out, 'not the least of these accomplishments is being able to understand, speak, read, write, reason, and remember academic content in a language other than English'.

Students who are learning the language of instruction are often not able to express what they have learned in the second language (Genesee and Hamayan, 1994). They may have difficulty understanding what they are being asked to do, and they usually need more time than their English-speaking peers because they often think and work in two languages. When they write in English, their teachers sometimes focus as much, or more, on their incomplete knowledge of English as on the information they are trying to communicate. Therefore, approaches to assessment may need to be modified in order to compensate for these problems and allow students to demonstrate learning in ways that do not depend totally on their proficiency in English.

The Cummins model

Cummins (1984, 1996) proposes a model for designing learning activities and assessment tasks for students who are learning the language of instruction. The model consists of four quadrants created by the intersection of two continua:

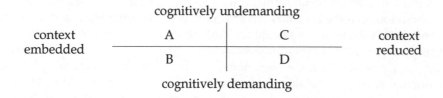

The 'context embedded/context reduced' continuum indicates the degree of contextual support that is provided. For example, at the far left of the continuum, the language is embedded in a meaningful context, and meaning is supported by direct face-to-face interaction, visual cues, etc. At the other end of this continuum, the linguistic information is not accompanied by these extralinguistic cues to meaning.

The 'cognitively demanding/cognitively undemanding' continuum indicates the demands that are placed on the learner's thinking processes. Towards the top of the continuum, the learner already has the necessary knowledge and the required level of language proficiency, and the task is relatively simple: e.g., factual recall is easier than making inferences. At the other end of the continuum, tasks are beyond the learners' present stage of proficiency and require the student to process a great deal of information at the same time.

To support learning and allow students to demonstrate what they know, teachers can use this framework to plan instruction and assessment. Students in the beginning stage of second language acquisition need to work on tasks in quadrant A in order to develop what Cummins calls Basic Interpersonal Communication Skills, or BICS (1984, 1996). Beyond the beginning stage, learners need to begin developing Cognitive Academic Language Proficiency, or CALP (Cummins, 1984, 1996). Teachers can support these students by providing learning activities and assessment tasks in quadrant B, where increasing cognitive demands are made on them while comprehension is supported through the use of familiar language, frequent opportunities for oral interaction, visual cues, visual organizers, etc. Students who have received appropriate long-term support and are approaching native-speaker levels of proficiency are ready to be challenged by tasks in quadrant D, where there is much less extralinguistic support. Tasks in quadrant C are not appropriate for any student: tasks that are neither cognitively demanding nor embedded in a meaningful context do not promote learning.

See Cline and Frederickson (1996) for more detailed suggestions on how to apply the Cummins model to instruction and assessment.

Teachers can adapt their assessment procedures in some of the following ways:

- **Use alternative assessment procedures.** Genesee and Hamayan (1994) suggest a variety of alternatives to formal tests in classroom-based assessment, such as observation, conferences, and student journals. For example, in a one-to-one conference you can ask a student to demonstrate comprehension or knowledge using using concrete or visual representations: e.g. *Point to . . . Give me . . . Show me . . . Draw . . . Find the page about . . . Where is the picture of . . . ?* etc. Bilingual peers can translate for beginning learners of English. Also, you can assess performance on tasks that involve several different aptitudes or talents, such as demonstrations, oral and written reports, graphic displays, videotapes and audiotapes, concrete models, or bilingual submissions.
- **Use a performance-based assessment model** to support learning and provide practice and feedback before final assessment.

A model for performance-based assessment

Use this process to implement performance-based assessment in your classroom:

(1) Show the learners a variety of models of performance: sample stories, lab reports, research projects, essays, and other written products; samples of practical work and artistic creations; videotapes of oral presentations and dramatic or musical performances; demonstrations of practical skills and of physical performance in sports and fitness activities, etc. Include models of various levels of performance.

(2) Encourage the students to discuss and rank the models and identify the elements of a good performance on that task.

(3) Share the criteria and rating system you used in assessing the models. For each item being assessed, a simple rating scale of 1/2/3, corresponding to 'Very good', 'OK' and 'Needs improvement', is easy to understand and administer. Whatever rating scale you use, discuss what makes the difference between descriptions such as 'OK' and 'Very good' on a specific aspect of performance.

(4) Provide plenty of opportunity for guided practice.

(5) Provide constructive feedback on process as well as product. Base the assessment on your observation, as well as students' notes or logs.

(6) Invite students to assess their work, and submit their best performance for summative assessment. For example, if they do three projects in a year, they might choose one to submit for assessment of their performance as 'self-directed learners'.

- **Use portfolio assessment.** A portfolio is a file or a box containing evidence of a student's progress. Portfolios involve teachers and students in collecting and assessing examples of performance and growth over a period of time. They may include samples of work, as well as response journal or learning log entries, records of conferences, teacher's observation comments or checklists, self- and peer assessment forms and checklists, as well as more traditional test and quiz papers. Portfolios give a more complete view of the learner, especially if they are collected across the curriculum at the secondary level, where subject teachers otherwise gain only a limited perspective on each student's performance and capabilities. Portfolios may include material in the first language: this acknowledges the student's proficiency and encourages continuing development in that language. Over the course of a year, samples in the portfolio usually show significant growth in English, in ways that are less discernible through traditional tests and exams. Portfolios also provide opportunities for parents to be involved in the selection and assessment of their children's work. Many writers on the education of linguistically and culturally diverse students recommend portfolio assessment as a more equitable way of gathering information about students' learning (Trumbull and Farr, 1996; Genesee and Hamayan, 1994; Freeman and Freeman, 1991).
- **Use assessment information to adjust instruction**. If the students are not 'getting it', investigate why. Perhaps the students are bringing knowledge or experience to the task that is different from what you might have expected from 'mainstream' students; perhaps the content conflicts with the students' knowledge, value systems, or sense of identity; perhaps the teacher talk or the learning resources are not comprehensible; perhaps the students have not had enough opportunity to rehearse and internalize new concepts through focussed oral interaction with their peers; or perhaps the assessment task required a level of proficiency in English that the students do not yet have.

Informed decision-making

Met (1994: 172–173) provides an illuminating example of how a teacher's knowledge of the students' linguistic, cultural, and educational backgrounds can help in making informed decisions about feedback and instruction. In a science lesson on the natural habitat of frogs, a second language learner states that most frogs live in trees. According to Met, the teacher could respond in several different ways, depending on what he or she knows about the student's background:

- *accept the student's response without comment*
- *respond with positive reinforcement*
- *probe to see if the student has misunderstood the lesson*
- *conclude that the student said tree because that is the only word for natural habitats the student knows, and therefore, the teacher decides to provide additional vocabulary options in her response*

- *conclude that the student has said tree because in Puerto Rico, where this student comes from, there is a common tree frog (coqui), and therefore, for this student, the answer is correct*
- *decide that further instruction using pictures and visual aids is needed to ensure that students are aware that frogs have several natural habitats and that students have the verbal skills to discuss them.*

- **Recognize that most newcomers need a 'silent period'** of observation in order to adjust to the new environment and figure out classroom routines. Also, many learners require a period in which they can absorb language without being required to produce it. What the teacher sees in class is 'the tip of the iceberg'; students who do not have the productive command of English to demonstrate learning may be learning more than you think. In a few months they may surprise you with the amount of content they have learned. Where marks must be given, it would be a good idea to weight the marks towards the end of the year or semester.
- **Encourage students to produce assignments and write tests in their first language** if they are not yet able to do the task in English. A bilingual teacher or trained tutor can help you to assess the student's performance.
- **Focus on content rather than language** when you want to assess what a student knows. Learn to 'see through the errors' as Law and Eckes suggest (1995: 47).
- **Provide the time that second language learners need** to process ideas in two languages during written tests and examinations. Give more time, or ask the students to answer fewer questions within the time allotted. Avoid multiple-choice and true/false questions that involve a lot of reading, or 'trick questions' that depend on comprehension of subtle differences in vocabulary.
- **Reduce the language barrier** and provide support for students' written responses. For example, students can match captions to visual representations of information, or complete a cloze passage with words or phrases selected from a list. Charts and other visual organizers help students to display knowledge or demonstrate their thinking without having to produce large amounts of language.

Cloze:

Students choose words from the list to complete the sentences and demonstrate their knowledge of the concepts and the specialized vocabulary.

located	**population**	**surrounded**
urban	**temperate**	**rural**

Most Canadians live in _____ areas, and about 30 percent of the Canadian _____ lives in the big cities of Toronto, Vancouver, and Montreal. These cities are _____ in the southern part of Canada, where the climate is _____ .

resources   products   service
produce   depend   manufacturing

Many jobs in Canada _____ on natural _____ such as trees, fish, and oil. In the cities, many people work in the _____ industries, making _____ in factories. _____ industries such as finance, communications, and government are also important in urban areas.

If students can complete this cloze passage, they have understood the key concepts and learned how to use important transition words to link ideas.

if   and   as a result
because   therefore   in order to
although   so   so that

I am a frog. I need to live in or near water _____ I have to keep my skin moist. _____ I sometimes move away from the water, I don't go very far, and I always stay where it is damp. This is _____ I have to keep my skin moist _____ to breathe properly.

_____ I stayed away from water for too long, my skin would dry up. _____, I would probably die. _____, I always stay in or near wet places.

Visual organizers:

Students can add key words to the boxes in this chart to demonstrate their understanding of key events leading up to World War 1. To provide more support, teachers can provide a set of words and phrases to choose from.

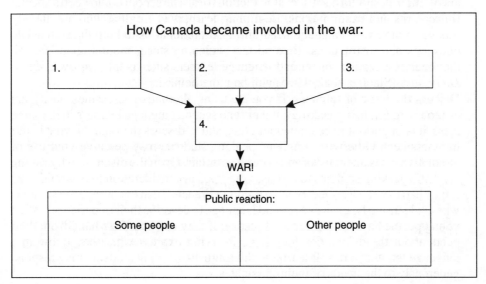

- **Provide practice tests** for students to work through in groups before taking a test. The next day, students can take an individual test that is the same or almost the same as the practice test. For example, in mathematics, the problems on a practice test may be the same as those on the individual test, with only the number values changed.
- **Give clear and simply-worded instructions** in assignments, tests and examinations. Avoid, or paraphrase and explain words such as 'identify', 'describe', 'list', 'discuss'. Avoid passive verbs, and give some clear guidance to the students.

Plain language instructions

Instead of this . . .	Try this . . .
Identify the major causes of World War 1.	What were the four major causes of WW1?
Describe the levels of government and their functions.	What are the three levels of government in Canada? What do they do?
Explain how triangles can be classified.	What are the 2 ways of classifying triangles?

- **Encourage older students to use dictionaries** in tests and examinations. Dictionaries are no substitute for knowledge, but they are essential tools of literacy and scholarship. Perhaps all students, second language learners and native-speakers of English, should have access to dictionaries. The school could keep a special set for tests and examinations. Beginning learners of English who are already literate in their first language need bilingual dictionaries to help them translate questions and instructions. Beyond the beginning stage, monolingual English dictionaries designed for second language learners such as the *Collins Cobuild Dictionary* (Sinclair et al., 1995) will be more helpful.
- **Discuss the issue of fairness.** If you are using alternative assessment tasks and criteria with English-speaking students and second language learners in the same class, it is important to be open about this, and to discuss the issue of what is fair in assessment. Otherwise, English-speaking students may perceive your use of alternative assessment tasks and criteria as unfair. Open the discussion by asking English-speaking students to discuss what special consideration they would need if they had to write a project or a lab report in French. Then encourage the students who are learning English as a second language to describe their experiences. Most young people have a keen sense of justice; if they can hear first-hand from their peers about the difficulties they have in trying express what they know in a language that they are still learning, the English-speaking students may respond generously to the needs of their classmates.

- **Assess the process of learning,** through the use of observation tools that do not assume a high level of proficiency in English. For example, use criteria such as being prepared for class, keeping materials organized, keeping a vocabulary notebook, helping with group presentations by providing concrete or visual material, helping to take care of the classroom, and so on. You will have more opportunities to do this when students are working in groups or at activity centres.

Observation checklist: the learning process

Use the form on p. 264 to help you observe and assess each student's involvement in the process of learning. You can fill in the form several times during the term or semester for each student in the class, using Ú or x. Leave blank all that do not apply. Explain the form to the students at the beginning of the year or course, and show the individual student the form each time you fill it in. Keep the form on file until the end of the assessment period. You can use the form in parent/teacher interviews, and/or send copies home. The form can be translated into the languages of the school so that it is meaningful to parents.

Note: Students can demonstrate involvement and participation in languages other than English.

ASSESSMENT OF LANGUAGE AND LITERACY DEVELOPMENT

Most procedures that are commonly used to assess students' language development have been developed for native-speakers of the language, and are therefore inappropriate for students who have not had the same access and exposure to English as their peers. Assessing the language development of students who are learning English as a second language involves gathering information about their level of proficiency in the first language, as well as their progress as learners of English.

First language assessment

Many students in the multilingual classroom have language skills that are more highly developed in a language other than English. For this reason it is important to gather information about each student's first language development, using some of the procedures described earlier in this chapter — not only for initial assessment when the student arrives at the school, but regularly thereafter to promote maintenance and continued development of the first language and to communicate support for bilingualism. For example, if you keep a portfolio to track each student's growth in reading and writing, collect samples in each student's home language as well as in English.

The following comparison of a student's performance in her first and the second language demonstrates how informative it can be to compare first and second language development. This student from Iran had been in an English-speaking

Observation Checklist: The Learning Process Class: _____ Month/term: _____ Student: _____ Teacher: _____					
Date:					
Came to class on time					
Brought all books and equipment					
Had homework ready					
Had an organized notebook or binder					
Got started promptly					
Paid attention					
Participated in all activities					
Tried new ideas					
Used time well					
Listened to others					
Co-operated with others					
Offered or asked for help					
Treated everyone with respect					
Made a contribution to group work					
Respected other people's ideas					
Worked well with people of other backgrounds					
Worked independently					
Handed work in					
Helped with classroom tasks					

grade six classroom for several months when the sample was collected. She was unable, or unwilling, to do more than write out the alphabet. Her handwriting appears undeveloped for her age, and she mixes upper and lower case letters. On the basis of this sample, the only assessment to be made about this student's proficiency in English is that she cannot write to communicate in English.

This sample of the same student's writing in Farsi was collected at the same time as the English sample. The Farsi sample gives a much clearer picture of the student's literacy development. It is obvious even to teachers who do not read Farsi that her handwriting is well developed, and that she is able to write continuous prose and edit her own work (see the insertion in the last line). According to the Farsi-speaking educator who assessed the sample, the student's literacy skills in Farsi are well developed and above the expected age or grade level. You can learn a lot simply from looking at a first language sample, but if you can get it assessed by a trained volunteer or a trained student from the senior grades you will learn a lot more.

You can collect information about reading in the first language by having a conversation about reading, asking about the student's experiences and preferences. You may find that a child who is a beginning reader in English can already read signs and simple stories in Chinese, or has learned to read the Qu'ran in Arabic. You may find that a secondary school student whose reading comprehension level in English is at the early elementary level has read Tolstoy or Dostoevsky in Russian, or likes to read about astronomy in Spanish, or enjoys the poetry of Rabindranath Tagore in Bengali.

Law and Eckes (1995) recommend using a home language interview and a primary language literacy questionnaire with students whose first language is not English. The Primary Language Record, developed for use in elementary schools in Britain, could be adapted for use in other contexts (Barrs *et al.*, 1988). With beginning level learners of English, conduct interviews and conferences with the assistance of a bilingual volunteer or peer.

Assessment of proficiency in English

When you assess a student's proficiency in English, judge the performance using criteria that are relevant to the process of second language acquisition. It is not usually appropriate to use criteria that compare second language learners with students who are native-speakers of English; you may find out how far they lag behind their English-speaking age peers, but it is more useful and more equitable to use assessment criteria that compare learners of English with each other (McKeon, 1994). See 'Initial Assessment and Placement' in Chapter 3 for specific suggestions on assessment tasks and criteria.

LARGE SCALE ASSESSMENT

The purpose of large scale testing is to assess the effectiveness of an entire education system. Including recently arrived students in such assessment is often inappropriate: their participation reveals little about the education system since they have not been involved in it. Also, large scale assessment often involves the use of standardized tests, which are usually normed on the performance of native speakers of English. Even where performance-based tasks are used for large scale assessment, the tasks and the performance standards are usually designed for native speakers of English.

When a school district is planning large scale assessment, the following conditions for the inclusion of recently arrived students and second language learners may be appropriate:

(1) The students are recent arrivals who have been in full-time schooling prior to arrival, and whose previous education has provided them with the opportunity to acquire the knowledge of English, subject knowledge, and academic skills being tested. For example, some students may have advanced background in

mathematics, and understand English well enough to follow the directions and word problems on the test. However, it is not appropriate to include their results in the overall reporting on the test, even though including their results might help to boost the results for the school or district. If they have been in the country for less than a full school year, their performance cannot be considered reflective of the instruction they have received in their new country. The results can be shared with the students and their parents, and can assist the school or school district in identifying the strengths and needs of specific groups of students or individuals, and in designing appropriate educational programs for them.

(2) The students have been in the new educational environment for *at least one school year,* **and** have acquired a level of proficiency in English that will enable them to *participate meaningfully.* Their results can be disaggregated from those of the general school population in order to identify needs and develop norms that compare second language learners with each other. These norms can be related to length of residence and/or exposure to English, and other factors that may be relevant. Such norms would be helpful in assessing the students' continuing needs and the effectiveness of the program of instruction they are receiving.

(3) Students who are in the early stages of second language acquisition have opportunities to demonstrate their proficiency in their own language. For example, their performance on writing tasks can be assessed by bilingual educators, using the same standards as those used to assess the English submissions.

CONCLUSION

Schools in multicultural communities need to use linguistically and culturally appropriate ways of assessing the linguistic and educational background of students who have recently arrived from other countries, or who first start learning English when they begin school. In addition, procedures are needed for ongoing curriculum-based assessment. These procedures take into account the students' linguistic and cultural backgrounds and life experiences and assist teachers to adjust instruction. It is important to take into account opportunity to learn in developing learning outcomes and standards, and to use alternative assessment strategies and criteria for students who are learning the language of instruction. At the same time, all students have a right to appropriate instructional programs, in school and beyond, to help them reach high standards of proficiency in English and to reach a level of academic achievement that will enable them to participate effectively in society as lifelong learners, as informed citizens, and as productive workers.

The following checklist can be used to assess the implementation of equitable and effective assessment practices in the school.

CHECKLIST: ASSESSMENT IN THE MULTICULTURAL SCHOOL

The checklist is organized as a series of indicators under two topic headings: 'Assessment of Academic Knowledge and Skills', and 'Assessment of Language and Literacy Development'.

The rating system can be used and interpreted as follows:

yes = whenever appropriate
not yet = this is an area that may need special attention
n/a = not applicable, or not available at this time

Assessment of academic knowledge and skills

yes not n/a
    yet

❏ ❏ ❏ Teachers use alternative assessment tasks to assist students to demonstrate what they have learned.

❏ ❏ ❏ Teachers use performance-based assessment to provide practice and feedback before final assessment.

❏ ❏ ❏ Teachers use portfolio assessment to track student progress.

❏ ❏ ❏ Teachers use assessment information to adjust instruction.

❏ ❏ ❏ Newcomers are not pressured to participate or produce work until they are able to do so.

❏ ❏ ❏ Students have opportunities to demonstrate learning in their first language.

❏ ❏ ❏ Teachers focus on content rather than language in assessing students' knowledge.

❏ ❏ ❏ Students receive the time they need to complete tests and examinations in their second language.

❏ ❏ ❏ Teachers reduce the language barrier in assessment: for example, by providing cloze passages and visual organizers instead of traditional essays and question-and-answer tests.

❏ ❏ ❏ Students have opportunities to work together on practice tests.

❏ ❏ ❏ Instructions on tests and examinations are clear and simply worded, leaving no doubt as to what is required.

❏ ❏ ❏ Students have access to dictionaries in tests and examinations.

❏ ❏ ❏ Teachers discuss with all students the reasons for using a variety of assessment tasks and criteria.

❏ ❏ ❏ Teachers assess the process of learning as well as the product.

❏ ❏ ❏ Only those students who have sufficient knowledge of English and experience with the content or skills being assessed are included in large scale assessment.

Assessment of language and literacy development

yes not n/a
    yet

❑   ❑   ❑   Teachers maintain a portfolio for each student.

❑   ❑   ❑   Samples of work in the first language as well as English are included in the portfolio.

❑   ❑   ❑   Teachers collect information about students' reading experiences in the first language as well as in English.

❑   ❑   ❑   Teachers use criteria relevant to second language learning in assessing and reporting on the English language and literacy development of students who are learners of English.

❑   ❑   ❑   In large scale literacy assessment, students who are in the early stages of second language acquisition have opportunities to demonstrate their proficiency in their own language.

❑   ❑   ❑   In large scale assessment, the results for students who are learning the language of instruction are disaggregated in order to identify needs and develop norms that compare second language learners with each other.

FURTHER READING AND RESOURCES FOR TEACHERS

Anthony, R.J., Johnson, T.D., Mickelson, N.I., and Preece, A. (1991) *Evaluating Literacy: A Perspective for Change.* Portsmouth, NH: Heinemann. The authors provide a critique of common assumptions about assessment and evaluation, and provide an ecological model of assessment and evaluation that includes the context and purpose of the assessment. Includes many examples of curriculum-related assessment and evaluation activities.

Cline, T. and Frederickson, N. (eds) (1996) *Curriculum Related Assessment, Cummins and Bilingual Children.* The articles in this book show how to apply Cummins' conceptual framework to curriculum-related assessment.

Cummins, J. (1996) *Negotiating Identities: Educational Empowerment in a Diverse Society.* Ontario, CA: California Association for Bilingual Education. Cummins explains how traditional educational practices and assessment procedures are largely responsible for academic failure among some cultural groups, and suggests some intervention strategies for reversing this failure.

Farr, B. P. and Trumbull, E. (1996) *Assessment Alternatives for Diverse Classrooms.* Norwood, MA: Christopher-Gordon Publishers, Inc. The authors provide a philosophical framework for the development of equitable approaches to assessment in linguistically diverse schools and school districts, and make suggestions for alternative assessment strategies.

Freeman, Y. S. and Freeman, D. E. (1991) Portsmouth, NH: Heinemann. *Whole Language for Second Language Learners*. The section on portfolio assessment (pp. 2120–225) provides practical advice for teachers.

Genesee, F. and Hamayan, E.V. (1994) *Classroom-based assessment*. In Genesee, F. (ed.) *Educating Second-Language Children: The Whole Child, The Whole Curriculum, the Whole Community*. New York, NY: Cambridge University Press. This chapter provides useful guidelines and practical examples of language and content integration.

Goodman, K.S., Goodman, Y.M., and Hood, W.J. (eds) (1989)*The Whole Language Evaluation Book*. Portsmouth, NH: Heinemann, and Toronto: Irwin Publishing. A collection of articles and vignettes on how to evaluate students' growth in reading, writing, and second language learning, using a variety of alternatives to standardized tests.

Hart, D. (1994) *Authentic Assessment: A Handbook for Educators*. Don Mills, Ontario: Addison-Wesley. A helpful guide to recent developments in assessment. Explains key concepts and terms, and provides many examples of assessment tasks, rating sheets, record sheets, and

Law, B. and Eckes, M. (1995) *Assessment and ESL: On the Yellow Big Road to the Withered of Oz*. Winnipeg, Manitoba: Peguis Publishers. Provides detailed advice on the assessment of ESL students; includes many samples of student work, as well as assessment forms and checklists.

O'Malley, J.M. and Pierce, L.V. (1996) *Authentic Assessment for English Language Learners*. Reading, MA: Addison Wesley. A very helpful guide for teachers and administrators, this book provides background information on authentic assessment as well as practical models of alternative forms of assessment that allow second language learners to demonstrate what they know and what they can do.

References

Abella, I. and Troper, H. (1982) *None is Too Many: Canada and the Jews of Europe: 1933–1948.* Toronto: Lester and Orpen Dennys.

Ada, A.F. (1988) The Pajaro Valley experience: working with Spanish-speaking parents to develop children's reading and writing skills in the home through the use of children's literature. In Skutnabb-Kangas, T. and Cummins, J. (eds) (op. cit.)

Alexander, K., and Glaze, A. (1996) *Towards Freedom: The African-Canadian Experience.* Toronto: Umbrella Press.

Alladina, S. (1995) *Being Bilingual: A guide for parents, teachers and young people on mother tongue, heritage language and bilingual education.* Stoke-on-Trent, England: Trentham Books.

Allport, G. (1954) *The Nature of Prejudice.* Cambridge, MA: Addison-Wesley.

Anthony, R.J., Johnson, T.D., Mickelson, N.I., and Preece, A. (1991) *Evaluating Literacy: A Perspective for Change.* Portsmouth, NH: Heinemann.

Aronson, E., Blaney, N., Stephan, C., Sikes, J., and Snap, M. (1978) *The Jigsaw Classroom.* Beverly Hills, CA: Sage.

Badets, J. and Chui, T.W L. (1994). *Canada's Changing Immigrant Population.* Toronto: Statistics Canada and Prentice Hall, 1994.

Baker, C. (1995) *A Parents' and Teachers' Guide to Bilingualism.* Clevedon, England: Multilingual Matters.

Banks, J. A. (1988a [1981]) *Multiethnic Education: Theory and Practice.* Second edition. Newton, MA: Allyn and Bacon Ltd.

Banks, J.A. (1988b) Approaches to multicultural curriculum reform. *Multicultural Leader,* 1: 2.

Banks, J.A. (1993) Multicultural education: development, dimensions, and challenges. *Phi Delta Kappan,* 75, (1): 22–28.

Banks, J.A. (1994) Transforming the mainstream curriculum. *Educational Leadership,* 5, 2, 4–8.

Barrs, M., Ellis, S., and Hester, H. (1988) *Primary Language Record Handbook for Teachers.* London: Centre for Language in Primary Education.

Bigelow, B., Miner, B. and Peterson, B. (eds) (1991) *Rethinking Columbus.* Milwaukee, WI: Rethinking Schools.

Bigelow, B., Christensen, C., Karp, S., Miner, B. and Peterson, B. (eds) (1994) *Rethinking Our Classrooms: Teaching for Equity and Justice.* Milwaukee, WI: Rethinking Schools.

Bilingual Education Office (1986) *Beyond Language: Social and Cultural Factors in Schooling Language Minority Students.* Los Angeles, CA: Assessment, Dissemination and Assessment Center, California State University, Los Angeles.

Black, N.F. (1913) *English for the Non-English.* Regina, Saskatchewan: Regina Book Shop Limited. Cited in Cummins and Danesi (1990): op. cit.

Black, S. (1992) On the wrong track. *Executive Educator,* 14, 2, 46–49.

Blackledge, A. (1994) *Teaching Bilingual Children.* Stoke-on-Trent, England: Trentham Books.

Blakey, L., Hattiangadi, M., and Stanton, S. (1995) *Our Wonderful World.* Toronto: Ginn.

Borovilos, J. (1990). *Breaking Through: A Canadian Literary Mosaic.* Scarborough, Ontario: Prentice-Hall Canada.

Borovilos, J. (1995). *Breaking Free: A Cross-Cultural Anthology.* Scarborough, Ontario: Prentice-Hall Canada.

Borovoy, A. (1989) Racism in Ontario. Keynote Address, given at the North York Board of Education on 14 February, 1989.

Bowman, B. (1993) Reaching potentials of minority children through developmentally and culturally appropriate programs. In Bredekamp, S. and Rosengrant, T. (eds) *Reaching Potentials: Appropriate Curriculum and Assessment for Young Children* : pp. 128–127.

Boykin, A.W. (1978) Psychological/behavioral verve in academic/task performance: pre-theoretical considerations. *Journal of Negro Education,* 47, 343–354.

Braddock, J.H. and Slavin, R.E. (1995) Why ability grouping must end: achieving excellence and equity in American education. In Pool, H. and Page, J.A. (eds) op. cit.: pp. 7–20.

Brandt, R. (1994) On educating for diversity: a conversation with James A. Banks. *Educational Leadership,* 51:2, 28–31.

Brophy, J.E., and Good, T.L. (1974) *Teacher–Student Relationships: Causes and Consequences.* New York, NY: Holt, Rinehart, and Winston.

Brown, H.D. (1992) Sociocultural factors in teaching language minority students. In P.A. Amato-Richards, and M.A. Snow, (eds) *The Multicultural Classroom: Readings for Content-Area Teachers* , White Plains, NY: Longman: pp. 73–92.

Burke, M.A. (1992). Canada's immigrant children. *Canadian Social Trends,* 24, 15–20.

Burnett, J. and Irons, C. (1993) *Mathematics in Many Cultures.* San Francisco: Mimosa Publications.

Burns, P. and Roe, B. (1993) *Burns/Roe Informal Reading Inventory* . Fourth Edition. Boston: Houghton Mifflin

Campbell, P. (1983) Helping young readers become book critics: here's how. *Bulletin, Council for Interracial Books for Children,* Vol. 14 No. 5.

Canadian Task Force on Mental Health Issues Affecting Immigrants and Refugees (1988) *After the Door has been Opened: Mental Health Issues Affecting Immigrants and Refugees in Canada.* Ottowa: Department of the Secretary of State of Canada, Multiculturalism Sector.

Canadian Teachers' Federation (1990) *Responding to the Needs of Immigrant and Refugee Children.* Ottawa: Canadian Teachers' Federation.

Caplan, N., Choy, M. and Whitmore, J. (1992) Indochinese refugee families and academic achievement. *Scientific American,* February, 36–42.

Carey, E. (1997) Poor kids far behind well-off classmates. *Toronto Star,* April 18: p. A1

Carter, B., and Mok, W.Y. (1992) *Newcomer Children: Rights, Needs and Adjustment.* Ottawa: Employment and Immigration Canada.

Chamot, A. and O'Malley, M. (1994) *The CALLA Handbook: Implementing the Cognitive Academic Language Learning Approach.* Reading, MA: Addison-Wesley.

Chartrand, Paul. (1992) Aboriginal peoples, racism and education in Canada: a few comments. In *Racism and Education: Different Perspectives and Experiences.* Ottawa: Canadian Teachers' Federation.

Citizenship and Immigration Canada (1995a) *A Broader Vision: Immigration Plan.* Ottawa: Minister of Supply and Services Canada.

Citizenship and Immigration Canada (1995b) Speaking Notes for the Honourable Sergio Marchi, M.P., Minister of Citizenship and Immigration, for the Annual Levels Report. House of Commons, November 1 1995.

Clark, R.M. (1983) *Family Life and School Achievement: Why Poor Black Children Succeed or Fail.* Chicago: University of Chicago Press.

Clarke, J. H. (1990) *Patterns of Thinking: Integrating Learning Skills in Content Teaching.* Needham Heights, MA: Allyn and Bacon.

Clarke, J., Wideman, R., and Eadie, S. (1990) *Together We Learn: Co-operative Small Group Learning.* Scarborough, Ontario: Prentice-Hall.

Clayton, J.B. (1996) *Your Land, My Land: Children in the Process of Acculturation.* Portsmouth, NH: Heinemann.

Clegg, J. (ed.) (1996) *Mainstreaming ESL: Case Studies in Integrating ESL Students into the Mainstream Curriculum.* Clevedon, England: Multilingual Matters.

Cline, T. and Frederickson, N. (eds) (1996) *Curriculum Related Assessment, Cummins and Bilingual Children.* Clevedon, England: Multilingual Matters.

Cloud, N. (1994) Special education needs of second language students. In F. Genesee, (ed.): op. cit., pp. 243–277.

Coelho, E. (1991a). *Caribbean Students in Canadian Schools: Book 2.* Markham, Ontario: Pippin Publishing Limited.

Coelho, E. (1991b) *Jigsaw.* Markham, Ontario: Pippin Publishing Limited.

Coelho, E. (1992) Jigsaw: integrating language and content. In C. Kessler, (ed.) op. cit., pp. 129–152.

Coelho, E. (1994) *Learning Together in the Multicultural Classroom.* Markham, Ontario: Pippin Publishing Limited.

Coelho, E., and Winer, L. (1991) *Jigsaw Plus.* Markham, Ontario: Pippin Publishing Limited.

Coelho, E., Winer, L., and Winn-Bell Olsen, J. (1989) *All Sides of the Issue.* Hayward, CA: Alemany Press.

Cohen, E. (1986) *Designing Groupwork: Strategies for the Heterogeneous Classroom.* New York, NY: Teachers College Press.

Cohen, E. (1990) Teaching in multiculturally heterogeneous classrooms: findings from a model program. *McGill Journal of Education,* 26, 1, 17–23.

Collier, V. P. (1989) How long? a synthesis of research on academic achievement in a second language. *TESOL Quarterly,* 23,3: pp. 509–529

Corson, D. (1990) *Language Policy Across the Curriculum.* Clevedon, England: Multilingual Matters.

Corson, D. (1993) *Language, Minority Education and Gender: Linking Social Justice and Power.* Clevedon, England: Multilingual Matters.

Cummins, J. (1984) *Bilingualism and Special Education: Issues in Assessment and Pedagogy.* Clevedon, England: Multilingual Matters.

Cummins, J. (1996) *Negotiating Identities: Education for Empowerment in a Diverse Society.* Ontario, CA: California Association for Bilingual Education.

Cummins, J. and Danesi, M. (1990) *Heritage Languages: the Development and Denial of Canada's Linguistic Resources.* Toronto: Our Schools/Ourselves.

Cummins, J. and Sayers, D. (1995) *Brave New Schools: Challenging Cultural Illiteracy.* Toronto: OISE Press.

Curtis, B., Livingstone, D.W., and Smaller, H. (1992). *Stacking the Deck: the Streaming of Working-Class Kids in Ontario Schools.* Toronto: Our Schools/Our Selves.

Davies, L., Logan, M., Paige, C. and Williams, J. (1990) *Book Time.* North York, Ontario: North York Board of Education.

Day, F.A. (1994) *Multicultural Voices in Contemporary Literature: a Resource for Teachers.* Portsmouth, NH: Heinemann.

de la luz Reyes, M. (1992) Challenging venerable assumptions: literacy instruction for linguistically different students. *Harvard Educational Review,* 62, 4, 427–445.

Dei, G. (1996). Black/African-Canadian students' perspectives on school racism. In Alladin, M.I. (ed.) *Racism in Canadian Schools.* Toronto: Harcourt Brace & Company Canada, Ltd.

Delgado-Gaitan, C. (1991) Involving parents in the schools: a process of empowerment. *American Journal of Education* 100, 20–46.

Delpit, L. (1986) Skills and other dilemmas of a progressive Black educator. *Harvard Educational Review* 56, 4, 379–385.

Delpit, L. (1988). The silenced dialogue: power and pedagogy in educating other people's children. *Harvard Educational Review,* 58: 43, 280–298.

Delpit, L. (1995) *Other People's Children: Cultural Conflict in the Classroom.* New York, NY: New Press.

Department of Education and Science (1985) *Education for All: Report of the Committee of Inquiry into the Education of Children from Ethnic Minority Groups* (The Swann Report). London: HMSO.

Derman-Sparks, L. and the A.B.C. Task Force. (1989). *Anti-Bias Curriculum: Tools for Empowering Young Children.* Washington, DC: National Association for the Education of Young Children.

Disman, M. (1983) Immigrants and other grieving people: insights for counselling practices and policy issues. *Canadian Ethnic Studies* XV, 3, 106–118.

Dunn, R., Beaudry, J. and Klavas, A. (1989) Survey of research on learning styles. *Educational Leadership,* 46, 6, 50–58.

Edelson, J.L. and Roskin, M. (1985) Prevention groups: a model for improving immigrant adjustment. *Journal for Specialists in Group Work,* 10, 4, 217–224.

Edmonds, R. (1979) Effective schools for the urban poor. *Educational Leadership* 37, 15–23.

Edwards, V. (1996) *The Other Languages: a guide to multilingual classrooms.* Reading: Reading and Language Information Centre, University of Reading.

Employment and Immigration Canada (1992) *Immigration Statistics 1991.* Ottawa: Minister of Supply and Services Canada.

Enright, S. and McCloskey, M. L. (1988) *Integrating English: Developing English Language and Literacy in the Multilingual Classroom.* Reading, MA: Addison-Wesley.

Erickson, T. (1989) *Get It Together: Math Problems for Groups.* Berkeley, CA: Regents of the University of California.

Esling, J. (ed.) (1989) *Multicultural Education and Policy: ESL in the 1990s.* Toronto: Ontario Institute for Studies in Education.

Farr, B. P. and Trumbull, E. (1996) *Assessment Alternatives for Diverse Classrooms.* Norwood, MA: Christopher-Gordon Publishers, Inc.

Ferguson, T. (1975) *A White Man's Country: An Exercise in Canadian Prejudice.* Toronto: Doubleday Canada Limited.

Finders, M. and Lewis, C. (1994) Why some parents don't come to school. *Educational Leadership* 51, 8, 50–54.

Fleras, A. and Elliott, J. (1992) *Multiculturalism in Canada.* Scarborough, Ontario: Nelson Canada.

Freeman, Y. S. and Freeman, D. E. (1991) *Whole Language for Second Language Learners.* Portsmouth, NH: Heinemann.

Freire, M. (1989) Refugee families and their children: a psycho-social analysis. Paper presented at the Canadian Psychiatric Association Meeting, 1989.

Fullilove, R. and Treisman, P.U. (1990) Mathematics achievement among African American undergraduates at the University of California, Berkeley: an evaluation of the mathematics workshop program. *Journal of Negro Education,* 59, 3, 463–478.

Garcia, J. (1993) The changing image of ethnic groups in textbooks. *Phi Delta Kappan,* 75: 1, 29–35.

Geddis, C. (1995) Personal interview, July 1995.

Genesee, F. (ed.) (1994) *Educating Second-Language Children: The Whole Child, The Whole Curriculum, the Whole Community.* New York, NY: Cambridge University Press.

Genesee, F. and Hamayan, E.V. (1994) Classroom-based assessment. In Genesee, F. (ed.): op. cit., pp. 278–300.

George, P.S. (1988) Tracking and ability grouping: which way for the middle school? *Middle School Journal,* 20, 1, 21–28.

Gibbons, P. (1993) *Learning to Learn in a Second Language.* Portsmouth, NH: Heinemann.

Gilad, L. (1990) *The Northern Route.* St John's, Newfoundland: Institute of Social and Economic Research, Memorial University of Newfoundland.

Gilbert, S. and Gay, G. (1985) Improving the success in school of poor black children. *Phi Delta Kappan,* 67, 2, 133–137.

Gill, D. and Levidow, L. (eds) (1987) *Anti-Racist Science Teaching.* London: Free Association Books.

Golden, R. (1992) *Dangerous Memories: Invasion and Resistance Since 1492.* Chicago: Chicago Religious Task Force on Central America.

Goodlad, J. (1984). *A Place Called School: Prospects for the Future.* New York: McGraw Hill.

Goodman, K.S., Goodman, Y.M., and Hood, W.J. (eds) (1989) *The Whole Language Evaluation Book.* Portsmouth, NH: Heinemann, and Toronto: Irwin Publishing.

Gould, S. J. (1981). *The Mismeasure of Man.* New York, NY: W.W. Norton & Co.

Graham, P. (1987) Black teachers: a drastically scarce resource. *Phi Delta Kappan,* 68, 8, 598–605.

Green, P.A. (1985) Multi-ethnic teaching and the pupils' self-concepts. In Department of Education and Science (*The Swann Report*) (op. cit.): pp. 46–56.

Gregory, E. (1996) *Making Sense of a New World: Learning to Read in a Second Language.* London: Paul Chapman Publishing Limited.

Guild, P. (1994) The culture/learning style connection. *Educational Leadership,* 51, 8, 16–21.

Hale-Benson, J. (1986) *Black Children: Their Roots, Culture, and Learning Styles.* Baltimore: Johns Hopkins University Press.

Hamayan, E.V. (1994) Language Development of Low-Literacy Students. In Genesee, F. (ed.): op. cit.

Handscombe, J. (1989) Mainstreaming: who needs it? In Esling, J. (ed.) op. cit: pp. 18–35.

Harris, V. J. (ed.) (1993) *Teaching Multicultural Children's Literature in Grades K–8.* Norwood, MA: Christopher-Gordon Publishers, Inc.

Hart, D. (1994) *Authentic Assessment: A Handbook for Educators.* Don Mills, Ontario: Addison-Wesley.

Hawkins, E. (1987[1984]) *Awareness of Language: An Introduction.* Revised Edition. Cambridge: Cambridge University Press.

Hawkins, E. (ed.) (1984, 1985) *Awareness of Language.* Cambridge: Cambridge University Press.

Heath, S.B. (1983) *Ways With Words: Language, Life, and Work in Communities and Classrooms.* Cambridge: Cambridge University Press.

Heath, S.B. (1986) Sociocultural contexts of language development. In Bilingual Education Office, op. cit.: pp. 142–186.

Helmer, S. and Eddy, C. (1996) *Look at Me When I Talk to You.* Toronto: Pippin Publishing.

Henry, F., and Greenberg, E. (1985) *Who Gets the Work? A Test of Racial Discrimination in Employment.* Toronto: Social Planning Council of Metropolitan Toronto.

Herberg, E. N. (1989) *Ethnic Groups in Canada: Adaptations and Transitions.* Scarborough, Ontario: Nelson Canada.

Hess, M. (1989) *Children, Schools and Poverty.* Report for the Canadian Teachers' Federation Ad Hoc Committee on Children and Poverty.

Hilliard, A. (1989) Cultural style in teaching and learning. *Education Digest* 55, 4, 21–23.

Hilliard, A. (1994) Teachers and cultural styles. In Bigelow et al. (eds): op. cit., p.127.

Hodson, D. (1993) In search of a rationale for multicultural science education. *Science Education* 77, 6, 685–711.

Hyerle, D. (1996) *Visual Tools for Constructing Knowledge.* Alexandria, VA: Association for Supervision and Curriculum Development.

Irvine, J. (1991). *Black Students and School Failure: Policies, Practices, and Prescriptions.* New York, NY: Greenwood Press; Westport, Connecticut: Praeger.

Jobe, R. (1993) *Cultural Connections.* Markham, Ontario: Pembroke.

Johnson, D. and Johnson, R. (1991) *Learning Together and Alone.* Needham Heights, MA: Allyn and Bacon.

Kagan, S. (1986) Cooperative learning and sociocultural factors in schooling. In Bilingual Education Office, op. cit.: pp. 231–298.

Kaprielian-Churchill, I., and Churchill, S. (1994) *The Pulse of the World: Refugees in Our Schools.* Toronto: OISE Press.

Kessler, C. (ed.) (1992) *Cooperative Language Learning.* Englewood Cliffs, NJ: Prentice-Hall.

Kezwer, P. (1995) *Worlds of Wonder: Resources for Multicultural Children's Literature.* Toronto: Pippin Publishing Limited.

Kim, Y.Y. (1988) *Communication and Cross-Cultural Adaptation.* Clevedon, England: Multilingual Matters.

Klesmer, H. (1994) Assessment and teacher perceptions of ESL student achievement. *English Quarterly,* 26,3, 8–11.

Kohn, A. (1993) *Punished by Rewards: the Trouble with Gold Stars, Incentive Plans, A's, Praise, and Other Bribes.* Boston: Houghton Mifflin.

Kozol, J. (1991) *Savage Inequalities: Children in America's Schools.* New York, NY: Crown Publishers, Inc.

Krater, J., Zeni, J., and Cason, N.D. (1994) *Mirror Images: Teaching Writing in Black and White.* Portsmouth, NH: Heinemann.

Krause, M.C. (1986) *Multicultural Mathematics Materials.* Reston, VA: National Council of Teachers of Mathematics.

Kunjufu, J. (1988) *To Be Popular or Smart: the Black Peer Group.* Chicago: African American Images.

Ladson-Billings, G. (1994) *The Dreamkeepers: Successful Teachers of African American Children.* San Francisco, CA: Jossey Bass.

Law, B. and Eckes, M. (1990) *The More Than Just Surviving! Handbook: ESL for Every Classroom Teacher.* Winnipeg, Manitoba: Peguis Publishers.

Law, B. and Eckes, M. (1995) *Assessment and ESL: On the Yellow Big Road to the Withered of Oz.* Winnipeg, Manitoba: Peguis Publishers.

Lewis, M. and Wray, D. (1995) *Developing Children's Non-Fiction Writing.* Leamington Spa, UK: Scholastic.

Lewis, M. and Wray, D. (1996) *Writing Frames: Scaffolding children's non-fiction writing in a range of genres.* Reading, UK: Reading and Language Information Centre, University of Reading.

Lewis, S. (1992) *Stephen Lewis Report on Race Relations in Ontario.* Toronto: Government of Ontario.

Lincoln, C. A. and Higgins, N.M. (1991) Making schools work for all children. *Principal,* 70:3, 6–8.

MacLear, K. (1994) The myth of the 'model minority': re-thinking the education of Asian Canadians. *Our Schools, Ourselves* 35, 5, 3, 54–76.

Malarek, V. (1987) *Haven's Gate: Canada's Immigration Fiasco.* Toronto: Macmillan of Canada.

Mansour, V. (1991) 'Guatemala's children: Old before their time, they work from dawn to dusk amid the ravages of war' *Toronto Star,* July 8.

Marlow, J. and Culler, K. (1987) How we're adding racial balance to the math equation. *The Executive Educator,* 4, 9, 24–25.

Massey, I. (1991) *More Than Skin Deep: Developing Anti-Racist Multicultural Education in Schools.* London: Hodder and Stoughton.

Matas, D., with Simon, I. (1989) *Closing the Doors: The Failure of Refugee Protection.* Toronto: Summerhill Press.

McArthur, T. (ed.) (1992) *Oxford Companion to the English Language.* Oxford: Oxford University Press.

McCloskey, M.L. and Stack, L. (1992) *Voices in Literature: Silver*. Boston: Heinle and Heinle.

McCloskey, M.L. and Stack, L. (1993) *Voices in Literature: Gold*. Boston: Heinle and Heinle.

McCloskey, M.L. and Stack, L. (1996) *Voices in Literature: Bronze*. Boston: Heinle and Heinle.

McGee Banks, C. (1993) Restructuring schools for equity: what we have learned in two decades. *Phi Delta Kappan,* 75: 1, 42–48.

McKenna, G. (1989) *Transcript of Remarks from 'Sharing the Responsibility: The Education of Black Students in Toronto Schools'* (plenary address). Toronto: Toronto Board of Education.

McKeon, D. (1994) When meeting 'common' standards is uncommonly difficult. *Educational Leadership* 1, 8, 45–49.

McKissack, P. (1986) *Flossie and the Fox*. Toronto: Fitzhenry and Whiteside.

Met, M. (1994) Teaching content through a second language. In Genesee, F. (ed.): op. cit., pp. 159–182

Miner, B. (1994). Taking multicultural, anti-racist education seriously: an interview with educator Enid Lee. In Bigelow et al. (eds): op. cit., pp. 19–22.

Ministry of Education (1980) *Race, Religion and Culture in Ontario School Materials: Suggestions for Authors and Publishers*. Toronto, Ontario: Ministry of Education.

Ministry of Education (1983) *Black Studies: A Resource Guide for Teachers*. Toronto, Ontario: Ministry of Education.

Ministry of Education and Training (1993) *Antiracism and Ethnocultural Equity Education in School Boards*. Toronto: Ontario Ministry of Education and Training.

Ministry of Education and Training (1995) *The Common Curriculum: Policies and Outcomes, Grades 1–9*. Toronto: Ministry of Education and Training.

Morgan, H. (1980) How schools fail black children. *Social Policy,* January/February: pp. 49–53.

Multilingual Resources for Children Project (1995) *Building Bridges: Multilingual Resources for Children*. Clevedon: Multilingual Matters.

Nehaul, K. (1996) *The Schooling of Children of Caribbean Heritage*. Stoke-on-Trent: Trentham Books.

Nelson Canadian Dictionary of the English Language (1997). Toronto: Nelson Canada.

Ngugi, wa Thiong'o (1985 [Ngugi, James. 1964]) *Weep Not, Child*. London: Heinemann.

North York Board of Education (1987) *Multicultural, Multiracial Leadership Camp: a Program in Multicultural and Anti-Racist Education*. North York, Ontario: North York Board of Education.

North York Board of Education (1989) *Guidelines for Assessing Learning Materials*. North York, Ontario: North York Board of Education.

Oakes, J. (1985) *Keeping Track: How Schools Structure Inequality*. New Haven: Yale University Press.

Oakes, J. (1986) Keeping track, part 1: the policy and practice of curriculum inequality. *Phi Delta Kappan,* 68, 1, 12–17.

Oakes, J. (1995). Two cities' tracking and within-school segregation. *Teachers College Record* 96, 4, 681–690.

Ogbu, J. (1983) Minority status and schooling in plural societies. *Comparative Education Review* 27, 168–190.

Ogbu, J. (1992) Adaptation to minority status and impact on school success. *Theory Into Practice,* 31:4, 287–295.

Ogbu, J. (1995) Cultural problems in minority education: their interpretations and consequences — part one: theoretical background. *The Urban Review,* 27:3, 189–205.

Ogbu, J. and Matute-Bianchi, M. (1986) Understanding sociocultural factors: knowledge, identity, and school adjustment. In Bilingual Education Office, op. cit., pp. 73–142.

Oliver, E.I. (1994) *Crossing the Mainstream: Multicultural Perspectives in Teaching Literature*. Urbana, IL: National Council of Teachers of English.

O'Malley, J.M. and Pierce, L.V. (1996) *Authentic Assessment for English Language Learners*. Reading, MA: Addison Wesley.

Opoku-Dapaah, E. (1995) *Somali Refugees in Toronto: a Profile*. North York, Ontario: York Lanes Press.

Page, J.A. and Page, F.M. (1995) Tracking and its effects on African-Americans in the field of education. In Pool, H. and Page, J.A. (eds), op. cit., pp. 71–78).

Page, N. (1995) *Sing and Shine On!* The Teacher's Guide to Multicultural Song Leading. Portsmouth, NH: Heinemann.

Parker-Jenkins, M. (1995) *Children of Islam: A Teacher's Guide to Meeting the Needs of Muslim Pupils*. Stoke-on-Trent, England: Trentham Books.

Parkin, F. and Sidnell, F. (1992) *ESL is Everybody's Business*. Markham, Ontario: Pembroke Publishers Limited.

Peterson, B. (1994) Songs that promote justice. In B. Bigelow, C. Christensen, S. Karp, B. Miner and B. Peterson *Rethinking Our Classrooms* (p. 38).

Philp, M. (1997) Poor already behind by time they reach school. *Globe and Mail,* April 29: p. A1.

Pine, G. and Hilliard, A. (1990) Rx for racism: imperatives for America's schools. *Phi Delta Kappan,* 71, 8, 593–600.

Polakow-Suransky, S. and Ulaby, N. (1990) Students take action to combat racism. *Phi Delta Kappan,* 71, 8, 601–606.

Pool, H. and Page, J.A. (eds) (1995) *Beyond Tracking: Finding Success in Inclusive Schools*. Bloomington, IN: Phi Delta Kappan Educational Foundation.

Porter, J. (1991) *New Canadian Voices*. Toronto: Wall and Emerson.

Pressley, M., and Associates (1990) *Cognitive Strategy Instruction that Really Improves Children's Academic Performance*. Cambridge, MA: Brookline Books.

Radwanski, G. (1987) *Ontario Study of the Relevance of Education, and the Issue of Dropouts.* Toronto: Ministry of Education.

Richard-Amato, P., and Snow, M. (eds) (1992) *The Multicultural Classroom: Readings for Content-Area Teachers.* White Plains, NY: Longman.

Rigg, P. and Allen, V. G. (eds) (1989) *When They Don't All Speak English.* Urbana, IL: National Council of Teachers of English.

Rigg, P. and Enright, S. (eds) (1986) *Children and ESL: Integrating Perspectives.* Washington, DC: TESOL.

Rosenthal, R., and Jacobson, L. (1968) *Pygmalion in the Classroom: Teacher Expectations and Pupils' Intellectual Development.* New York, NY: Holt, Rinehart and Winston.

Rutter, J. (1994) *Refugee Children in the Classroom.* Stoke-on-Trent, England: Trentham Books.

Samway, K.D. and Whang, G. (1996) *Literature Study Circles in a Multicultural Classroom.* York, Maine: Stenhouse Publishers.

Samway, K. D., Whang, G., and Pippitt, M. (1995) *Buddy Reading: Cross-Age Tutoring in a Multicultural School.* Portsmouth, NH: Heinemann.

Scarcella, R. (1990) *Teaching Language Minority Students in the Multicultural Classroom.* Englewood Cliffs, NJ: Prentice Hall.

Schniedewind, N. and Davidson, E. (1998) *Open Minds to Equality: A Sourcebook of Learning Activities to Affirm Diversity and Promote Equity.* Needham Heights, MA: Allyn and Bacon.

Shade, B. (1982) Afro-American cognitive style: a variable in school success? *Review of Educational Research,* 54: 2, 219–244.

Shan, S., and Bailey, P. (1991) *Multiple Factors: Classroom Mathematics for Equity and Justice.* Stoke-on-Trent, UK: Trentham Books Ltd.

Sharan, Y. (1990) Group Investigation: expanding cooperative learning. In Brubacher, M., Payne, R., Rickett, K. (eds). *Perspectives on Small Group Learning.* Oakville, Ontario: Rubicon Press.

Sinclair, J., (ed.) (1995) *Collins Cobuild English Dictionary.* London: Harper Collins.

Skelton, C. (1997) Students get more to choose. *Globe and Mail,* Monday June 23.

Skutnabb-Kangas, T. and Cummins, J. (eds) (1988) *Minority Education: from Shame to Struggle.* Clevedon, England: Multilingual Matters.

Slavin, R. (1983) *Cooperative Learning.* New York: Longman.

Slavin, R. (1990) *Cooperative Learning: Theory, Research, and Practice.* Englewood Cliffs, NJ: Prentice-Hall.

Solomon, P. (1992) *Black Resistance in the High School: Forging a Separatist Culture.* Albany: State University of New York Press.

Spangenberg-Urbschat, K. and Pritchard, R. (eds) (1994) *Kids Come in All Languages.* Newark, Delaware: International Reading Association.

Statistics Canada (1992) *Immigration and Citizenship.* Ottawa: Supply and Services Canada.

Stenmark, J.K., Thompson, V., and Cossey, R. (1986) *Family Math/Matemática Para la Familia*. Berkeley, CA: Regents, University of California.

Sue, S. and Padilla, A. (1986) Ethnic minority issues in the united states: challenges for the educational system. In Bilingual Education Office: op. cit., pp. 35–72.

Swartz, E. (1992) Multicultural education: from a compensatory to a scholarly foundation. In Grant, C. (ed.) *Research and Multicultural Education: From the Margins to the Mainstream*. London: Falmer Press.

Tizard, J., Schofield, W.N. and Hewison, J. (1982) Collaboration between teachers and parents in assisting children's reading. *British Journal of Educational Psychology,* 52, 1–15.

Toronto Star (1994) 'Immigrants do not commit more crimes.' July 23.

Toronto Sun (1997) 'Flood of refugees swamping Canada.' February 10: p. 1, p. 4.

Toronto Star (1997) 'Scholarships promote harmony.' June 24: p. E2

Troper, H. (1979) An uncertain past: Reflections on the history of multiculturalism. *TESL Talk,* 10, 7–15.

Troyna, B. and Siraj-Blatchford, I. (1993) Providing support or denying access? The experiences of students designated as 'ESL' and 'SN' in a multi-ethnic secondary school. *Educational Review,* 45, 1, 3–11.

Walker, R. (1990). Multiculturalism in the teaching of music. In D'Oyley, V. and Shapson, S. (eds) *Innovative Multicultural Teaching* Toronto: Kagan and Woo Limited.

Washington, V. (1980) Teachers in integrated classrooms: profiles of attitudes, perceptions, and behavior. *Elementary School Journal,* 80, 4, 193–201.

Watt, D.L.E. and Roessingh, H. (1994) Some you win, most you lose: tracking ESL student dropout in high school (1988–1993). *English Quarterly,* 26, 3, 5–7

Wheelock, A. (1994) *Alternatives to Tracking and Ability Grouping*. Arlington, VA: American Association of School Administrators.

Whitaker, C. (1989) The disappearing Black teacher. *Ebony,* January issue, 124–126. Cited in Pine and Hilliard, op. cit.

Wisconsin Department of Public Instruction (1991) *Strategic Learning in the Content Areas*. Madison, WI: Wisconsin Department of Public Instruction.

Wong, M.G. (1980) Model students? Teachers' perceptions and expectations of their Asian and white students. *Sociology of Education,* 53, 236–246.

Wong Fillmore, L. (1991) When learning a second language means losing the first. *Early Childhood Research Quarterly,* 6, 323–346.

Yao, E. L. (1985) Adjustment needs of Asian immigrant children. *Elementary School Guidance and Counselling,* 19:3, 222–227.

Yau, M. (1995) *Refugee Students in Toronto Schools: An Exploratory Study*. Toronto: Toronto Board of Education.

Yolen, J. (1992) *Encounter*. New York, NY: Harcourt Brace Jovanovich.

Young, R. M. (1987). Racist society, racist science. In D. Gill and L. Levidow (eds) *Anti-racist Science Teaching* (pp. 16–42).

Zapata, J. (1988) Early identification and recruitment of Hispanic teacher candi-
    dates. *Journal of Teacher Education,* January/February, p. 19. Cited in Pine
    and Hilliard, op. cit.
Zaslavsky, C. (1994) Bringing the world into the math class. In Bigelow et al. (eds):
    op. cit., pp. 76–78.
Zaslavsky, C. (1996) *The Multicultural Math Classroom: Bringing in the World*
    Portsmouth, NH: Heinemann.

Index

ability grouping 185
aboriginal people 2, 4, 98, 103
academic skills and knowledge 64, 199
Acadians 3
acculturation 26, 28, 29, 31
adaptability 50
additive bilingualism 86
'add-on' approach 202
adjustment (*see also* acculturation) 26, 31,
    43, 49, 82, 108
advocate 105
African Americans 110, 111, 168, 171, 180
African American Vernacular English 87,
    152
African Heritage Month 103
analytical learners 161
anti-Semitism 8
antiracism 102-104, 118, 183, 195-207, 212,
    244
artists 103, 212
arts education 207, 210-216
Asian immigrants 7
Asian students 183
assessment 61-80, 105, 188, 251-270
assimilation 18-20, 29
awards 102, 109

background knowledge 236
Basic Interpersonal Communication Skills
    (BICS) 257
behavioural preferences 160
bias 118, 205, 221, 243
Bible 238
bilingual dictionaries 78
bilingual education 65, 68, 80, 83, 85-87,
    106, 107, 110, 254, 267
bilingual resources 114

bilingual skills 148
bilingual support 148
Black English Vernacular 87, 152
Black students 183
Book Time 127
British North America Act 6

camps 46
Caribbean English Creole 152
celebrations 102
Central American students 45, 46
chants 174
children's literature 221
Chinese 7, 47, 110, 111, 171
choice 32
Christmas concert 205
citizenship 51
classrooms 37, 64, 136, 138, 152
cloze test 75, 173, 260
co-operative learning 140-146, 152, 161,
    164, 165, 166, 177, 188, 210
Cognitive Academic Language Proficiency
    (CALP) 257
cognitive style (*see* learning styles) 162
cognitively demanding/undemanding 257
colleges and universities 252
colonization 2-4
community groups 49, 108, 121, 124, 124,
    235
community languages 55, 58, 59, 95, 97, 98,
    128, 217
competition 164, 165, 210
computer studies 218
conceptual frameworks 236
context embedded/context reduced 257
convergent thinking 174
cooking 202

284